FOOD LOVERS'
GUIDE TO®
DALLAS &
FORT WORTH

FOOD LOVERS' SERIES

FOOD LOVERS'
GUIDE TO®
DALLAS &
FORT WORTH

The Best Restaurants, Markets
& Local Culinary Offerings

1st Edition

June Naylor

Guilford, Connecticut

Copyright © 2014 by Morris Book Publishing, LLC

Editor: Amy Lyons
Project editor: Julie Marsh
Layout artist: Mary Ballachino
Text design: Sheryl P. Kober
Illustrations by Jill Butler with additional art by Carleen Moira Powell and
MaryAnn Dubé
Maps: Trailhead Graphics Inc. © Morris Book Publishing, LLC

ISBN 978-0-7627-8111-9

Printed in the United States of America
10 9 8 7 6 5 4 3 2 1

To Marshall, for gamely and generously giving your appetite, road-warrior sensibilities, and love.

Contents

Recipes, 225

Appendices, 243

Index, 254

About the Author

Sixth-generation Texan June Naylor has been a food and travel journalist and dining critic for more than 20 years, and she's penned three cookbooks with noted Texas chefs. Culinary travel assignments have led her to Thailand and France, New Zealand and Argentina, and throughout the southwestern United States. She has served as a Regional Panelist for the James Beard Foundation Restaurant Awards committee and is a member of Les Dames d'Escoffier. While writing about food and travel for the Fort Worth–based luxury magazine called *360 West,* she also contributes stories to *American Way, USA Today, Dallas Morning News, Texas Highways,* and *Texas Monthly,* while also running a culinary events company in Fort Worth. She is also a founding member of Foodways Texas, a nonprofit dedicated to the preservation and celebration of the food history and culture of the Lone Star State. A lifelong student of food, June took her first cooking class at age 8, in Dallas, and has enjoyed classes around the globe ever since. June is the author of other books from Globe Pequot Press, including *The Insiders' Guide to Dallas/Fort Worth, Texas Off the Beaten Path,* and *Quick Escapes from Dallas/Fort Worth.*

Acknowledgments

Writing about restaurants, culinary evolutions, interesting characters, and almost everything edible in the world of food never fails to thrill me. I equate excellent food—that can be a superb pot of pinto beans as easily as it might be an impossibly delicate *crudo*—with art, and I have immense admiration for those who celebrate food on a plate or on a page. Since I first read work by M. F. K. Fisher and Calvin Trillin, I longed to write about food. I owe much to editors (and friends) who have provided encouragement and expertise, particularly that from beloved faux sisters and rays of sunshine, Trish Rodriguez Terrell and Barbara Rodriguez. Meda Kessler and Patricia Sharpe have given me both friendship and guidance along the way, too. Helping specifically with this book, I must thank Pat again, as well as the nicest BBQ snob I ever met, Daniel Vaughn. Cynthia Wahl, my Texas Toast partner, has been invaluable. Dotty Griffith, my long lost cousin, contributed her esteemed Dallas insight, while Fort Worth pals, Crystal Willars Vastine and Josie Villa Singleton, along with the galavanting Food Truck Foodie, Stephanie Hawkes, shared theirs. At Globe Pequot, I owe thanks to Amy Lyons, whose patience astounds, and to Julie Marsh, Lynn Zelem, and Tracee Williams, who kept this book going in the right direction. The chefs, cooks, and restaurateurs who work hard every day to give customers their best deserve more credit than I can ever supply. I'm indebted to you for giving me so much worthy material. Finally, I must thank my beloved road warrior/soul mate, Marshall Harris, for his love, support, enthusiasm, tireless appetite, understanding of what makes food meaningful, and willingness to eat anything. My greatest debt is to my parents, who taught me at a very, very early age that good, handmade food is one of life's eternal joys.

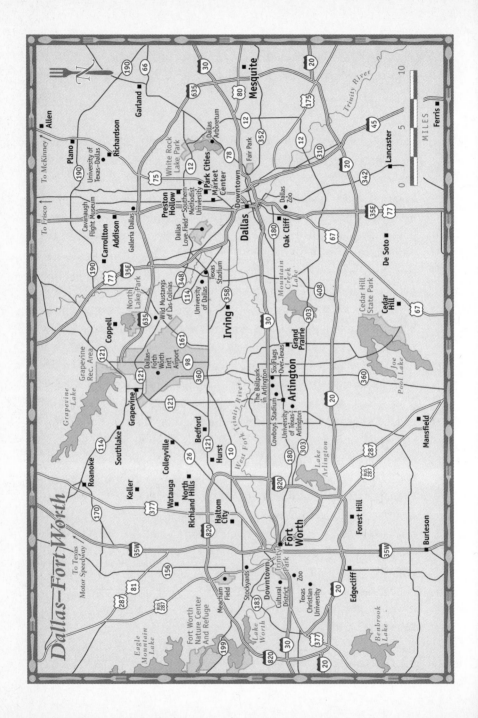

Introduction

Dallas has certainly evolved since it was founded as a trading post on the banks of the Trinity River. Just a few delectable days spent inspecting the food scene today shows you how Big D came to own a distinct and enviable chunk of real estate in the culinary world. Even before Southwestern cuisine brought the city's dining scene to national fame, there was Helen Corbitt, who expanded the Neiman Marcus brand into the epicurean stratosphere. She blazed a trail made even more exciting in recent years by Dallas culinary stars such as Dean Fearing, Stephan Pyles, Kent Rathbun, and Katherine Clapner, who prove every day that Dallas has a palate to be reckoned with.

Dallas continues to thrill taste buds with its Tex-Mex, barbecue, and steaks, but appetites also reach beyond such familiar realms of comfort food these days. Dallas now offers an abundance of farm-to-table eating offerings and impressive efforts within the Slow Food movement. Plan a cuisine-centric trip around Dallas just to nibble, taste, sip, and nosh. On visits to markets, artisan shops, wine cellars, and restaurants, you'll find flavors you didn't expect, and you'll get acquainted with personalities behind all this new energy on the Dallas food scene. Here are some of the appetizing ideas to explore.

Fancy Food, Relaxed Mood: Until recently, Dallas was considered a dress-for-dinner kind of town. But Chef Dean Fearing changed all that, defying the coat-and-tie protocol by declaring that **Fearing's** (p. 102), his restaurant in the glamorous Ritz-Carlton, would have no dress code. At Fearing's, with its seven dining venues, Dean still serves up ample portions of the Southern-accented, feel-good food for which he became famous at the **Mansion Restaurant** on Turtle Creek (p.

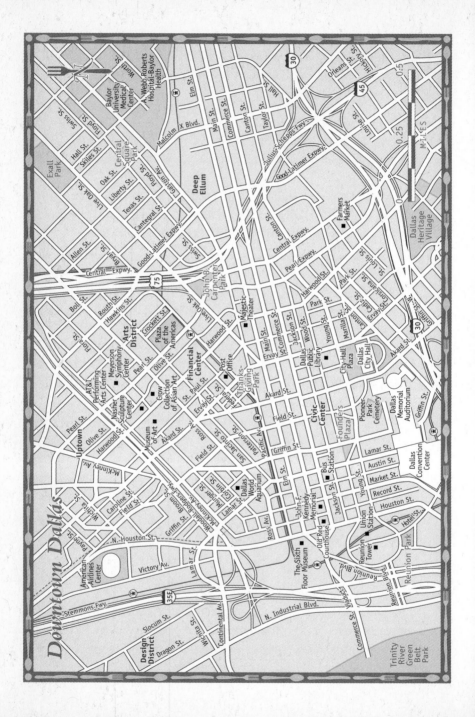

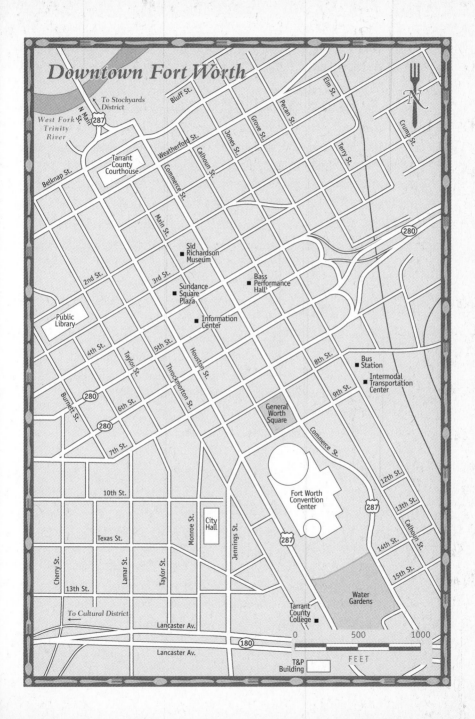

103)—and yes, Dean's Tortilla Soup with South of the Border Flavors (p. 231) remains as fabulous as ever.

Farm to Market: Since 1941 the Dallas Farmers Market has been a go-to place for the freshest produce you can find, and much of it comes from around the state. Open from 8 a.m. daily, it's one of the largest of its kind in the nation. Local producers fill Shed No. 2 and happily hand you samples of fruits and vegetables to taste for yourself. In 2014 the market will undergo significant change for the better, as a private company will make $65 million in improvements.

How It's Made: Long before it became fashionable to buy and eat artisan cheeses, Paula Lambert opened her little cheese company in Dallas's Deep Ellum neighborhood. Since opening in 1982, the **Moz-**  **zarella Company** (p. 74) has grown in impressive ways, winning international awards and earning accolades from major national publications. Paula, one of numerous Dallas cuisine personalities deeply entrenched in the Slow Food movement, tells wonderful stories as she shows you around her intimate cheese-making business, and she'll sign copies of her much-lauded cheese cookbooks. Nearby in Lakewood, Times Ten Cellars offers a variety of wine crafted on-site from Texas grapes; its wine bar is a divine place to wind down after a winery tour.

Stocking Up: Jimmy's Grocery, an old-school Italian grocery famous for its meats and handmade pastas, is a surprise in East Dallas. The astounding Italian sausage sandwich with red and yellow peppers, onions, and melted cheese washes down well with a $1 shot of espresso to fortify you browsing aisles laden with Prosecco, exceptional wines from Piedmont and Tuscany, and more olive oils than you've ever seen. At the new landmark **Whole Foods Market** (p. 181) on Park Lane, find surprisingly divine raw food dishes and DIY cupcake center, along with a cool wine bar, live music venue, and expansive gluten-free food choices.

Classic Dallas: The Rosewood **Mansion Restaurant** on Turtle Creek (p. 103) entered a new era in hiring Bruno Davaillon from Mix Las Vegas. His otherworldly five-course tasting menu with ingenious wine pairings from sommelier Michael Flynn will have you floating on clouds. Stephan Pyles continues to produce swoon-worthy fare at his namesake restaurant (p. 46), where ceviche tastings are as popular as his signature cowboy rib eye with red chile onion rings. A few blocks away, Stephan tantalizes with tapas-style dining at his new **Samar** (p. 40), a place for exotic finds from his journeys to Spain, Morocco, and India. Nearby, Stephan's new **Stampede 66** (p. 96) puts unheard-of spins on fried chicken, Texas chili, tacos, and margaritas.

Old-Fashioned New Goodness: Bishop Arts District is the lovingly revived, restored quarter in Oak Cliff, offering a walkable neighborhood of pubs, restaurants, coffeehouses, and bistros. Visit **Bolsa** (p. 121) for flatbread topped with smoked salmon and local cheeses, washed down with a cocktail brimming with fresh ingredients; **Tillman's Roadhouse** (p. 123) for venison chili; **Hattie's** (p. 113) for shrimp and grits; **Eno's** (p. 111) for extra-thin pizza and handcrafted beer; and **Dude, Sweet Chocolate** (p. 124) for artisan sweets.

Texas Trilogy: Start the day with a Tex-Mex breakfast in the Dallas Farmers Market's El Mercado Mexican Restaurant; graze on a lunch of smoked pork ribs and sliced beef brisket at the legendary **Sonny Bryan's** (p. 46) on Inwood, which celebrated its century mark in 2010; head to **Wild Salsa** (p. 43) for a tequila tasting before making an evening of a bone-in rib eye and a Texas Cabernet at **Chamberlain's** (p. 177), **The Place at Perry's** (p. 94), **Nick & Sam's** (p. 91)—or any of Dallas's born-and-bred prime beef palaces.

Over to the Wild West: In Fort Worth, 30 miles west of Dallas, you find joys in a hamburger that's hardly changed since grocers at a humble store called **Kincaid's** (p. 204) first started serving them more than 40 years ago. Also in Cowtown, an institution for comfort food is **Paris Coffee Shop** (p. 205), which has cured innumerable ills since the 1930s with its monster biscuits at breakfast, as well as extraordinary chicken-fried steak and chicken and dumplings at lunch. And surely there's no place but downtown Fort Worth where you can walk 5 blocks in any direction and find a fabulous cut of prime beef. From the intersection of Main and 6th—not far from the cattle-drive path cut through town by the legendary Chisholm Trail—you can be seated in front of a flawless steak in seconds at **Del Frisco's** (p. 178), Ruth's Chris, **Reata Restaurant** (p. 197), or **Capital Grille** (p. 81).

Many are the evenings in Fort Worth, however, when you just want to meet over drinks and snacks, and the hottest gathering spot in downtown for just that is **Grace** (p. 189). Chef Blaine Staniford keeps things interesting with a bar menu offering crispy-fried oysters with baby spinach and black pepper butter, burrata mozzarella with grilled rustic bread, and a sophisticated artisan *salumi* and cheese selection. In West 7th, **Waters** (p. 200) serves assorted fresh oysters sent overnight from the world's oceans. Over on Magnolia, Vance Martin has won legions of fans at **Lili's Bistro** (p. 192) with his signature Gorgonzola fries, green chile polenta bites, and the sautéed calamari.

In Fort Worth, your sweet tooth gets love from Chef Gwin Grimes, who uses all-natural, locally sourced ingredients for her stunning shortbread cookies, as well as her cranberry scones, buttery pumpkin bread and cherry oat bars and brownies at **Artisan Baking Company** (p. 205). **J. Rae's** (p. 209) cute storefront on Foch Street keeps everyone

tickled pink with adorable specialty sugar cookies, as well as red velvet, lemon-coconut, and chocolate-chocolate cupcakes, but it's the white chocolate cheesecake that puts you in a real swoon. At **Black Rooster Bakery** (p. 207), the brownies with walnuts, tart lemon squares, pecan pie bars, and old-fashioned cinnamon-pecan coffee cake give you a new understanding of decadent.

Perhaps most telling about the finery found in handmade, downhome eats in Dallas and Fort Worth is the lavish praise from a somewhat unexpected source: In 1998, the James Beard Foundation bestowed its Regional Classics Award on **Joe T. Garcia's Mexican Restaurant** (p. 204) in Fort Worth, and in 2000, the same award went to **Sonny Bryan's Smokehouse** (p. 46) in Dallas. The restaurants have a combined 165 years of experience in making Texans and their bellies mighty happy.

Bear in mind that all descriptions in the following pages are current at press time. The nature of the restaurant business, unfortunately, is subject to momentary change. Good, popular restaurants don't always last, but we aimed to include restaurants that we believe will be around a long while.

Do note also, as you peruse these pages and whet your appetite, this guide is not meant to be an exhaustive laundry list of available food. Selections included in the book represent the best to be found among various cuisine categories and in assorted areas of the Metroplex. Good choices in places to eat abound, and it's impossible to include every worthwhile option. Just trust that the suggestions populating these pages were carefully cultivated.

Whatever path your palate chooses, you enlighten it in unforgettable ways with new discoveries in these premier epicurean cities.

How to Use This Book

By and large, the book is organized according to geographic areas: Neighborhoods are divided into Downtown, which includes also nearby areas of the Arts District, Design District, Market, and Medical Centers; Deep Ellum and East Dallas—and by the latter we mean virtually everything east of North Central Expressway, also called US 75; Uptown, the area reaching northward from Downtown all the way to the Park Cities, including Oak Lawn and Cedar Springs; Oak Cliff, the section of town just south and a smidge west of Downtown; Park Cities, the area encompassing Highland Park and University Park; North Dallas, which includes Preston Hollow, Far North Dallas, Addison, Irving, Frisco, Plano, Richardson, and McKinney; and Fort Worth and its suburbs, including Arlington, Colleyville, Grapevine, Haltom City, Keller, Roanoke, and Southlake.

The chapter entries are further arranged according to the following categories:

Foodie Faves

A broadly defined section, this covers everything from hot, chef-driven destinations to the most humble of holes-in-the-wall.

Landmarks

Big D and Fort Worth grew into their food personalities behind the strength of these powerhouses and old-timers.

Specialty Stores, Markets & Producers

Here you'll find our favorite independent markets, boutique shops, ice creameries, coffeehouses, bakeries, and so forth. Where there are cooking schools, these are included, too.

Price Codes

The following system generally determines the pricing, according to the price of a single entree, without any drink, tip, or tax. It's just an estimate.

$	less than $10
$$	$10 to $25
$$$	$25 to $35
$$$$	more than $35

Getting Around

Mass transit is slowly making itself familiar to residents in the Dallas–Fort Worth area. Buses and trains are operated by the Dallas Area Rapid Transit (DART; dart.org; 214-979-1111); the light rail routes carry you all over the Dallas area. DART works with the volunteer-run McKinney Avenue Transit Authority to operate the historic M-Line trolley, which offers free, daily service in Uptown.

In Fort Worth, the bus service, called the T (the-t.com; 817-215-8600), operates routes around town. Connecting downtown Dallas and Fort Worth, the Trinity Railway Express (TRE; trinityrailwayexpress.org) makes stops at Victory Plaza and Union Station in Dallas and at Dallas–Fort Worth (DFW) Airport.

Dallas is encircled by I-635, or the LBJ Freeway, and I-20. The other major highways are US 75 (North Central Expressway, sometimes called the Central Expressway) from the north, US 67 from the southwest, US 80 from the east, and US 175 and I-45 from the southeast, which links to Houston.

There are bicycle rental options in Dallas and Fort Worth, and bike lanes on major streets are becoming more common. But as the area sprawls in a way that mimics Houston and Los Angeles, moving around by car is preferable unless you're limiting yourself to one specific area. Car rentals are abundant for visitors, of course.

Keeping Up with Food News

While it would be terrific if we could just step outside and follow our noses to the next fabulous place to eat, it's a wonderful fact that there are so many good sources available for great foodie information—right at our fingertips.

The abundance of reliable, savvy food reporters, critics, observers, and gossips in our Dallas–Fort Worth midst keeps you well informed. If you're curious about a restaurant you've heard about, wondering what an established restaurant might be doing that's new, or trying to figure out where to find your favorite kind of food, all you have to do is reach for your laptop or smart phone.

Here's a look at the websites, blogs, and publications most likely to share valuable information about great eating in North Texas. You can look for updates on these publications' Facebook pages, too.

360 West Magazine, **360westmagazine.com.** This luxury life-style monthly keeps a close watch on the culinary scene, offering news about restaurants in business for a long while, as well as a look ahead to what's on the horizon. Chef recipes, new gadgets, cookbooks, and trends are showcased, too.

D Magazine, **dmagazine.com.** The slick Dallas monthly always features a few dining reviews. A few times a year, editor Nancy Nichols and her crew offer special dining features, sometimes sussing out the best burgers or desserts or neighborhood favorites. Follow Nancy and her crack dining staff at sidedish.dmagazine.com for daily—and, some-times, hourly—updates.

Dallas Morning News, **dallasnews.com** Dining critic Leslie Brenner dishes up a weekly restaurant review, as do a couple of con-tributors to the newspaper. For a daily dose of what's happening in the food world, read Leslie and her colleagues' reports at eatsblog.dallasnews.com.

The Dallas Observer, **dallasobserver.com.** Critic Scott Reitz brings humor and irreverence to the review process for refreshing change, which is what we want from the alternative weekly. The paper's blog, which is fun to read, is at blogs.dallasobserver.com/cityofate/.

Edible DFW, **ediblecommunities.com/dallasfortworth/.** This community-based publication covers local foods in the Dallas–Fort Worth area. It's a good behind-the-scenes view of people making everything from meats to eggs, cheeses, honey, vegetables, and baked goods. Published quarterly, it's also good for cooks who love new recipes.

Fort Worth Foodie, **fwfoodie.com.** A quarterly magazine in Fort Worth, this publication looks at restaurants, chefs, and food producers in our area. Good ideas for entertaining and cooking are included, as is lovely food photography.

Fort Worth Star-Telegram, **star-telegram.com.** The Friday edition of this daily contains some dining reviews, which you'll find also online at dfw.com. Be sure to watch for restaurant news updates from longtime observer Bud Kennedy in his dfw.com column called Eats Beat, dfw.com/eatsbeat/.

Modern Luxury, **modernluxury.com.** An upscale monthly for the well-heeled consumer, this magazine takes an extensive look at a different restaurant each month. Longtime area critic Mark Stuertz is among the most entertaining writers.

Here's a sampling of the strictly online sources:

Crave DFW, **cravedfw.com.** Anything and everything you wanted to know (and possibly didn't) is posted on this busy site.

Culture Map Dallas, **dallas.culturemap.com.** Judicious and ambitious, this crew delves into all corners of the DFW food and drink world. The reading is always enlightening.

Eater Dallas, dallas.eater.com. The Dallas–Fort Worth edition of the national blog does a credible job of keeping up with what to eat, and what the critics around the area are saying. It's often a good stop to find a roundup of information.

Escape Hatch Dallas, escapehatchdallas.com. Bon vivant Mike Hiller, a far-wandering travel scribe, reports on Dallas-area food interests that he finds rewarding.

Urban Daddy, urbandaddy.com/home/dal. If it's stylish or otherwise intriguing, Urban Daddy will give it a good look and put its flair on the reporting.

Foodie Festivals & Events

Each month brings new ways to celebrate the eating culture in the Dallas–Fort Worth area. Frequently, there are high-quality food celebrations that are one-off in nature. For news on those, you'll need to keep your eyes on the food blogs (see above) for the most up-to-date information.

Here are some of the best culinary gatherings that happen each year. Note that a few of them may move from one month to another in a given year.

January

ZestFest, zestfest2011.com. Fashioned for foodies who like it hot, this weekend of fiery foods takes place at the beautiful Irving Convention Center. Cooking demos by celebrity chefs, music performances, interactive contests, and thousands of food samples are on tap.

February

Empty Bowls, tafb.org. A fund-raiser for Fort Worth area food banks, this benefit sells out annually. When you buy your ticket, you get a locally handcrafted bowl (to keep), and you enjoy excellent soups, breads, and desserts made by local restaurants. This event is held at Amon G. Carter Jr. Exhibits Hall in the Will Rogers Memorial Center, Fort Worth.

March

Empty Bowls, ntfb.org. This Dallas fund-raiser benefits local food banks, and like its Fort Worth counterpart, it sells out annually. In exchange for your ticket purchase, you get a handcrafted bowl (to keep) created by a local artist, and you enjoy excellent soups, breads, and desserts made by local restaurants. The Dallas event is held at the Meyerson Symphony Center.

Fort Worth Food + Wine Festival, fortworthfoodandwine festival.com. Fort Worth's first cuisine-centric festival is held citywide at restaurants, markets, and public spaces, starring chefs, winemakers, brewers, and more. More than 20 events make this a weekend-long event.

Savor Dallas, savordallas.com. Staged at venues across Dallas and Irving, this taste-a-thon covering one weekend lets you eat and drink anything and everything delicious to be found in Dallas County.

A Weekend Escape In Grapevine

A significant growth spurt in this busy burg—a growing, historic town right next to DFW Airport, now packed with galleries, live entertainment venues, and winery tasting rooms—means you now need a weekend escape to drink in all the fun Grapevine serves.

You could spend all your time just eating: All along Main Street, find homegrown restaurants and bistros. Claim a bar stool or a cozy two-top at the warm, welcoming **Into the Glass** (322 S. *Main St.*, *76051*; *817-422-1969*; *intotheglass.com*), tucked into one of the shotgun spaces along vintage Main Street. Among the more innovative dishes served in Grapevine, the brie nachos with cranberry salsa and the beef tenderloin with a side of Gorgonzola grits are most likely to start a riot. You can wash those down with any of 80 wines by the glass or bottle, typically boutique-style selections from Europe, South America, and the West Coast. At **Farina's Winery & Café** (420 *S. Main St.*, *76051*; *817-442-9095*; *farinaswinery* *.homestead.com*), start with a plate of assorted cheeses, grapes, tapenade, and grilled garlic bread, followed with chicken Marsala, baked white fish in a roasted garlic-lime sauce, or shrimp scampi, served up with wines crafted by the owners. New to Grapevine, at the south end of downtown, **Winewood** (1265 *S. Main St.*, *76051*; *817-421-0200*; *thewinewood.com*) provides a sleek, wood-and-stone setting in which to linger over a starter of seared ahi tuna on wonton chips in mango vinaigrette, followed by a plate of hickory-grilled salmon swabbed with poblano cream sauce. Look for live music in the evening at all three restaurants.

Sip the afternoon and evening away, if you like. As its name suggests, Grapevine's connection to the wine business is significant, thanks to the presence of eight wineries in town. A delight especially in temperate months, the tasting room at **La Buena Vida Vineyards** *(416 E. College St., 76051; 817-481-9463; labuenavida .com)* spills out onto an expansive stone patio that's soothing with fountains and shaded by vine-laced arbors, providing a lovely place to sip wines and listen to live music. At **D'Vine Wine** of Grapevine *(409 S. Main St., 76051; 817-329-1011; grapevine.dvinewineusa .com)*, right in the middle of the vintage thoroughfare, wine tastings happen at a very busy, convivial bar through the day and into the early evening. Live music is staged on weekends. This is a place to bottle wine with custom labels for birthday parties, family gifts and business groups. Between all that eating and drinking, check out **Grapevine Mills** *(3000 Grapevine Mills Parkway, 76051; 972-539-9386; visitsealife.com/grapevine)*, an outlet mall that's also home to Sea Life, a 45,000-square-foot, walk-through aquarium stocked with plenty of scary sharks and a mesmerizing octopus named Ringo. Your days can easily fill with leisurely moseying between art galleries, starting with **Morgan Dane** *(701 S. Main St., #101, 76051; 817-488-6822; morgandaneartgallery.com)*, home to paintings, pottery, and sculpture by local artists; and ending with a look at the painstakingly curated collection in **Great American West Gallery** *(332 S. Main St., 76051; 817-416-2600; greatamericanwestgallery .com)*, a new, impressive space within a Victorian bank building and possibly the only gallery in Texas dedicated solely to Western art. Be sure to leave ample time to craft your own handblown glass art piece at **Vetro Glassblowing Studio & Gallery** *(701 S. Main St., #103, 76051; 817-251-1668; vetroartglass.com)*.

April

Central Market's Passport, centralmarket.com. Each year, **Central Market** (p. 72) chooses a different country to explore for a fortnight of cooking classes, tastings, demonstrations, parties, and more. Chefs and winemakers representing the designated country are flown in for special gatherings for the public. In past years, Spain, France, and Brazil have been honored. Fun for all ages is guaranteed.

Chocolate Fest, chocolatefestgrapevine .com. A two-day party honoring any and all things chocolate: there's a wine-and-chocolate event one evening, as well as an art show with chocolate tastings to fill an afternoon.

May

Dallas Wine & Food Festival, dallaswinefest.com. Staged at various venues around Dallas, this festival focuses on local and national culinary talent as well as award-winning wines.

Taste Addison, addisontexas.net. For three days, foodies will enjoy goodies from more than 60 Addison restaurants that will be serving generous samplings of their menus at reduced prices. On the side, there's national musical entertainment, celebrity chef demonstrations, and wine-tasting seminars, carnival rides, midway games, award-winning children's entertainment, and more. Held in Addison Circle.

June

Beastro, fortworthzoo.org. To raise money to support the Fort Worth Zoo's educational programs, this food-focused party provides supporters with some of the best appetizers, entrees, and desserts in town. There are open bars throughout the park, with live entertainment on tap, too.

July

Bastille on Bishop, gooakcliff.org. The Bishop Arts District speaks with a French accent for one evening, with crepe stands, a mussels cooking competition among area chefs, plenty of French wine, music, games, and more.

Taste of Dallas, tasteofdallas.org. This party, more than 30-plus years strong, benefits the American Heart Association, among other charities. For a filling weekend, there are cooking demos, culinary marketplace, a grand tasting, restaurant kiosks, kids' food events, art, and music. It happens at Fair Park.

August

Restaurant Week, krld.com. To liven up an otherwise quiet time in the restaurant world, KRLD Radio and Central Market team up to stage Restaurant Week in more than 100 restaurants across the DFW area, all to benefit local food banks and a children's home. You get a three-course meal for $35 at any of the renowned restaurants, representing a significant savings if you dined at any of them any other time. Some restaurants participate in a four-course offering for just a few dollars more, and some restaurants extend the Restaurant Week offering through much of the month of August, too. Reservations are absolutely necessary, well in advance.

Food Trucks

The Dallas–Fort Worth food truck scene became official in late spring 2011. Earlier in the year, food trailers began to operate in Fort Worth, hoping to serve the crowds coming to the Metroplex for the 2011 Super Bowl. Vague city regulations across Tarrant County (where Cowboys Stadium, host to the big game, is located) put a damper on expectations, and most of those businesses did not survive the winter. A few months later, Dallas began to amend city policies so that trucks could park for longer than 30 minutes in any one location—on the condition that trucks be larger than a trailer and operate within very specific health codes.

The Dallas food truck scene exploded in late August 2011 when Sigel's Liquor Store on Greenville Avenue hosted the first food truck festival. Ten trucks opened at 4 p.m., and by the end of the night 2,000 people had visited the location; the food trucks had arrived!

Whether you're seeking Asian fusion or gourmet hot dogs, creative cupcakes or a gluten-free meal, one of the DFW trucks has what you are craving. Gastro Bomber, a Fort Worth–based truck, serves pub style food with a side of comfort, bringing "Sheppard Pie Balls," bacon wrapped tater tots (affectionately named "Pig's Toes"), and "Irish Nachos" to the streets. Lucky Ducky Dogs is taking hot dogs outside the comfort zone with dogs made from duck, alligator, and black beans. Rockstar Bakeshop gets creative with their rock music–named whoopee pies with menu items like "Champagne Supernova" (strawberry champagne cake and champagne buttercream frosting) and "The Presley" (vanilla cake, marshmallow frosting, peanut frosting, and banana chips).

How does the DFW truck scene compare to Austin's, which is huge? Austin's trailers park in one place, usually all the time. In comparison, the trucks in Dallas are mobile, operating at different locations daily, usually in one location for lunch and one for dinner. (Fort Worth's often work the same way.) The Dallas trucks, by law, must spend the night at a registered commissary. Klyde Warren Park in downtown Dallas has become a daily stop for several trucks, and the Truck Yard near downtown at 5624 Sears Street typically hosts three trucks daily. Fort Worth boasts two parks where the trucks rotate each day at lunch and dinner, Fort Worth Food Truck Park near West 7th Street and Clear Fork Food Truck Park in the university area operating year-round. On weekdays at lunchtime, Fort Worth's Thistle Hill, a historic home in the hospital district, immediately south of downtown, hosts four or five trucks. As the Metroplex is so large and trucks have fans in all areas, the trucks will continue to roam in order to serve customers.

While Dallas and Fort Worth city regulations have stabilized, most suburbs continue to evaluate and develop their policies on how the food trucks can best suit their city culture. The truck owners, in order to operate in each city, have to get permits and comply with a litany of regulations. Watch for new parks in places like Denton, Plano, Arlington, North Richland Hills, and Bedford.

Food truck owners run a complex business. The operators work as hostess, cook, busboy, manager, and more. Successful trucks typically have a business plan before rolling out, and most of the best usually have two or more owners who share duties, with someone focused on marketing and locations and someone else handling inventory. As the business is weather-dependent, smart owners have enough in savings to get through cold, rainy winters and, more important, hot summers when no one wants to be outside.

Above all, successful trucks have great food. In cities like Dallas and Fort Worth where customers have access to good food near their homes or businesses, a mediocre menu on a food truck won't sell. As with any business, high quality food and good customer service keep the clientele loyal.

Stephanie Hawkes blogs about everything food truck on DFW Food Truck Foodie. *Follow her posts and keep track of food truck locations and menus at dfwfoodtruckfoodie.com, facebook.com/dfwfoodtruck foodie, and Twitter: @dfwtruckfoodie.*

September

State Fair of Texas, bigtex.com. Starting in later September and continuing well into October, the largest state fair in the nation offers everything you'd expect, from rodeos to horse shows to myriad music and dance events. But every single day, there's a different cooking competition for nonprofessionals. One day it's breads, then it's chocolate, followed by eggs, pasta, Tex-Mex, Italian, cake, pies, and so forth. Ribbons and bragging rights are awarded. Next door to the Culinary Arts Kitchen, there's usually a celebrity-chef event underway, starring noted chefs from the area, offering cooking demonstrations.

October

Traders Village BBQ Cook-Off, Traders Village, 2602 Mayfield Rd., Grand Prairie; 972-647-2331; tradersvillage.com. Among the larger events of its kind in the state, this contest attracts 100 cookers preparing more than 600 items for judges to sample. The prize money is in the thousands, bringing in competitors from around the country.

November

Greek Festival, St. Demetrios Greek Orthodox Church, 2020 NW 21st St., Fort Worth; fortworthgreekfestival.com. For one weekend, there's a giant lunch and dinner opportunity for those who love Greek food. Enjoy spanakopita, souvlaki, Athenian chicken, moussaka, leg of lamb, gyros, and much, much more. There are pastries you can take home, too. Plenty of music and dancing are served up as well.

December

Meat Fight, meatfight.com. What started as a backyard contest between friendly chefs has grown into an event for anyone who loves grilled and smoked meats. Dozens of Dallas and Fort Worth chefs compete for best pitmaster honors in making brisket, pulled pork, sausage, and more categories. Held in Deep Ellum, the fun benefits the Multiple Sclerosis Society.

Downtown Dallas & Surrounding Districts

Time once was downtown Dallas hummed with energy and commerce. Skyscrapers shot upward in the earlier 20th century, and the banking center of the Southwest became a giant in the business world. Exciting hotels downtown included the Adolphus, built by beer baron Adolph Busch as his Texas home. Private clubs offered the finest dining in Dallas, as the city was "dry" for many years, and affluent diners had to buy memberships at exclusive clubs—these included the Petroleum Club, Lancers Club, Cipango Club, and numerous others—if they wanted a cocktail before dinner or a fine imported wine with their meals.

Neiman Marcus began its life in downtown Dallas, and Helen Corbitt put the world-renowned retailer on the culinary map with her cooking at the famed Zodiac Room. Everyone who was anyone dined at the Zodiac, and bragged loudly about it. Other fine-dining establishments opened in downtown hotels—the Baker and the Statler Hilton were among the more popular options—and the occasional fancy, independent restaurant, such as Brennan's of New Orleans, kept people in the downtown-dining mindset. But as was the situation across the country, the downtown area fell into a lull when suburbs began to boom in the 1960s. Finding a good place to eat downtown, aside from those private clubs, became difficult for many years.

That trend was reversed, fortunately, in the 1990s, and excellent eating has become easy to find in downtown and the immediate environs ever since. Today your downtown dining options run the gamut from bacon-and-egg cafes and gastropubs to exceptionally upscale destinations, and everything in between. And for residents of downtown, most of whom live in condos and apartments in fabulously renovated office buildings and former department stores, there exist plentiful choices on downtown's streets and in adjacent areas.

The nearby dining districts found within this chapter also include the Dallas Arts District, which sits on the northeast corner of downtown and is home to multiple art museums and performing arts venues; the Design District, on the northwest corner of downtown, where the city's wealth of art galleries, interior design businesses and finer antiques dealers sit; and, also at the northwest corner of downtown, the vast Dallas medical quarter, home to some of the nation's leading medical research and treatment facilities, and the adjacent market center, a collection of apparel, home interiors, and gift-market halls that bring in commerce from around the world on a never-ending schedule.

Foodie Faves

Avila's, 4714 Maple Ave., Dallas 75219; (214) 520-2700; avilasrestaurant.com; Mexican; $$. Behind an exterior that's easy to overlook, good recipes are at work. Starting with a relatively thick, slightly nubby salsa blending tomato and jalapeños, served with crisp corn tortilla chips, it's easy to move along to a bowl of pozole, a stew-like hominy-chicken blend in a chile-fired stock, served with sides of chopped radish, white onion, jalapeños, and finely shredded cabbage. Mole poblano–covered enchiladas consist of tender corn tortillas

THE EVOLUTION OF DALLAS BARBECUE

Over a century ago, Elias Bryan set up a barbecue stand in Dallas, but it took until 1953 for his grandson Sonny to open his eponymous barbecue joint on Inwood Road. **Sonny Bryan's Smokehouse** (p. 46) soon came to define barbecue in Dallas. A sauce-drenched chopped beef sandwich alongside a heap of bracelet-sized onion rings, enjoyed while hunched over one of the ancient school desks inside the original Sonny Bryan's, has become a rite of passage for those new to Dallas and to countless famous visitors.

While Sonny Bryan's was the definition of Dallas barbecue to many, it's another Dallas joint, Dickey's, that may define what Texas barbecue is to those beyond the borders of the Lone Star State. With hundreds of locations in forty-three states, much of the country may get their first bite of smoked brisket from a Dickey's location, the first of which is still operating on the corner of Henderson and Central Expressway, where it opened in 1941. For decades Dallas's barbecue scene was happy to live in a sauce-laden obscurity, compared to the famous joints in Central Texas. Those with big names were satisfied to keep resting on their reputations rather than push for excellence in their smoked meats. While weekend journeys to barbecue meccas like Lockhart and Taylor have been commonplace, no one viewed Dallas as a destination for barbecue—that is until the opening of **Pecan Lodge** (p. 39) and Meshack's in 2009 and **Lockhart Smokehouse** (p. 116) in 2011.

Both Meshack's and Pecan Lodge arrived on the scene without fanfare. It took several months for visitors to discover that Meshack's was smoking some excellent brisket and some of the area's best ribs. Four years later, they are still selling out of meat every day that they're open. Pecan Lodge went from a small joint with a loyal following to instant stardom and hour-long lines after a trip from Guy Fieri and his show *Diners, Drive-Ins and Dives*. It is now the city's most popular barbecue joint on the four days per week that it's open. The brisket, smoked over mesquite, is lusciously fatty, tender, and smoky. Homemade sausage is a menu staple, while the highly sought-after beef ribs (not too common in these parts) sell out quickly. Get in line early.

Lockhart Smokehouse is the destination for true Central Texas-style eating. Meat is ordered by the pound and served on butcher paper. Sauce and sides are secondary while the oak-smoked brisket and shoulder clod take top billing along with sausage from the legendary Kreuz Market in Lockhart, Texas. It's here that you'll find some under-represented cuts like smoked pork chops and mammoth beef short ribs as well as daily specials that range from cabrito and lamb, and even to whole hog, on occasion.

No dining genre in Dallas would be complete without an upscale version, even when talking barbecue. White tablecloths adorn the tables at **Smoke** (p. 122) in West Dallas, but the walls are hung with campy, 1970s family portraits, and thankfully, you'll still smell like smoke when you leave. A wider menu from Smoke chef Tim Byres features veal sweetbreads and foie gras, along with the more familiar brisket and ribs. His homemade sausages alone are worth the trip, but don't let your table go without a Big Rib. It's a massive beef short rib smoked to meltingly tender and served with the popular hominy casserole.

After decades of being associated with a couple of legends that haven't aged very well, Dallas is now brimming with quality barbecue options. Thanks to Pecan Lodge and others, any new joints in Dallas will have plenty to live up to.

Daniel Vaughn, aka The BBQ Snob, started his journey as a barbecue expert with his blog, Full Custom Gospel BBQ. *Now the barbecue editor for* Texas Monthly *magazine, he is also the author of* The Prophets of Smoked Meat: A Journey Through Texas Barbecue, *a 2013 release from Anthony Bourdain's new imprint, Ecco.*

filled with shredded chicken and green chile beneath a deep brown blanket of slightly sweet velvet, and stout tamales, served as a trio, are packed with tender pork chunks inside lush masa jackets. Try shrimp enchiladas with black beans on the side. Be prepared to wait for a table at peak hours, when the blue-hued interior hung with heavy wood- and tin-framed mirrors can be packed.

The Café at the Perot Museum, 2201 N. Field St., Dallas 75201; (214) 428-5555; perotmuseum.org; American; $$. Wolfgang Puck's catering division pops up frequently in the museum world, and the extraordinary new Perot Museum of Nature & Science claims the more impressive of these. Because the museum is so very high profile (it opened in December 2012), this particular Puck cafe has ramped up the offerings. You find local ingredients in the pizzas, pastas, sandwiches, soups, freshly prepared burgers, hot dogs, and other goodies. Check out the Grab & Go section, which includes sushi among its options. The cafe sits just off the museum lobby, with a magnificent view of the plaza outside.

Cafe des Artistes, 1722 Routh St., Dallas 75201; (214) 217-6888; cafedadallas .com/wp/; French; $$. Opened in fall 2012 in 1 Arts Plaza in the Dallas Arts District, the brasserie from Dallas's large Lombardi restaurant group reminds us a little of Balthazar in New York's SoHo, only with a newer feel. There's a sense of the classic European style, with marble-top tables, brass chandeliers, velvet draperies, and cushy red mohair banquettes, along with cafe tables on the sidewalk that look identical to those all over Paris. Quickly, word spread that this was a great place for dinner after the symphony or opera, as the restaurant is a few steps away from the Meyerson Symphony Center, Winspear Opera House, and Wyly Theatre. Even better, many of the performers from those venues are finding the late-night spot a good place to hang, even gathering around the piano for impromptu shows. Our favorite time to go is Sunday brunch, when the short rib hash, topped with poached eggs, and the salmon Benedict go down so very easy with Bloody Marys, with beignets for dessert. Other preferred dishes so far include *moules frites,* sautéed prawns in garlic and lemon with red chile flakes, and lobster risotto. Take someone special.

The Cedars Social, 1326 S. Lamar St., Dallas 75215; (214) 928-7700; thecedarssocial.com; American; $$. When craft cocktails became the rage, this innovative, stylized midcentury-modernesque spot in the newly revived South Lamar district just south of downtown proper capitalized on the trend—and immediately set the bar pretty high. While much of the attraction remains the bar scene, the food keeps pace in notable ways, never risking the status of afterthought. A case in point is a green salad that brings together leafy goodness from local farmer Tom Spicer, burrata cheese, heirloom tomatoes, and a dressing of balsamic reduction with basil oil; atop that, you can add hanger steak or a crab cake, among other options. Small, sharable plates include truffle mac and cheese, salmon tartare with roasted salsa, short rib tacos, and Kobe meatballs. For something on the big side, you can pick between items like Berkshire pork rack with cassoulet or Akaushi strip loin with caramelized shallots. Oh, and those drinks? A Texas Fizz blends gin, freshly squeezed orange juice, lemon juice, confectioners' sugar, and club soda; and an Alive & Well combines vodka, lemon verbena vermouth, fresh ginger, and club soda. That doesn't happen everywhere.

Cook Hall, 2440 Victory Park Ln., Dallas 75219; cookhalldallas .com; Gastropub; $$. Opened in late 2012 in the W Dallas Victory Hotel, replacing Craft, this warm and inviting spot in an otherwise uber-modern and rather austere hotel brings together good things in food and drink. At the bar, you can build your own drink for the cost of the base alcohol, plus $3 for a do-it-yourself kit. You'll see lots of recipes for drinks, too, to give you inspiration. Among goodies to enjoy with libations, pork belly sliders appease the meat lover, with juicy bacon on crusty buns, which are just as sumptuous as they sound. Other sharing dishes, which are the focus of Cook Hall, include fried oyster sandwich, crispy duck tacos, Welsh rarebit with fried egg, and pasta with braised short ribs. That's not all: West Coast oysters, charcuterie, chicken soup, and shellfish stew are also stars on the gastropub menu. In all, it's a hangout, but with lots of style.

Dallas Chop House, 100717 Main St., Dallas 75201; (214) 736-7300; dallaschophouse.com; Steak House; $$$$. Found on the ground floor of a bank building that was designed by the legendary Philip

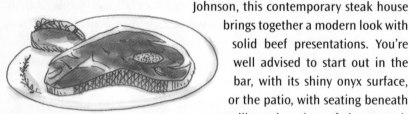

Johnson, this contemporary steak house brings together a modern look with solid beef presentations. You're well advised to start out in the bar, with its shiny onyx surface, or the patio, with seating beneath a trellis and a view of downtown's Main Street Garden. Starters to consider include the grilled shrimp over jalapeño grits with an avocado relish; tenderloin steak tartare; beef carpaccio; and crispy fried sweetbreads with a chipotle cilantro sauce. The filet mignon comes in two sizes, as does the rib eye, and you can get that steak adorned with assorted treatments, including a Cajun crawfish shrimp sauce; a sharp mustard au poivre; classics like béarnaise or hollandaise; or Maytag blue butter. When its fancy appeal may have been a bit intimidating to people reacting to a tough economy, the savvy restaurant owners began implementing kinder, gentler approaches to dining, including a four-course tasting menu for $45; and prime rib specials on the weekend.

El Fenix, 1601 McKinney Ave., Dallas 75202; (214) 747-1121; elfenix.com; Mexican; $–$$. More than a few Dallasites might raise an eyebrow at seeing El Fenix included in a book that proclaims to serve the discerning diner in Big D. But three excellent reasons exist to defend its inclusion: First, it's the restaurant credited with creating the much-loved combination plate, long a standard at all Tex-Mex restaurants; next, it's absolutely packed every day at lunch; and finally, it's been around since 1918—which is saying quite a lot. The cavernous restaurant exhibits bright murals and colorful detail, offers quick and efficient service, and serves solid, dependable Tex-Mex specialties. Warm tortilla chips are super light and crisp, brought in baskets with bowls of thin, tomato-based salsa. Favorite plates include pairings of enchiladas, tacos, tamales, chalupas, Spanish rice, and refried beans. One smaller plate with a lot of flavor is the half order of deluxe nachos: crisp tortilla chips topped with beans, cheese, fajita chicken or beef. and jalapeño slices. Find the restaurant especially convenient to the new Perot Musuem of Nature & Science.

The French Room, 1321 Commerce St., Dallas 75201; (214) 742-8200; hoteladolphus.com/dining; French; $$$$. Inside the elegant Adolphus Hotel, smack in the middle of downtown proper, the French Room's setting makes you feel as though you've landed in a pre-French Revolution period movie. Cherubs painted on the sky blue ceiling, floating amongst billowy clouds, overlook the dining room, which is girded with much baroque detail, as is the Adolphus as a whole. Exceptionally elegant, this has been the scene of many a celebration, engagement, and VIP entertaining. Updated seasonally, the menu typically offers appetizers like house-smoked salmon, sautéed escargot in truffle celery root cream, seared ahi tuna and foie gras torchon, lemon-butter-poached lobster, and a selection of caviars—if you want a tasting, that's $475 per 90 grams' worth. Mains include wild striped bass over swiss chard with lobster, Nova Scotia halibut marinated in coconut-miso, duck breast with pear tart, and Colorado rack of lamb with sweet garlic potato gnocchi. The French Room is known for its soufflés, but dessert might also include chocolate-hazelnut crunch torte with salted caramel ice cream.

FT33, 1617 Hi Line Dr., Dallas 75207; (214) 741-2629; ft33dallas .com; American; $$$. Perhaps the most ballyhooed of all Dallas openings in 2012, a year of plentiful restaurant debuts, this creation in the newly hot Design District brings "season-inspired modern cuisine" to the fore. Owner-chef Matt McCallister fiddles around with his menu every day, but guests quickly came to expect an innovative presentation of locally procured ingredients with each minute menu tweak. Typical among beginnings is the pork jowl plate, ample slices of juicy bacon laced with black truffle and sprinkled lightly with caraway crumble, propped up next to a creamed parsnip fluff, with a slick of fermented mango crossing through. An arrangement of roasted turnip, radish, and carrot over an onion *sofrito* and wheat berries with a sprinkling of micro herbs along the edges satisfies the vegetable freak. Among the interesting fish dishes is a black fin snapper, a smooth, light fillet settled into an earthy ham broth and decorated with red peas and a touch of fennel. A plate of lamb stars a cut of lamb breast and a thick, very pink rib from a rack, served over plump barley with a tart yogurt sauce and a sweetish carrot puree. A smartly crafted wine list and a menu of specialty cocktails rounds out an experience enjoyed in a dapper setting; this a very contemporary interior blending warmth and industrial notes through use of reclaimed barn wood, concrete, steel, marble, oil drum lids, birch tables, and granite.

Fuel City Tacos, 801 S. Riverfront Blvd., Dallas 75207; (214) 426-0011; fuelcitywash.com; Mexican; $. Yes, this is a truck stop—but unlike any you've ever experienced. It's also a combination convenience store, drive-through beer shop, and killer taco stand. Orders are placed at the taco-stand window at the northern end of the store, and whether you pull up at 3 a.m. or 3 p.m., you'll find folks sitting in their cars, gobbling from little carryout boxes. Tops is the picadillo, ground beef with bits of potato seasoned with a dab of garlic and a lot of black pepper. It's tucked into a double layer of small white-corn tortillas and topped with chopped onion and cilantro. A wedge of Mexican lime comes on the side. The tiny container of green chile salsa is both superfluous and irresistible. (It goes just as well on the amazingly tender beef fajita taco, another good option.)

Grab cold drinks from the cooler inside—a Mexican Coke, made with real cane sugar, or a super-fizzy Topo Chico sparkling water hits the spot. Sitting in the shadows of downtown among strip clubs and liquor stores, Fuel City isn't in the prettiest part of Dallas, but it draws a cross section of Dallas's population. The patio on the north side of the building seats 70 at picnic tables.

The Greek, 1722 Routh St., Dallas 75201; (214) 999-1311; thegreekonearts.com; Greek; $$. New in late 2012 to 1 Arts Plaza, this casual gathering place comes from the owners of Ziziki's (p. 101), a long-time popular destination dining spot in Travis Walk. The Greek puts a little twist on favorite items, such as the burger, which is retooled as smashed lamb meatballs on pita. Early menu hits also include flatbreads, sharable plates of spreads (artichoke hummus—yum), as well as boards laden with myriad meats or cheeses, with olives, Dijon, fig jam–stuffed peppers, and breads. Mixologist Jason Kosmas has crafted a cool drinks menu, too, featuring delights like the Constantinople, blending Metaxa, chai vermouth, and pomegranate juice. This cool joint is perfect for pretheater; it's just a block down from the AT&T Performing Arts Center.

Herrera's Café, 4024 Maple Ave., Dallas 75219; (214) 528-9644; herrerascafe.com; Mexican; $–$$. The incarnations of Herrera's may be as numerous as the generations that have become addicted to its grassroots Tex-Mex goodness. This is not fancy food, not prescribed for heart-healthy diets, and probably not for the otherwise faint of heart. Lots of gooey, melted cheese characterizes many a dish, the majority of which fall into the "flat food" category: crispy tacos, enchiladas, tamales, rice, and beans. There are burritos, too, as well as chiles rellenos, egg dishes, and fajitas. Daily specials start at $4.99. From a mind-boggling menu, there are all-day breakfast plates, steak topped with an enchilada, and more than 35 combination plates, including the stunning Rupert Special, a plate of two cheese enchiladas, one guacamole tostada, 1 bean tostada, and rice and beans. Hangover remedies include Crazy Nachos, as well as *menudo*. A good selection of Mexican and domestic beers is available, as are margaritas—with happy hour prices including a $4 frozen margarita in the late afternoon on weekdays.

Lee Harvey's, 1807 Gould St., Dallas 75215; (214) 428-1555; leeharveys.com; Bar/Burgers; $. If you love the dive bar with a killer hamburger, and you need something different from **Adair's** (p. 68), you'll want to find Lee Harvey's. It's hidden away just south of downtown proper, not far from South Lamar, in a rundown neighborhood that's showing signs of hipster-driven recovery. Upon approach, you'll think we're crazy to recommend what appears to be a beat-up house as a place to eat. Inside, you find you've stepped into a 1960s time warp, with period beer signs and an old-fashioned bar where you can belly up for a super cold can of Bud or Pabst Blue Ribbon—or most any kind of bottle beer you'd like. The burgers, BLTs, and grilled cheese sandwiches are the real reason for seeking out this locals' haunt, though; cooked to order on an age-seasoned griddle, these cholesterol nightmares will give your taste buds unmitigated comfort—and ample guilt, if you're a waistline watcher.

Maple & Motor, 4810 Maple Ave., Dallas 75219; (214) 522-4400; **Burgers; $–$$.** How rapidly this small joint tucked away between the market/medical district and Love Field rose from upstart to bona fide contender for Dallas's best burger. One bite and you're sure the griddle must have generations of experience behind it. Go for broke and get the really dolled-up cheeseburger, a freshly fashioned, flavorful patty topped with thick, crunchy bacon, grilled jalapeño slices, and fried egg, cradled by an expertly grilled bun, which will wow you as no burger has in years. The counter staff may advise you to have this bad boy cut in half for easier handling. Though it sounds like way too much is going on in this burger, you'll be able to taste the individual components, each rich in its own distinction. Other items deserve notice as well: the loaded Tater Tots, smothered in cheese and chopped bacon, were likened to having "the essence of the baby Jesus in them" by one devout patron; and onion rings bear crunchy, seasoned jackets around the sweet white vegetable ring. Campy vintage beers, such as Schlitz and Pabst Blue Ribbon, round out a full selection of brews, and fountain drinks include root beer and orange sodas made down in Dublin, Texas. Avoid the peak noon hour, when crowds overwhelm this tiny space. Better to try for a late lunch or anytime during the evening hours.

The Meddlesome Moth, 1621 Oak Lawn Ave., Dallas 75207; (214) 628-7900; mothinthe.net; Gastropub; $$. Pioneering the trend of dining and drinking in the Design District, the Moth serves 40 draught beers, 2 live ales, and more than 80 bottled beers. The true beer geek will love the Moth's motto: If you've seen it in a commercial, we don't serve it. The food's certainly a cut above most places specializing in beer, too, as is the gastropub trend, of course. Salads, for instance, include a cobb made with prosciutto, roasted chicken, and other goodies; and a crab and shrimp chop. There's a list of mussels preparations, including Thai, Catalan, and Diablo; and potpies in variations like steak and mushroom or rabbit. Plates for sharing range

 from fried sweetbreads, steak tartare, and shrimp and grits, to roasted quail, pâté, and baby back ribs. Not into meats? Vegetable plates include zucchini chips, fried tofu, and toasted mushrooms farro. Each menu item is noted with the perfect beer pairing, too. But back to the brews: If you can't decide what to drink, definitely opt for the flights, each including five 5-ounce pours or special selections that might include Texas, Europe, Malt of the Eat, Captain Keith, Hop Head, and Belgian. The interior of the Moth is worth the trip alone: The stained-glass windows are rescued from the original Hard Rock Cafe in Dallas, which was a landmark; and the place itself is just sophisticated in ways that you don't expect a beer place to be. When you realize the owner is Shannon Wynne, whose Flying Saucer concept has been such a hit for years, you get why the Moth is special.

Nasher Cafe by Wolfgang Puck, Nasher Sculpture Center, 2001 Flora St., Dallas 75201; (214) 242-5118; nashersculpturecenter .org; American; $–$$. This cafe makes a lot of sense for people who want to spend a lazy afternoon roaming the extraordinary collection

PRESERVING A PIECE OF HISTORY

When Luna Tortillas—in the beautiful 1938 building on the north side of downtown—closed, everyone fond of the architecture in this cool old structure worried what might become of it. Whereas Dallas doesn't tear down its vintage buildings as much as it once did, there was still concern that the industrial space wouldn't go to good use. Turns out, fears were unfounded, as heritage-minded restaurateurs made sure the building enjoyed TLC and brought in great food, besides. Found next door to the Perot Museum of Nature & Science, Meso Maya *(1611 McKinney Ave., Dallas 75202; 214-484-6555; mesomaya.com; Mexican; $$)* and its adjacent street-side taqueria called La Ventana, opened in late 2012. Adding wrought iron sconces, carved wooden accents, and an exterior wall with a 60-foot-long colorful, hand-painted mural featuring a beautiful señorita and a Mexican landscape, Meso Maya has a menu starring native Mexican ingredients, such as maize, cacao, chiles, agave, squash, chayote, nopales, plantains, and regional rice. Among starters, the *queso fundido* blends Mexican cheeses with green poblano chile strips, caramelized onion, spinach, and mushrooms into a gooey pool (it's really, really sinfully good) that you pull by the forkful into handmade corn tortillas. Light and flavorful, the *sopa de lima* is a light chicken broth in which float bits of avocado, chayote (squash), melted Chihuahua cheese, cilantro, and a scattering of tortilla strips. Favorite entrees include beef brisket tacos; shrimp tacos; tortas—that's the big Mexican hoagie—filled with either roasted pork with pickled onions and black beans or fire-roasted chicken, bacon, Chihuahua cheese, avocado, and tomato; and pan-roasted striped bass with squash, red cabbage, and mushrooms atop a bed of rice with mango relish garnish. Do leave room for buttermilk crepes filled with caramelized plantains, goat-milk caramel, and pecans, with vanilla-bean ice cream on top. Other location: 11909 Preston Rd., Dallas 75230.

of contemporary sculpture at this exquisite indoor-outdoor museum. You're not going to find the city's most innovative cuisine here by any means, but it will keep you fueled and from having to leave in search of sustenance. An Italian turkey sandwich comes topped with provolone, sundried-tomato pesto aioli, lettuce, and tomato, and the portobello burger layers mushroom with smoked Gouda, caramelized red and yellow bell peppers, and garlic-herb aioli on challah, while the salad offerings include one mixing green beans with chickpeas and red beans, crumbled feta, and toasted pine nuts over baby greens, and one with roasted red and green grapes, sliced pears, veggies, and toasted hazelnuts. You can find chips, cookies, and soups here, as well. Note that the cafe is open only from 11 a.m. until 4 p.m.

Oak, **1628 Oak Lawn Ave, Dallas 75207; (214) 712-9700; oakdallas .com; American/Upscale; $$$–$$$$.** One of the hottest tables in town, dinner at Oak has helped elevate the Design District to a happening evening neighborhood. The kitchen's talented team delivers a list of surprising jewels on your plate. Runaway hits include the starter dish of Moroccan octopus, tender and sliced and arranged with sumptuous pieces of pork jowl, bright and crisp radish slices, cool cilantro, and a ripple of zippy aji chile sauce; and gnocchi decorated with lamb sweetbreads and cauliflower. Mains to fall in love with include the beef cheek with quark spaetzle, carrots, and cipollinis in a red-wine braise; and Scottish salmon with dandelion greens and pistachios. Panko-crusted brussels sprouts are the side of choice. At lunch, the yellow-fin tuna niçoise salad with a quail egg pleases, as does the shrimp Bolognese. Peanut butter cheesecake and a polenta financier with caramel corn crunch are indulgences, indeed. Check out a very smart wine list, with offerings from around the world. Do reserve a table in advance for weekends, when sharply dressed, well-heeled clientele fill the booths and tables—crafted from oak, naturally—in this airy, contemporary space.

Off-Site Kitchen, 2226 Irving Blvd., Dallas 75207; (214) 741-2226; offsitekitchen.net; American; $. Outside-the-box-thinking in dining was missing in Dallas for such a long time, but it's coming into focus with places like Off-Site Kitchen. Thanks to the smarts of chef-about-town Nick Badovinus, who created a tiny take-out joint with exceptional, approachable food. There are a few picnic tables outside, but you can cart the food off to a picnic—or just eat in your car. You won't want to stall. Ground-on-site Black Angus burgers sit atop exquisite rolls from **Village Baking Co.** (p. 150) and get treatments like roasted jalapeño-smoked bacon relish or barbecued onions and swiss cheese. Barbecue sandwiches include slow-cooked pork shoulder with Carolina slaw; cracked-pepper brisket; and corned beef with cherry pepper sauerkraut. Sides include Very Sloppy Cheese Fries (you've been warned, OK?) and fries with garlic salt, while sweets range from cherry cola pie to chocolate-Oreo pudding. Cold beer is available, too.

Oishii, 2525 Wycliff Ave., Dallas 75219; (214) 599-9448; dallasoishii .com; Japanese/Pan-Asian; $$. It's very hard to beat the lunch specials here, where weekday specials range from the sushi lunch platter and the sashimi salad to kung pao chicken and pad thai. You can always find a light but satisfying bowl of pho, the traditional Vietnamese beef noodle soup; and vermicelli bowls filled with grilled pork or shrimp. In the evening, start off with pot stickers, chicken satay, cool Vietnamese spring rolls, crab soup with Chinese asparagus, or tart squid salad. Pork short ribs in spicy salt, baby bok choy in garlic sauce, coconut sea bass, Peking duck, and the hot-and-sour firepot draw the most raves. Sushi lovers can choose from a long list of

nigiri sushi, with choices ranging from green mussel to spicy tuna; maki rolls like spider, rainbow, and caterpillar; and the house specialty rolls, including the Dynamite, a Cajun roll topped with baked crawfish and spicy sauce, and the Uptown, a crab-salmon-avocado-cucumber roll topped with tuna, wasabi cream, and Sriracha sauce. Though perched in a slightly awkward location between Lemmon Avenue / Cedar Springs and the market district, and almost under the Dallas North Tollway, this bright, friendly spot—always brimming with a passionately loyal clientele—is worth seeking out.

Original Market Diner, 4434 Harry Hines Blvd., Dallas 75219; originalmarketdiner.com; American; $. Another certified hidden jewel that always evokes the response, "Where's that? Never heard of it," when we talk about the reliable comforts found at this traditional bacon-and-egg cafe. Tucked away behind the market halls, close to the University of Texas (UT) Southwestern Medical Center and the Design District, this 1950s diner was a drive-in at its opening. Run by several generations of the family owning the place, it's been updated enough to keep pace with trending tastes. At breakfast, for instance, there's the Belgian waffle and there's banana-bread french toast. There's a Greek omelet with gyro meat and feta, and there's a Mexican egg burrito. Eggs Benedict can be the traditional version, or you can get it Texified, with poached eggs, cheddar, and sausage beneath that hollandaise blanket. Lunches may be as old-fashioned as meat-loaf sandwich or tuna salad on toast, as substantial as beef stroganoff or stuffed cabbage rolls, or as virtuous as a Mediterranean salad topped with salmon. In any case, do leave room for a piece of pie: The diner is loved for its coconut cream pie and its lemon icebox pie. Be prepared to wait in line on the weekend at breakfast.

Pecan Lodge, 1010 S. Pearl Expy., Dallas 75201; pecanlodge.com; **Barbecue; $–$$.** Thank heaven this place burst onto the scene in 2010: Dallas honestly didn't have much in the way of great barbecue before—most of the good stuff in our part of the world is in Central Texas, so we were downright thrilled when Justin Fourton decided to open his place in the Dallas Farmers Market. How good is it? Daniel Vaughn, the barbecue blogger for *Texas Monthly* and creator of his magnificent *Full Custom Gospel BBQ* blog, offers high praise for this place, and he's been to no fewer than 500 barbecue places in the state. Further, Pecan Lodge sells out most every day it's open—and that became common even before Guy Fieri and *Diners, Drive-Ins and Dives* aired the Pecan Lodge segment in May 2012. Every food critic in the region has gone wild for Pecan Lodge, too, thanks to mesquite-smoked beef brisket, pork ribs, pulled pork, sausage, beef ribs, and sides like mac and cheese, fried okra, and West Texas pinto beans. Other specialties include the Hot  Mess, a sea-salt-crusted sweet potato stuffed with smoked brisket, chipotle cream, cheese, butter, and green onions. Gilding the lily means enjoying banana pudding for dessert. Pecan Lodge is only open Thurs through Sun, and it closes at 3 p.m., or when the barbecue is gone.

Pyramid Restaurant & Bar, 1717 N. Akard St., Dallas 75201; pyramidrestaurant.com; **American; $$$$.** Longtime Dallasites remember when the illustrious restaurant inside the fancy-schmancy Fairmont Hotel was the Pyramid Room—it's where everyone went on the very most special occasions. The old continental dining concept had run its course, and it was elaborately reconceived in 2008. Still very much a fine-dining destination, its focus is much more modern, but with plenty of warmth: Dark mahogany floors and beautiful sculptures crafted from centuries-old wood adorn the interiors. The menu keeps current as well, with dishes crafted from local growers; there's even a 3,000-square-foot rooftop garden the chefs utilize for herbs and vegetables. Signatures include a rib eye steak from Niman Ranch, grilled with red wine butter and served with chive mashed potatoes, roasted mushrooms, and glazed carrots; foie gras torchon with apple ponzu gelée, bonito, and yuzu kosho on brioche; and lobster dumplings with enoki mushrooms and scallions. If you're staying over at the hotel—which, if you're enjoying a cultural weekend, is wonderfully close to museums—check out brunch, when the Italian Benedict, steak and eggs, huevos rancheros, and croque madame make getting up and dressed up more fun. A special touch: There's a chef's tasting room that you can book for parties of 2 to 22 people, and a personalized, nine-course tasting menu with special wine pairings will be crafted according to your specifications. Now that's very special.

Samar by Stephan Pyles, 2100 Ross Ave., Dallas 75201; (214) 922-9922; samarrestaurant.com; International; $$–$$$. Following his many travels through Spain, India, and the eastern Mediterranean, superstar chef Stephan Pyles brought home the flavors he enjoyed most on his journeys and reinterprets them at a sexy, cozy restaurant in the middle of the Dallas Arts District (and just 3 blocks east of his namesake restaurant; see p. 46). His exotic party lets you sample small plates, including the tapas he loved in Spain, the tandoori specialties he found in India, and the Arabic joys discovered from Lebanon, Turkey, Greece, and Morocco. We like to begin with blistered green Spanish chiles, grilled oysters, spinach samosas, grilled tomato bisque with lobster salad, or lamb lollipops; and continue with zucchini-feta fritters, halloumi-stuffed squash blossoms, and duck confit tagine. The spice bombs are distinctive but never too crazy. Pyles handles all ingredients with a deft hand. On a nice evening, ask to share a hookah pipe on the patio. If Pyles is in the house, have him tell you the story of his mad dash to Damascus to purchase the decor's light fixtures.

SER Steaks + Spirits, 2201 N. Stemmons Freeway, Dallas 75207; sersteak.com; Steaks; $$$$. The new premier restaurant high atop the massive Hilton Anatole in the Market Center area, and very handy to the Design District and medical centers, SER is a very high-end steak house opened in late 2012 to replace the late, great Nana. Pronounced "sear"—get it . . . as  in, to sear a steak?—the upstart was widely considered an instant hit, though more than a few Dallasites wondered if we truly needed yet another fancy place to enjoy beautifully prepared prime beef. Apparently, Big D says, "Bring it," and Chef Anthony Van Camp does just that, and with so much more than steaks: Yes, he does offer a 45-day-aged prime rib eye topped with tomato chutney, and a Wagyu (Japanese-style lean beef) steak, but diners wishing for non-meat offerings get spoiled by a selection of fish like line-caught salmon and day-boat sea scallops, and poultry options that include pan-roasted duck breast. Smaller dishes include lobster bisque, local arugula salad topped with Marcona almonds, grilled Atlantic calamari, and foie gras "sliders." A sampling of local cheeses includes very popular choices from nearby Waco and Dublin. For dessert, you may need nothing more than an espresso and the stunning views of the Dallas skyline from your table.

Tei-An Soba House, 1722 Routh St., Dallas 75201; (214) 220-2828; tei-an.com; Japanese; $$. Though Dallas has enjoyed its share of Japanese restaurants over the years (long-timers will recall Sakura on Maple Avenue, which gave us our first taste of tempura in the very early 1970s), the majority of Asian dishes we became familiar with involved sushi and yakitori. Thanks to chef Teiichi Sakurai, who opened Tei-An

in 1 Arts Plaza to much acclaim, we finally had a noodle shop bearing most stylish overtones. Sakurai makes his soba noodles on-site, found in myriad combinations with fish and vegetables. Each creation looks like a prized piece of art, and we're happy to say that everything tastes as fabulous as it appears. True Japanese cuisine aficionados keep this restaurant high atop their favorites list, thanks to dishes such as Dungeness crab with uni risotto; abalone salad with fresh herbs; soba-coated Dover sole with uni, Parmesan, and truffle; tempura-fried *matsutake* (an exotic mushroom); and whole crispy *renko dai* (pink snapper). For dessert, there's sole dumpling with black honey. If it sounds a bit too outlandish, check out the restaurant's Facebook page, where the kitchen posts its gorgeous food photos almost daily; you get a strong sense of its imagination and sublime executions. The daring palate is amply rewarded.

Terrace Bistro and SODA Bar, **NYLO Dallas South Side, 1325 S. Lamar St., Dallas, 75215; (214) 421-1080; nylohotels.com/ dallas/; American; $$.** You'll feel as though you've stepped into a SoHo salon at this restaurant, tucked into a corner just off the lobby of the uber-fashionable new contemporary hotel on South Lamar. Paintings hanging on a wall styled from repurposed lumber provide a distinct contrast to Asian details found in an ornate mirror and brasserie-type lighting and banquettes along other walls. Treats at breakfast include buttermilk pancakes stuffed with blueberries or pecans, and a grilled peanut butter–banana sandwich. At lunch you can go light with grilled asparagus topped with a fried egg or seafood ceviche, or you can wrap your fists around a bistro burger topped with aged cheddar and grilled onions on challah. At dinner, the steak frites, roasted pork belly, and glazed duck breast over polenta sound best. For something lighter, with possibly the best view in Dallas, head to the rooftop to the SODA Bar, where you gaze across a swimming pool, fire pit, and deck toward the bright lights of downtown. You do so while sipping a signature beverage, such as The Frenchie, a mix of Ketel Citron, Frangelico, cranberry juice, and lemonade, while nibbling on a vegetable wrap, grilled shrimp skewers, steak tacos, or a BLT burger.

Wild Salsa, 1800 Main St., Ste. 100, Dallas 75201; (214) 741-9453; wildsalsarestaurant.com; Mexican; $$. If you're looking for a diversion from Tex-Mex, this serves as a worthy consideration. Foods on the menu come from various regions of Mexico, with some melding of influences from other parts of Latin America. Inside the carved wooden doors at the entrance, past the brilliantly colored Day of the Dead–inspired murals, among the Mexican folk decor, you can sit either on the bar side or restaurant side of the establishment. Either way, you'll want to dig into the Acapulco ceviche, nuanced with a little coconut to offset the citrus marinade on the fish, and the shrimp-bacon quesadillas, with a side of guacamole. Among tacos, our favorites are the ones containing fresh fish and the tender *lengua* (tongue—try it, it's amazingly good). Sensational tortas, or sandwiches, are those with beef *barbacoa* filling. Among beverages, enjoy the nonalcoholic *aguas frescas,* particularly the banana flavor and the watermelon. Wines come primarily from Spain and Chile, but the cocktail of choice is the lovely Paloma, a drink blending silver tequila with grapefruit juice, agave nectar, and hibiscus grenadine.

Landmarks

Five Sixty by Wolfgang Puck, Reunion Tower/Hyatt Reunion, 300 Reunion Blvd., Dallas 75201; (214) 741-5560; wolfgangpuck .com; Asian; $$$$. The name refers to the height of the landmark structure, crowned with the lighted ball, next to the Hyatt Reunion. The first Puck restaurant in Dallas features a glass pavilion entrance

Stephan Pyles and Matt McCallister: A Tale of Two Chefs

Stampede 66 (p. 96) is rootsy, over-the-top, and rollicking. **FT33** (p. 30) is avant-garde, minimalist, and cool. Stampede 66 could have only sprung from Texas soil. FT33 could exist in any international city. Two of the hottest tickets in Dallas, the restaurants opened within about a month of each other in 2012 and are as different as night and day. Yet the two have a deep connection: Their respective chef-owners, Stephan Pyles and Matt McCallister, were once Master and Grasshopper.

The professional relationship began in 2006 when McCallister, a novice with a burning desire to make it big in the culinary world, brashly approached Pyles, one of the most famous chefs in Texas and the country. McCallister wanted to study at his feet. Pyles wasn't so sure. The kid had no formal culinary education and his only experience aside from cooking with his mom was working at an Italian deli that served food at night in Scottsdale, Arizona, where he grew up. So, thinking he would never hear from him again, Pyles asked McCallister to convince him why hiring him would be a good idea. The missive he received in reply landed McCallister an interview and eventually a job as lowly line cook at Pyles' eponymous restaurant.

Thus began a four-and-a-half-year apprenticeship. The guru—who was a cofounder of Southwestern Cuisine in the mid-80s, had written four cookbooks and had been honored at the age of 39 as Best Chef in the country by the prestigious James Beard Foundation in 1991—was an exacting taskmaster. But his acolyte had the benefit of youth and energy and was willing to study late at night after he got off an exhausting shift. He bought a copy of the main cookbook from the Culinary Institute of America and memorized it from front to back.

Eventually the hard work paid off, and he rose step-by-step through the ranks until ultimately, he became executive chef. Teacher and student found a particular bond in their mutual appreciation for "molecular gastronomy," a bag of culinary tricks that had been perfected in restaurants like El Bulli, outside Barcelona. At Fuego, as Pyles christened a special chef's table that could be reserved by small groups, he and McCallister would personally prepare dazzling seventeen-course modernist cuisine dinners. Liquid Popcorn and Caramel Foam were two of Fuego's specialties.

But star pupils grow up, and it was not long before McCallister was ready to spread his wings. In 2011 the youngster embarked on a series of short apprenticeships at famous restaurants around the country. In October 2012, after returning from stints at, among others, the French Laundry in Napa, Daniel in New York City, and Alinea in Chicago, he opened sleekly contemporary FT33, to "introduce diners to unorthodox pairings and innovative modern cuisine." He was 31 years old.

Pyles, meanwhile, reached back to his West Texas boyhood to find the template for his own next stage: the restaurant that would be the capstone of his career. He drew on two main wellsprings of inspiration: his classic French training and fond memories of his folks' truck-stop cafe in Big Spring. As he said in a blog post, " . . . we are developing a whole new modern take on classic Texas cuisine." Opened in November 2012, Stampede 66 is his most personal and most ambitious restaurant yet.

A person looking to make reservations at either restaurant cannot but be struck by a curious fact. Having gone their separate, very distinctive ways, Master and Grasshopper are now competing for the same dining dollar a mere two miles apart in central Dallas. Funny how that happens sometimes.

Patricia Sharpe is executive editor and longtime food editor of Texas Monthly *magazine.*

on the street level, where diners hop on the elevator to ride 50 stories to a 200-seat dining room inside a giant twinkly ball. Up there, you get 360-degree view of Dallas while supping on a menu with Asian influences and sipping wines from a 400-label list, with domestic choices as well as those from Europe, South American, and Australia and New Zealand. Across a floor of dark, smooth river rocks from the sushi bar, the long, silver-and-ivory lounge features a glass-topped bar with round armchairs adjacent to a seating area with low cocktail tables. Our favorites include Tai Snapper Sashimi with Seaweed Salad in a Sesame-Lemon Dressing, as well as the robata-grilled Maine Lobster with Thai Basil–Yuzu Chile Pesto.

Sonny Bryan's Smokehouse, 2202 Inwood Rd., Dallas 75207; (214) 357-7120; sonnybryans.com; Barbecue; $. Just over 100 years old, Sonny Bryan's has always been the first name in beloved barbecue in Dallas. A big hit on one of Julia Child's visits, this is a tiny place where you sit in old, wooden school-style desks to eat smoked brisket, pork ribs, and sausage—and drink a cold beer. Crowds can be especially thick at lunch, when this little, old shack looks as though it will burst at the seams. If you can't find a place to eat inside, there are a couple of picnic tables outside on the parking lot. More than a few customers have been known to create an impromptu picnic in their cars or on their truck tailgates.

Stephan Pyles, 1807 Ross Ave., Dallas 75201; (214) 580-7000; stephanpyles.com; American; $$$$. Here's the namesake restaurant of one of Dallas's true culinary icons. The West Texas native is, along with fellow local legend Dean Fearing (see p. 102), one of the creators of Southwest cuisine that swept the region and nation in the 1980s. Pyles's

Arts District restaurant occupies a midcentury-modern building that housed a former insurance company; the owner-chef's exquisite feel for interior design turned the building into a showplace, making clever use of large, exposed bricks in tandem with contemporary touches in chandeliers and wood details to create a warm environment. There's plenty of iced shellfish on show in front of the exposed kitchen, where a team of chefs keep up with the whirl of orders coming from the main dining room and private dining areas. From Pyles's travels in Peru, you reap the benefits in the form of numerous ceviches, marinated fish creations that you can enjoy in sampler form, if you like. Pyles also creates a number of dishes from regional producers, and he offers the signature cowboy rib eye with red chile onion rings that became a monster hit at Star Canyon, one of the more renowned of the 18 restaurants he's opened over the past 30 years. See Chef Stephan Pyles's recipe for **Ecuadorian Shrimp Ceviche with Orange & Popcorn** on p. 228.

The Zodiac, 1618 Main St., Dallas, 75201; (214) 741-6911; neimanmarcus.com; New American; $$. Helen Corbitt put Dallas cuisine on the map in the 1950s when she came to Neiman Marcus to launch the Zodiac Room. As Stanley Marcus brought people from around the world to shop in his department store, Corbitt and her elegant meals, always accompanied by her exquisite popovers—still a mainstay on the Zodiac menu—invited Dallas ladies to lunch in style at his flagship store. There's more than the signature chicken salad today, of course, as the Zodiac serves more than its fair share of men, too: Seared ahi tuna salad, crab cake sandwich, braised pot roast, and Maine lobster ravioli round out the menu. Fine wines fill an ample list. Check out the walls, covered with vintage photography, and especially photographs of Stanley Marcus, the late store patriarch, whom is still referred to as "Mr. Stanley" by longtime employees. A special treat is a conversation with executive chef and cookbook author Kevin Garvin, only the third food director in NM's history, who oversees the dining room daily. Lunch daily; closed Sun.

Specialty Stores, Markets & Producers

Dallas Farmers Market, 1010 S. Pearl Expy., Dallas 75201; **(214) 939-2808; dallasfarmersmarket.org.** Since 1941, the Dallas Farmers Market has been a go-to place for the freshest produce you can find, and much of it comes from around the state. Open from 8 a.m. daily, it's one of the largest of its kind in the nation. Farmers in the various sheds love handing out samples of their produce, unloaded on-site from the backs of their trucks; when numerous producers are pushing their melons, berries, and tomatoes, the sampling can be positively abundant. You'll see several producers of local honey, and particularly that known as Zip Code Honey, which is said to be extremely effective in treating seasonal allergies that plague many Texans. You can tuck into a hearty snack at the end of Shed No. 1, where a roasted corn stand sells a cup of *elotes,* hot corn kernels cut right from the cob and mixed with mayonnaise and cheeses, which we like to top with chili powder or hot sauce. Cooking classes are held on several Saturdays through the year, with Dallas's top chefs teaching with market goods. The market is home also to **Pecan Lodge** (p. 39), an excellent BBQ eatery.

Frosted Art Bakery & Studio, 1546 Edison St., Dallas 75207; **(214) 760-8707; frostedart.com.** Gorgeous baking in the Design District looks as though it's strictly the creation in a fantasy. Bronwen Weber, owner and pastry chef, with her wildly inventive team conjure up not just extraordinary wedding cakes but also specialty cakes for birthdays and other special occasions. Her Alice in Wonderland spectacle is something to behold; her giant Valentine's cookie—something like an Ed Hardy heart tattoo—must be seen to be believed. Petit fours crafted to look like gift boxes are almost too pretty to eat. Frosted Art only sees patrons by appointment, but the custom work in cakes, cupcakes, cookies, and pies is worth a great deal of planning and collaboration for special occasions. You really can't have a party without these.

Opening Bell Coffee, 1409 S. Lamar St., Dallas 75215; (214) 565-0383; openingbellcoffee.com. Much more than a coffee stop, this destination in the booming just-south-of-downtown section of South Lamar does serve a fine cup of joe. For those who like flavored coffees, the hazelnut is especially popular. Buying fair-traded coffee, Opening Bell makes a mean caramel latte, too. But there's a lot more going on here: Situated on the bottom floor of South Side on Lamar, a renovated Sears Roebuck building that's been converted to apartment lofts, the coffee hangout begs for camping. It's comfortable, with plentiful sofas, tables, and chairs, so you'll see people studying and working during the day. Oh, and it's a bar, too: If you need your coffee with a kick, they'll make you a Black Irish, an iced mocha with a shot of O'Mara's Irish Cream. Or if you've come in to hear a local band or enjoy open-mike night, you can sip any of a number of imported or domestic beers (among the latter, there's locally made Ugly Pug and Texas's favorite, Shiner Bock). Wines are poured, as well. In the morning, your menu includes breakfast tacos, *kolaches* (the Czech pastry, a pillow of gently baked dough filled with sausage and/or cheese), bagels, and cinnamon rolls. At lunch and dinner, choices include Baja chicken enchilada soup and smoked ham or chicken salad sandwiches, as well as a number of sweets.

Tiff's Treats, 1001 Ross Ave., #102, Dallas 75202; (214) 720-0500; tiffstreats.com. Operating primarily as a cookie-delivery business, this is a storefront that you can visit while in the neighborhood—but you need to call ahead to place an order, because all cookies are baked to order, which takes 30 minutes. Warm, chocolate chip cookies are

LEARN TO COOK

3015 at Trinity Groves, *3015 Gulden Ln., Dallas 75212; (214) 939-3015; 3015dallas.com.* Professional chefs from the community teach classes in a wide range of cuisines. You can choose between hands-on instruction or demonstration classes, offered in a modern kitchen with state-of-the-art equipment. You'll take home a collection of recipes and enjoy an excellent meal, too.

Artisan Baking Co., *4900 White Settlement Rd., Fort Worth 76114; (817) 821-3124; artisan-baking-company.com.* Gwin Grimes's expertise in creating exquisite pastry and bread comes to life in her popular classes. Most are hands-on in approach, and each equips you with wonderful insight and recipes. You'll take home plenty of samples of your baked goods as well.

The Bastion, *2100 Hemphill St., Fort Worth, 76110; (817) 913-6972; bastionrestaurant.com.* Although this is technically a restaurant, it's the cooking classes that bring us back time and again. Generally, classes are offered on Thurs, Fri, and Sat evening, with themes that can include The Best of Provence, Tapas, International Breads, Simply Italian, and much more. Most last 3 hours and include a full meal. You can bring your own wine.

Central Market, *5750 E. Lovers Ln., Dallas 75206; (214) 234-7000; centralmarket.com.* Upstairs at the gourmet grocery store, there's a large cooking school with a daily schedule of learning activities. The typical offering is a demonstration-style class that accommodates 30 students, but there is a smattering of hands-on classes in the monthly schedule. You can opt for a class that shows you how to create an entire Italian, French, or Spanish dinner, or a wine-and-food pairing evening or chocolate creations. Some classes focus entirely on tamales or pizza. Others teach you knife skills. Teachers are often the store's chef staff, but quite often you'll catch a class taught by a local restaurant chef, and occasionally it's a famous chef on a cross-country book tour. Reservations are strongly advised; classes often sell out weeks in advance. Other area Central Market stores with cooking schools also keep a full schedule of classes, but each posts a different schedule monthly. Find one convenient to you among these: 4651 West Freeway, Fort Worth 76107, (817) 989-4700; 320 Coit Road, Plano 75075, (469) 241-8389; and 1425 E. Southlake Blvd., Southlake 76092, (817) 310-5665. You can find them at centralmarket.com, where you can register for classes online.

Culinary School of Fort Worth, *6100 Camp Bowie Blvd., Fort Worth 76116; (817) 737-8427; csftw.com.* This is a professional school for people wanting to enter the industry, or for those who want to cook as well as anyone in a professional kitchen. Classes are arranged by the trimester and offer course loads of 22 to 28 hours, with classes in day or night schedules. Internships are available to students, and the students often cook at events for the public.

Dallas Farmers Market, *Market Resource Center, 1010 S. Pearl Expy., Dallas 75201; (214) 653-8088; aiwf.org/dallasftworth.* A very special offering at the Dallas Farmers Market is a seasonal schedule of cooking classes, taught by noted area chefs. What makes this such a find is that the classes are far more affordable than at any other class venue in town. Each class is $25 if purchased in advance, or $30 at the door. Themed classes recently offered have included One-Pot dishes, taught by Ke'O Velasquez, chef at **Urbano Cafe** (p. 67); Fresh Shellfish at the Market, taught by Michael Scott, Northwood Country Club; and Winter Vegetables from Lucia, taught by David Uygur, owner-chef at **Lucia** (p. 117). After the cooking demo, everyone enjoys lunch. It's a great way to meet new people and further the bond created by breaking bread together. The chefs typically utilize products from the market; it's fun to go find some new goodies downstairs in the sheds to take home and use after class is over. Classes are typically held Sat from 11:30 a.m. until 1 p.m.

Young Chefs Academy, *6333 Camp Bowie Blvd., Ste. 260, Fort Worth 76116; (817) 989-2433; youngchefsacademy.com.* Kids going to class here come to understand what it is to truly make meals from scratch. They're taught a great deal about safety in the kitchen, as well as good health practices and balanced nutrition and practical kitchen skills, using top-notch kitchen equipment. Classes are designed for kids as young as kindergarten and up through teenage years. Programs are scheduled by the week in summer and on weekends during the school year. Birthday party classes can be booked, too.

the huge draw at Tiff's, but there are also brownies and Blue Bell Ice Cream, the favorite ice cream of Texas from that creamery in Brenham. Additional locations are found in Addison, North Dallas, Plano, and Richardson.

Urban Market, 1409 S. Lamar St., Dallas 75215; (214) 421-0258; urbanmarketdallas.com. Found on the lower level of South Side on Lamar, the same old Sears Roebuck building housing **Opening Bell** (above), this handy market stands out as the only downtown grocery to date. There's a deli on-site, offering sandwiches made with locally baked **Empire Baking Company** (p. 105) products and Boar's Head meats and cheeses. The beverages department stocks 120 craft beers on a global menu, and there are wines from inexpensive to fairly pricey. Grocery-wise, all the basics are there, from dry goods to perishables, but the selection is in keeping with a smaller, European-style store. For busy area residents, there's a personal shopping program: You place an order, and it's delivered a couple of days later for a $25 charge. Salads and party trays fill a catering menu, too.

Deep Ellum & East Dallas

Just east of downtown Dallas, immediately on the other side of Central Expressway, lies a century-old district called Deep Ellum. It might as well be an extension of downtown, but it has a distinct personality all its own and opens the door to East Dallas, so we think it belong in its own chapter.

Originally called Deep Elm, the early African-American residents took to calling it Deep Ellum, and the name stuck. Considered one of the most historically important neighborhoods in Dallas, Deep Ellum holds Dallas's largest collection of commercial storefronts of the period. The buildings dating from the 1880s to very early 1900s, particularly the warehouses, have been converted to popular loft apartments and condos.

In the 1980s, Deep Ellum came back from neglect, as developers refurbished buildings to become home again to nightclubs, as well as art galleries, retail shops, restaurants, and coffeehouses. The quarter has its share of tattoo parlors, too, adding to the colorful quality of the area.

On either side of Deep Ellum, you find Fair Park, home of a fantastic collection of Art Deco buildings and the State Fair of Texas; and the Baylor Medical Center neighborhood. The latter unfolds to reveal Lakewood and other areas of near East Dallas. The Baylor area also leads to Lower Greenville, the reach of Greenville Avenue with plentiful dining. Greenville leads north, bordering the east side of Southern Methodist University. You'll find a great diversity to the selection of eating throughout this chapter. It's a wonderful reflection of Dallas's versatility.

Foodie Faves

Alfonso's, 718 N. Buckner Blvd., Dallas 75218; (214) 327-7777; alfonsositalianrestaurant.com; Italian; $$. Although fairly predictable, this old-school family Italian restaurant has stuck around for 30 years, watching untold hundreds of neighbors come and go. The modern storefront space is simple, as is the menu, which offers favorites that the regulars swear by. Toasted cheese bread and lemony crab claws rank among the popular starters, while antipasto salad and minestrone make the more reliable smaller plates. Pasta dishes include spaghetti, linguine, rotini, and penne with sauces ranging from marinara to Alfredo, as well as meatball and sausage. Veal dishes abound, with Florentine and Marsala among top picks. Pizza can be as simple as that with pepperoni and mushroom or more adventurous, with artichoke hearts and shrimp as toppings. Plenty of kids' choices keep the smaller diners happy, too. There's a full bar, along with beer and wine choices.

All Good Cafe, 2934 Main St., Dallas 75226; (214) 742-5362; allgoodcafe.com; American; $–$$. The grilled cheese—that's cheddar and Pepper Jack on sourdough—with roasted green chiles and Roma tomatoes, treated to a dose of chipotle-spiked mayo stays in the mind as a happy memory long after lunch is over. The only serious competition for best sandwich here is the Ultimate BLT, combining peppery bacon, lush tomato slices, green leafy lettuce, slices of avocado, and an herbed mayo on honey wheat. Dinner delights include meat loaf with mashed potatoes and a choice of fresh veggies, such as zucchini and squash, sautéed spinach, roasted corn and chiles, and black eyed peas. But breakfast is what sets All Good apart from most of its brethren: Starting the day with soft-scrambled eggs and sautéed tortilla strips in the Mexican morning dish called *migas* is a delight, thanks to exceptional salsa infused with cilantro, fresh tomatoes, jalapeños, and white onion. Sunny-side-up eggs on the huevos rancheros brings a smile to your face, particularly if you add some of that peppery bacon on the side. Thick buttermilk pancakes and the chicken-fried steak with eggs guarantee a couple of extra pounds—but so worth it. The palpable Austin feel to this joint, which doubles as a live music venue, makes this a favorite hangout near downtown.

Angry Dog, 2726 Commerce St., Dallas 75226; (214) 741-4406; angrydog.com; American; $–$$. As traffic in the Deep Ellum district has endured the ebb-and-flow that will occur in any long-standing neighborhood, Angry Dog has outlasted many, many a neighbor. Opened in 1990, this joint is a beloved bar meant to satisfy your jones for a good scotch, a fine list of excellent craft beer, and something pretty darn great to eat, on the side. One of its slogans, in fact, is "We began as a bar, then we got hungry." You will, too, the moment you smell tempting aromas wafting from the kitchen. Better-than-it-has-to-be bar food includes fried mushrooms, fried pickle chips and chips with Grifter's Queso (gooey cheese dip with ground beef, sour cream, guacamole, and a side of salsa), and cheese fries. Famous sandwiches include the all-beef kosher dog with plenty of toppings, the half-pound burger that's won its share of local awards, and a fried chicken sub topped with bacon and avocado. You can be a sissy and get a grilled tuna salad or chicken Caesar, and maybe no one will make fun of you. Sunday brunch here is good for whatever you did to hurt yourself the night before—just come as you are.

Baker's Ribs, 3303 Main St., Dallas 75226; (214) 748-5433; **bakersribs.com; Barbecue; $–$$.** A family-owned joint that opened more than 20 years ago, Baker's began in one of the dining booms that propelled Deep Ellum to prominence. Though the neighborhood has been up and down, Baker's has prevailed and kept a loyal clientele, much of which is a busy lunchtime crowd from downtown and the nearby Baylor Hospital district. When you sit down to a platter of this Texas barbecue, slow smoked over hickory right on the premises, you'll see why people make regular journeys to partake in the pleasures here. Pick your passion, either in sandwich or plate form, from a long list that includes smoked pork, chopped beef, spicy sausage, sliced beef brisket, ham, turkey, chicken, pork ribs, and even sloppy joe. Sides include coleslaw, potato salad, pasta salad, black bean–corn salad, green beans, mac and cheese, marinated tomatoes, and smoky pinto beans. Fried pies, handheld pastries packed with apricot, apple, cherry, pineapple, peach, and blackberry, among several filling choices, are the dessert of choice—if you have room. Several other locations are scattered around the Dallas–Fort Worth area.

Central 214, 5680 N. Central Expy., Dallas, 75206; (214) 443-9339; **central214.com; American; $$.** Just off the lobby of the Hotel Palomar, this contemporary restaurant goes a long way toward overhauling what we've long thought about boring hotel

restaurants. Chef Graham Dodds works with seasonal ingredients, sourcing locally and regionally grown goods, to keep an exciting, changing menu at the fore. Typical starters include goodies like roasted shishito peppers with romesco sauce; littleneck clams with melted leeks, bacon, and mushrooms; and kale salad with watermelon radishes, chunky ricotta salata, and artichoke hearts. Larger plates range from paella with striped bass to oxtail ragout. Gather some pals together for brunch, when Dodds's menu offers a grilled cheese sandwich with San

Marzano tomato soup, deep dish quiche with chorizo and chard, and duck confit hash over Yukon Gold potatoes, bacon, and a duck egg. The bar scene brings locals and visitors alike for creative concoctions like the 214 Gimlet, a mix of gin, St-Germain, lime juice, and cucumber, and Sage Passion, blending vodka, passion fruit, lemon, and sage leaves.

Company Cafe, 2217 Greenville Ave., Dallas 75206; (214) 827-2233; companycafe.net; American; $$. A stack of gingerbread pancakes makes us long for Grandma's hug, as do the handmade jams fetched from local markets. Breakfast brings a warm and fuzzy feeling with more menu selections at this tree-hugging spot on Lower Greenville, starting with the Deep Bowl, an amalgamation of goodness, including pepper-fired smoked venison sausage from the Texas Hill Country, piled atop baked sweet potatoes, sliced avocado, and two eggs, served over easy. For an especially healthy selection, consider the egg-white omelet plumped with lean bison, squash, and other veggies right from the market, with a side of gluten-free french toast. At lunch, the seasonal salad combines organic greens with cucumbers, pickled onions, blueberries, dried cranberries, goat cheese, and candied pecans, all of which goes nicely with a topping of smoked salmon. At dinner, the South meets the health nut with gluten-free chicken and waffles, a plate of olive oil–fried chicken with gluten-free waffles, the latter stuffed with bacon and roasted jalapeño.

Redeem your waistline with a side of sautéed broccolini or cauliflower mash. Just leave room for a gluten-free blondie sundae. Enjoy perusing the *New York Times* or a stylish magazine while you hang out over a cup of *kombucha* in this very contemporary storefront. Second location: 3136 Routh St., Dallas 75201.

Fireside Pies, 2820 N. Henderson Ave., Dallas 75206; (214) 370-3916; firesidepies.com; Italian; $$. The first of several Firesides to open in the Dallas–Fort Worth area, this pizza bistro screamed, "Something special is here," when lines began streaming  out the door for a table each evening. Now a mainstay in the Knox-Henderson district just off of North Central Expressway, Fireside is famous for its wood-fired ovens, cracker-crisp pizza crust, and innovative, sophisticated toppings that include any number of Italian meats and locally sourced cheeses. Among favorites is one topped with fire-roasted tomato sauce, a blend of mozzarella, fontina, fontinella, and Parmesan-Reggiano cheeses, thick slices of sweet chicken-fennel sausage, and creamy roasted garlic cloves. Salads get special treatment, too, such as the one mixing baby spinach and baby arugula, tossed with Danish blue cheese crumbles, shreds of tender, spicy pepperoni, black olives, sun-dried tomato halves, and a balsamic-mustard dressing. Simple, yet inspired. No wonder it's one of the coolest spots in town. Multiple locations in Dallas, Grapevine, and Fort Worth.

Garden Cafe, 5310 Junius St., Dallas 75214; (214) 887-8330; gardencafe.net; American; $–$$. Did you say you were wishing to find a place serving breakfast all day? Here it is. Well, serving until close at 2 p.m. weekdays and 3 p.m. on weekends. Garden Cafe may be a little hippie-dippy and all, but you can't possibly find a restaurant with a greater commitment to a connection to old-fashioned food. Home-style cooking includes the gregarious Country Boy Benedict, a plate of biscuits with two over-easy eggs, ham, gravy, and hash browns, and the more conscientious omelet, made with local, organic, free-range eggs, spinach, kale, mushrooms, tomato, and other veggies. Sweet potato pancakes and bowls of local, organic, steel-cut oatmeal have won dedicated fans, as has the Sunday dish of chicken and dumplings. Poetry readings, art events, and patio parties bring in plenty of patrons, too.

HG Sply Co., 2008 Greenville Ave., Dallas 75206; (469) 334-0895; HGSPLYCO.com; American; $$–$$$. New on Lower Greenville, this hot destination for clean food pleases even those who don't care whether their food is considered healthful. An especially casual neighborhood bar and grill, HG (hunter/gatherer) takes cues from the very popular Paleo diet. Most every dish includes natural and/or organic ingredients from small suppliers (the chicken is from Windy Meadows in Campbell, Texas; eggs, Vital Farms, Austin; etc.) and nothing tastes heavy. Favorites to date include the duck confit bowl with sweet potato hash, mushrooms, and Brussels sprouts; ginger-garlic hummus, dipped with chips made from apple, jicama, cauliflower, cucumber, and bacon; and grilled fresh fish atop fresh, organic salad greens. Even the bar program follows the healthy protocol—cocktails are crafted from fresh garden/market ingredients, never a mix. Like most of its neighbors on this street, the room is a deep shotgun space, with sidewalk tables most desirable in mild weather.

Hibiscus, 2927 N. Henderson Ave., Dallas 75206; (214) 827-2927; hibiscusdallas.com; American; $$$. One of the cluster of restaurants in the Knox-Henderson 'hood owned by a group called Consilient, this sophisticated dinner spot launched itself as a très trendy spot and has hung on to become a place where a loyal following comes not for the flash but for the fine food. Tempura green beans and asparagus with lemon aioli, chicken-fried quail, big-eye tuna tartare, and a salad of pear and goat's milk ricotta with red currants, pistachios, and arugula typify the starters. Burly mains range from short rib and bistro steak with fries to a 20-ounce bone-in rib eye, while slightly lighter

options include Alaskan halibut and scallops with salsa verde. The interior here is pretty but never fussy, so it's as good for a business dinner as it is a couple's night out. Enjoy a good bottle of wine while you're at it.

Il Cane Rosso, 2612 Commerce St., Dallas 75226; (214) 741-1188; ilcanerosso.com; Pizza; $–$$. The brick-and-mortar location of a popular new pizza phenomenon sits in Deep Ellum, in the shadows of downtown, Fair Park, and the Baylor hospital district. Crowds found this modest place with a welcoming patio quickly and went crazy; soon it was named the best pizza by most of the local press, and rightfully so. Baking pizza that meets the guidelines established by the Associazione Verace Pizza Napoletana, Il Cane Rosso prides itself in using a centuries-old dough recipe utilizing only flour, water, sea salt, and yeast. Baked in a wood-burning oven imported from Napoli, its thin, crunchy outer crust and chewy interior crust add up to pizza you'd surely find in heaven. Go for the simple version topped with San Marzano tomatoes, fresh mozzarella, and basil. Or get crazy and enjoy the Gus, topped with those aforementioned ingredients, plus Jimmy's Italian sausage and mushrooms. Sensational salads, a daily pasta dish, and calzone fill out the menu. Watch for Il Cane Rosso's mobile oven to show up at wine bars and brewpubs around town, too. Postings are on the website and Facebook.

John's Cafe, 1733 Greenville Ave., Dallas 75206; (214) 874-0800; johns-cafe.com; American; $. As old-school as you can hope to find, this breakfast-lunch spot on Lower Greenville is caught in a 1950s time warp—and that's a good thing. Crispy-edged hash browns, handmade biscuits, fluffy pancakes, and excellent sausage patties make this a favorite morning destination, while the gyros, mushroom-swiss burger, and club sandwich with sides of cheese fries and onion rings make it a place to return for lunch. The staff is friendly, as is the clientele, which sits together at community tables. Even if you arrive alone, you'll leave having made new friends.

Kalachandji's, 5430 Gurley Ave., Dallas 75206; (214) 821-1048; kalachandjis.com; Indian/Vegetarian; $. Named for the man worshipped as Supreme Personality of Godhead by legions of devotees in India since the 17th century, "the beautiful moon-faced one" now resides in Dallas and sits at the temple attached to this exceptionally popular vegetarian restaurant. Krishnas run the establishment, which has attracted a great following even among carnivores—the food is that good. In fact, there isn't a media outlet or website that has not named this the best place for healthful eating in Dallas in many years. And it's cheap, too: Instead of listing prices on the menu, Kalachandji's asks for a donation. Among favorite dishes are dal, the bean soup nearly like lentil; *pullao,* a rice preparation with vegetables, nuts, and spices; vegetable curry; *pakora,* the deep-fried vegetable plate; and a daily changing entree that may be lasagna, enchiladas, or quiche. You can even sign up for cooking classes here.

The Mecca Restaurant, 5815 Live Oak St., Dallas 75214; (214) 352-0051; themeccarestaurant.com; Coffee Shop; $. Yes, another long-adored bacon-and-egg joint that ranks among places in Dallas where you're sure to find a big crowd just about any day. Open since 1938, the Mecca recently moved from a rather rundown location on the far side of town to this Lakewood-area store, where it's still enjoying busy breakfast and lunch service. On the breakfast menu, the Big D Special is a rib eye steak or two pork chops with eggs cooked your way, hash browns or grits, plus toast or biscuit, for $13. Some folks just want the short stack of pancakes, topped with blueberries or bananas, while others swear by the giant cinnamon roll, nearly the size of a hubcap. At lunch, plates include the chicken-fried steak, fried chicken livers, fried chicken, or chopped sirloin steak with sides that range from mashed potatoes and green beans to pea salad and corn-bread dressing. Burgers with Tater Tots are popular, as is the fried catfish basket. Whatever you choose, you'll earn yourself extra time at the gym.

Mot Hai Ba, 6047 Lewis St., Dallas 75206; (972) 638-7468; **mothaibadallas.com; Vietnamese; $$.** Chef-owners Jeana Johnson and Colleen O'Hare rapidly won over even the toughest critics with their interpretation of northern Vietnamese food, specifically that which the two came to love in Hanoi while they toured the country on motorcycles. Favorite dishes include imperial rolls stuffed with pork and shrimp; chargrilled pork belly meatballs atop vermicelli with fresh, raw herbs; and fresh shellfish in preparations reflecting French and Vietnamese influences. The bar serves French wines and beer from Asia, France and Belgium. Exposed brick walls, steel tables, and wood accents in décor keep the spirit casual but chic.

Pepe's & Mito's, 2911 Elm St., Dallas 75226; (214) 741-1901; **pepesandmitos.com; Mexican; $–$$.** Here's another established eatery that has weathered a number of ups and downs endured by the Deep Ellum district. Good thing, too, because this solid Mexican cafe should stay put to keep its devotees happy. For starters, the shrimp cocktail, featuring big crustaceans in a Mexican cocktail sauce with pico de gallo and avocado slices, makes for a virtuous meal all on its own, and the albondiga soup, a traditional bowl of meatballs in a broth riddled with carrots, onion, potatoes, tomatoes, and chiles, spells comfort. Rib eye steak a la Tampiqueña pleases with its topping of a chipotle-cheese enchilada, and *pollo al mojo de ajo* hits high notes with its garlic-cilantro butter. Combo plates let you put together a mixture of enchiladas and tacos in varying styles. Service is quick and happy, and the setting is colorful and casual.

The Porch, 2912 N. Henderson Ave., Dallas 75206; (214) 828-2916; **theporchrestaurant.com; American; $$–$$$.** Another from the Consilient restaurant group that keeps opening trendy new spots in this 'hood, the Porch has outlasted its 15 minutes of fame as The It Place. What's enjoyable about this, of course, is that the Porch was always about substance, not just style. That it's stuck around means that its food remains the reason you want to be here. Yes, it's still an attractive place to meet and mingle, but what's coming out of the kitchen is ultimately as interesting as anything else here. At lunch, we like the turkey chili, buttermilk fried-chicken cobb salad, the chicken avocado BLT sandwich, and the grilled salmon over roasted corn. At dinner, we can sip a cocktail or two and enjoy brisket sliders and fried Port du Salut cheese, or go big with pork schnitzel, grilled flat iron steak, or pan-roasted chicken with Spanish chorizo. Sit at tall tables in the bar area or comfy booths in the main dining section. It's all good.

Royal Thai, 5500 Greenville Ave., Dallas 75206; (214) 691-3555; royalthaitexas.com; Thai; $$. Celebrating 20 years of business in a town as fickle as Dallas can be at times a very big deal. In the case of Royal Thai, the occasion of making this milestone can't possibly be surprising, as it's one of the more dependable, well-liked places around. Owners Gene and Jay Potchana cleverly have Jay's mom, Boonroam, to thank, as she bought her expertise from her well-liked restaurant near Bangkok to Dallas. The result—a pretty restaurant with soothing ambience and authentic Thai food—has been nothing but successful since the doors opened. Appetizers worth trying include the *tod mahn plah,* or fish patties with kaffir lime, curry, and chopped green beans, alongside a cucumber-red onion salad; chicken satay skewers; and the outstanding charbroiled beef salad. Among soups we recommend the *tom kha gai,* which brings together delicate chicken with lemongrass, mushroom, tomato, and chile flavors in a tart broth of coconut milk and chile paste. Dinner treasures, such as Royal Thai Swimming Angel, sliced chicken over sautéed spinach with Thai peanut sauce, and Pattaya Beach, a mix of shellfish with red curry, basil, cabbage, and snow peas, always have us plotting a return visit.

Sissy's Southern Kitchen & Bar, 292 N. Henderson Ave., Dallas 75206; (214) 827-9900; sissyssouthernkitchen.com; American/Southern; $$–$$$. Hitting all the right notes, this upstart landed just off North Central Expressway in early 2012 to much acclaim. At first, there was great curiosity as to how owner Lisa Garza, a *Top Chef* competitor, would do in her own place. Then lo and behold, everyone discovered that Garza had the goods—the food achieved excellence at moments. By the year's end, Sissy's was atop most of the best-new-restaurant lists. So far, stellar bites have come from Sissy's fried chicken, pickled shrimp, gumbo, squash casserole, deviled eggs, shrimp and grits, and Grandma's layered salad. At the bar, we're loving the mint julep, and who doesn't love a bucket of bubbly? The place is very stylishly old-fashioned, with hints of Charleston elegance and hospitality.

Start, 4814 Greenville Ave., Dallas 75206; (214) 265-1411; startrestaurant.net; American; $-$$. Make no mistake, this is not fast food—but it's served fast. The difference between this and other places dispensing food quickly? Start is about very healthy eating, period. Begun by a mom and dad who were worried about the dearth of quality, nutritious food available for people on the run, Start serves only scratch-made dishes created entirely of fresh, natural ingredients. At breakfast that's whole wheat pancakes with vegetarian sausage or a burrito filled with cage-free eggs and wood-smoked bacon, natural cheese, and salsa in a whole wheat tortilla. Lunch/dinner favorites include a whole wheat empanada filled with all-natural chicken, cheddar and goat cheese, and an addictive quinoa salad tossed with crunchy veggies, extra-virgin olive oil, and herbal vinaigrette. On a sunny day, you'll want to score a table on the deck.

Tei Tei Robata Bar, 2906 N. Henderson Ave., Dallas 75206; (214) 828-2400; teiteirobata.com; Japanese; $$–$$$. Soon after sushi bars began opening with regularity in Dallas, here came something

a little more unusual—a Japanese restaurant that wasn't trying to lure patrons with jacked-up rolls with contrived names and myriad, elaborate toppings that really don't belong on sushi. Instead, here was a civilized, stylish enclave with a very soothing sensibility and design, and one where the *robata,* or grill cooking typical in northern Japan, was the focus. From the cool, serene sake bar to the ceramic bowls in which dishes are often served, you could tell this place was different in the best possible way. Sashimi options may include fresh octopus, surf clam, flounder-wrapped sea urchin, and super *toro.* Grilled goodies might be sake-marinated black cod, baby yellowtail collar, whole black snapper, or whole giant prawn. Not into fish? There's probably something like yuzu-pepper-cured roasted duck breast and filet mignon. Grabbing a seat at the U-shaped bar surrounding the open kitchen is perfect for two dining together, but the booths are better for groups of three, four, and more.

Tried & True, 2405 N. Henderson Ave., Dallas 75206; (214) 827-2405; neighborhoodservicesdallas.wordpress.com; American; $–$$. One of Dallas's most illustrious chefs, Nick Badovinus, has struck again, and it could be gold. In late 2012, he opened the city's first bourbon bar, which also happens to sell a lot of delicious craft beers and cleverly spun, casual bar food. Like he's done when he was with the Consilient restaurant group and he's doing now with his own Neighborhood Services restaurant group, Badovinus is pouring his sense of fun and passion for simple but exceptional flavors into his work. The interior has elements that include retro motorcycle parts, music from—at various times—a CD jukebox and an old turntable, pool table, shuffleboard, and vintage beer signs, including those for Schlitz and others you'd probably forgotten. The menu is very Nick, with changing offerings that can be anything from corned beef tacos, cracked-pepper beef sandwich, and pizza to charcuterie. You'll see—it's just like the marquee says out front, "Honest Food."

Trinity Hall, 5321 E. Mockingbird Ln., Dallas 75206; (214) 887-3600; trinityhall.tv; Irish Pub; $–$$. Just a stone's throw from North Central Expressway, the collection of eateries, shops, and businesses at Mockingbird Station has seen its ups and downs. Perhaps half of the places in business at its opening about a decade ago are still around, many replaced a few times. But Trinity Hall, one of Dallas's few Irish pubs, has hung on nicely. The owners brought from across the pond several items for the interior—found in the bar back and other decor— to give authenticity to their homage to Trinity College in Dublin. The proprietors also honor their roots with musical concerts on-site that include the Irish harp concert, folk and ballad bands, Celtic dancing, and more. If you're itching for some sports, the TVs almost always broadcast soccer and rugby games from over there, too. A poker game is usually scheduled on Monday night, and team trivia quiz games fill the Sunday evening bill. Oh, and there's lots to eat and drink, as well: You'll find fish-and-chips and shepherd's pie, naturally, as well as lamb stew, pub curry stew, seafood casserole, burgers, and steaks. And because those sports broadcasts happen in the morning, there's a breakfast menu, too, including steak and eggs and a full Irish breakfast.

 Sipping pleasures include all the bar offerings you'd expect, plus a schedule of Irish whiskey and beer tasting events. See the website for a timely schedule. It's a great place, by the way, to eat and drink after a movie at the Angelika theater—one of the few in Dallas showing indie and art-house flicks—next door.

Twisted Root, 2615 Commerce, Dallas 75226; (214) 741-7668; twistedrootburgerco.com; Burgers; $–$$. Deep Ellum's return to destination dining status was helped a couple of years ago in part by the arrival of Twisted Root, a funky watering hole turning out an inspired menu of burgers, including those made with bison, antelope, lamb, ostrich, veggies, and more. Plenty of cachet came courtesy of a filming here by Food TV's *Diners, Drive-Ins and Dives,* so the lines can be fairly long at high noon. Nevertheless, you cannot go wrong with the half-pound burger topped with creamy blue cheese and jalapeños— to which you should add spicy pickle slices and Dijon-horseradish mustard. A runner-up is the turkey burger on a white bun, topped with chipotle sauce, guacamole, and a thick slice of cheddar. Curly fries and homemade sweet potato chips delight as sides. There's also "cold-ass" beer that comes five bottles to a bucket. Parking can be a challenge, but just keep searching for an available parking meter. And bring your sense of humor, too: The staff gives you a slip of paper with a celebrity name on it, and you'll have to face the music if you're chit says Britney Spears and your name is called on the loud speaker when your order is ready to pick up at the counter.

Urbano Cafe, 1410 N. Fitzhugh Ave., Dallas 75204; (214) 823-8550; urbanodallas.com; American; $–$$. Initially opened in Uptown as an upscale sandwich cafe, Urbano has matured into a restaurant with a focus on artful presentations. For starters, there's a lovely assortment of local artwork hanging on the walls at this contemporary, rather minimalist place. Then the food itself is design on a plate that also happens to taste really good. At lunch, that might be the Parmesan chicken panini with roasted tomato, romaine, and garlic-Parmesan dressing, a spinach cobb salad, or shrimp risotto with avocado, tomato, and herbs. At dinner, your choices could include an appetizer of Korean short ribs or prosciutto-wrapped figs, a grilled asparagus salad, seared duck over fontina grits, or seared salmon with herbed polenta crab fritters. Urbano is BYOB, so bring a nice bottle of wine and pay a $2 per person corkage fee to drink it with your meal.

You'll go away wondering what took you so long to visit this place; it's a hidden jewel you'll want to visit again.

Velvet Taco, 3012 N. Henderson Ave., Dallas 75206; (214) 823-8358; velvettaco.com; **Mexican; $.** Jumping on the taco bandwagon that has fully taken Dallas by storm, the Velvet version shows pride in its work, noting on its menu that though this taco may not change the world, "it's pretty freakin' great." And we can attest to that truth, and we're sure it's because VT makes its own tortillas, slow-roasts ingredients right in the kitchen, and puts everything together to order. Oh, and the fruits used in the margaritas and sangria are fresh, never frozen. Tacos to love include the one stuffed with rotisserie chicken, herbed goat cheese, smoked bacon, avocado, and basil cream; or the one with wild mushrooms, onion chutney, purple potatoes, and micro greens; or maybe the grilled flank steak, portobellos, white cheese, grilled red onion, and herb mixture. Oh wait, then there's the Bangkok shrimp taco, with red curry–coconut sauce, spinach, habanero, grilled pineapple, thai basil, and basmati rice. If you want your taco wrapped in lettuce instead of a tortilla, just ask. And for dessert, it's red velvet cake, of course.

Landmarks

Adair's Saloon, 2624 Commerce St., Dallas 75226; (214) 939-9900; adairssaloon.com; **American; $.** Those of us who grew up in Dallas knew the original Adair's over on Cedar Springs, just off Oak Lawn, and it was just as rugged a dive as the current, newer location in Deep Ellum. It's where we would take a new prospective sweetheart to see what he or she was made of; if he or she could handle the crowd, the questionable bathroom facilities, and the jalapeño perched atop the saloon's legendary burger, he/she was a real keeper. (If not, this sissy would probably need kicking to the curb.) Originally opened in 1963, Adair's is as well known for its pure honky-tonk atmosphere, its live music stage that's hosted the likes of the early Dixie Chicks and Jack Ingram, a jukebox alive with Hank Williams tunes, especially cold beer, strong drinks, a layering of graffiti unrivaled by any other place in town, and exceptional burgers. Said burgers speak of an ages-seasoned griddle, which also produces a fine BLT and a ham-and-cheese sandwich, all about five or six bucks. Popcorn's just a buck-fifty, and a cocktail is just three at happy hour. Note that when visiting any Deep Ellum business, watch the parking meter; you need to feed it, even at night, or Dallas's finest will issue you a stout parking ticket.

Campisi's, 5610 E. Mockingbird Ln., Dallas 75206; (214) 827-0355; campisis.us; Italian; $$. Longtime patrons of this 1950s-era restaurant still call it "The Egyptian," because the sign out front says just that. The sign was there when the Campisi family bought the place for their pasta-and-pizza restaurant and bar, and the name stuck. Once a place that seemed like a whiskey joint Frank and Dino would love, it's also the sort of loungey place that wiseguys would call home. Whether or not the latter ever was the case has always been debated, but what's certain is that Campisi's Egyptian still brings crowds in droves for its oval-shaped, thin-crust pizzas that are sliced into long strips, rather than wedges. The

story goes that the Campisis were the first folks to serve pizza in Dallas, and nobody's disputed it. Popular dishes also include the shrimp scampi, rich in butter, garlic and lemon, and the huge servings of lasagna. On a budget? Stop by on Tuesday night, when the spaghetti dinner, with salad and garlic bread, is $6.99. Numerous locations have opened around the Dallas area.

The Grape, 2808 Greenville Ave., Dallas 75206; (214) 828-1981; thegraperestaurant.com; French/American; $$–$$$. Opened on Lower Greenville in the early 1970s to launch a revival of a decaying neighborhood, The Grape has remained relevant like no other restaurant boasting such longevity in all of Dallas. As it did in its infancy, The Grape has made French bistro dining accessible for neighborhood folks and has never gone out of fashion. Though it's been updated in subtle ways, it remains cozy, with the building's original 1920s architectural details, and its intimacy makes you want to only bring someone very special along to dine with you. Chef Brian Luscher, who purchased the bistro with wife Courtney from the original owners a few years ago, keeps The Grape's hungry fans happy with classic mussels in white wine, crushed red pepper, and butter; jumbo lump crab cakes with lemon-tarragon aioli, duck leg confit, mustard-crusted salmon, and steak frites. Of course, there's always the classic mushroom soup The Grape served at its 1972 opening, and always will. Local food critics have lauded The Grape with superlatives recently, including "best brunch," among many others. Do check out the changing wine list, always filled with finds that show great care in sourcing.

Highland Park Cafeteria, 1200 N. Buckner Blvd., Dallas 75218; (214) 324-5000; highlandparkcafeteria.com; American; $. Opened in Highland Park in 1925, this landmark moved to its new location in recent years, with much consternation from its generations of loyal fans. Nobody need have worried, however, because the transition was rather seamless; even the framed photos of the nation's presidents, which line the walls where you queue up to grab a tray and see your plates served, made the move. More importantly, the recipes all survived the relocation, and if you close your eyes, you taste what customers have for nearly 90 years—homemade goodness. Those of us who have been eating there since childhood can attest that the aromas of freshly baked breads, roast beef, and pies have not changed one bit, and that the comforting flavors in the fried chicken, cucumber salad, collard greens, baked squash, chess pie, and coconut cake remain wonderfully the same.

Local, 2936 Elm St., Dallas 75226; (214) 752-7500; localdallas .com; American; $$$. Before anyone in Dallas was joining Slow Food or heard chefs talking much about sourcing locally produced foods, Chef Tracy Miller opened a restaurant in Deep Ellum where she did the strangest thing: She found and served dishes that starred products only if in season and mostly if grown somewhere nearby. She also put a lot of thought and care into the whole dining experience, serving guests a little bowl filled with warm, spiced nuts when they sat down and presented a small *amuse-bouche*—a soup—before the dinner courses began. Word of this smallish, contemporary, and very stylish bistro in a renovated hotel building spread like wildfire, and soon Miller's food and the legend of Local was read about in all the regional press, as well as in *Gourmet, Travel + Leisure,* and *Metropolitan Home* magazines, and the *New York Times.* Miller changes the Local menu several times a week, depending on what's freshest from her farmers, but you can count on the sort of inspiration that produced appetizers like three-cheese ravioli in teardrop tomato broth; balsamic-roasted candy-striped beets with local arugula and goat cheese from Paula Lambert at the **Mozzarella Company** (p. 74), just down the street; a burger basket starring Burgundy Pasture beef, gruyère, caramelized onion, and yellow tomato; and cornflake-crusted sea bass with creamy Meyer lemon risotto. Miller continues to give us reason to journey to Deep Ellum. And we hope she always will.

San Francisco Rose, 3024 Greenville Ave., Dallas 75206; (214) 826-2020; sanfranciscorose.com; American; $–$$. Open since 1977, the Rose lays claim to being the city's first sports bar—and who are we to argue? But rather than a dark place stinking of stale beer, the Rose blooms with comfort, familiarity, and warmth, in spite of the proliferation of more than 30 TVs throughout the joint. Drinks specials abound—there's always $4 well drinks and $12 buckets of beer, as well as draft beer for $3 on Thursday—but the food will keep everyone happy. Nick's Killer Nachos, sweet potato chips, and fried pickles rank among better appetizers, while the hickory burger and bacon-cheeseburger win good marks, too. The Saturday/Sunday brunch includes the Southern staple known as chicken and waffles, the popular Mexican breakfast dish called *migas,* and good old eggs Benedict. The patio is pet friendly, so be sure to bring Spot, too.

Specialty Stores, Markets & Producers

Central Market, 5750 E. Lovers Ln., Dallas 75206; (214) 234-7000; centralmarket.com. Created as a gourmet store by the San Antonio–based grocery chain H-E-B, this is the first Central Market to open in Dallas County. Designed in a fashion that emulates a European market by following a serpentine footpath, the store opens with a customer service desk, followed by an abundant produce department. There you will find more varieties of peppers, cucumbers, potatoes, onion, apples, citrus. and greens—in organic and regular varieties—than you knew existed. You bag your produce, weigh it, and key in the item codes to produce your own tickets that will be scanned at checkout. The meat and fish markets carry fresh, seasonal, and locally produced goods in massive quantities. There's a huge wine and beer department, and packaged goods shelves with all the olive oils, vinegars, condiments, and canned items you will ever need. A healthy living department stocks vitamins and other nutritional supplements, skin and body care items, essential oils, and locally made soaps. A big bakery, fabulous cheese department, and prepared foods section—with a huge takeout counter—wraps up the store tour by cash registers. Watch for a regular schedule of in-store events, featuring plentiful free demos and tastings. Other stores in North Dallas, Plano, Southlake, and Fort Worth. Note the Central Market Cooking Schools on page 50.

Deep Ellum Brewing, 2823 St. Louis St., Dallas 75226; (214) 888-3322; deepellumbrewing.com. Opened in late 2011, this brewery is just plain fun. The craft beers made on-site are downright wonderful, and the people running the show are all about good times. You can visit on Thursday evening (usually 6–8:30 p.m.) and Saturday afternoon (noon–3 p.m.) for a tour and tasting, which is a great time for bringing friends to try locally made brews. Deep Ellum's beers are found on a growing supply of local menus and are stocked at most grocery and liquor stores in town, too.

Jimmy's Food Store, 4901 Bryan St., Dallas 75206; (214) 823 6180; jimmysfoodstore.com. This old-school corner market famous for its butcher shop, handmade pastas, long rows of Italian sauces, and hard-to-find ingredients is something of a surprise in Dallas. The depth of olive oil, vinegars, olives, Prosecco, and excellent Italian wine supplies will steal your heart. At the back of the store, to one side of the meat market, you can order sandwiches from the deli. The hot Italian sausage sandwich with red and yellow peppers, onions, and melted cheese is immensely gratifying, as is the Cuban sandwich, hot and crunchy outside, all tender and spicy and tart inside. A shot of espresso is just a buck. There's a small seating area by the windows in front, as well as a slightly larger one in back, down the hall behind the deli.

Legal Grounds, 2015 Abrams Rd., Dallas 75214; (214) 824-5800. Lakewood's favorite coffee shop, owned by an attorney, features decor packed with legal volumes on bookshelves. Besides a place to get a fine cappuccino, Legal Grounds is also where you'll dig into scones, cinnamon rolls, pancakes, and french toast. If there's a complaint, the place is a little grubby, but the service makes up for any shortcomings.

Mokah Coffee Bar, 2803 Taylor St., Dallas 75226; (214) 651-0077; lifeindeepellum.com/mokah/. Attached to a Deep Ellum art gallery, this coffee bar serves a lovely espresso, drip coffee, and cups of loose-leaf tea. It's a roomy space, meant for art and music events, but there's a definite warmth that makes you want to hang out, even if nothing's going on. The staff is especially sweet, as well.

Mozzarella Company, 2944 Elm St., Dallas 75226; (214) 741-4072; mozzco.com. Long before it became fashionable to buy and eat artisan cheeses, Paula Lambert opened her little cheese company in Dallas's Deep Ellum neighborhood in 1982. Since then the Mozzarella Company has grown in impressive ways, winning international awards and earning accolades from major national publications. Paula travels frequently to Europe for greater inspiration, and she has penned two much-lauded cheese cookbooks. Favorites are the Hoja Santa, wrapped in aromatic leaves and hinting of mint and sassafras; the queso Oaxaca, a Mexican-style mozzarella; and the herb cacciota, plumbed with Texas basil or Mexican marigold mint.

Murray Street Coffee, 103 Murray St., Dallas 75226; (214) 655-2808; murraystreetcoffee.com. Perched on a quiet corner in Deep Ellum, this cool coffee hangout features a menu of espresso, drip coffees, maté, chais, teas, Italian sodas, and juices. We like bringing the laptop along to get some work done in this chill environment, where there's also a breakfast sandwich and granola parfait. Lunch eats include a veggie sandwich on Ezekiel bread.

Rudolph's Meat Market, 2924 Elm St., Dallas 75226; (214) 741-1874; rudolphsmarket.com. The very definition of a landmark, this family business has been selling meat to local customers since 1895. Aged beef; veal, lamb, and pork chops; poultry; and sausage filled the butcher cases, and the staff is well versed in what you'll need and how to prepare it. In fact, they'll even send you home with recipes.

Spiceman's FM 1410, 1410 N. Fitzhugh Ave., Dallas 75024; (214) 404-9104. Tom Spicer operates a small retail operation next to **Jimmy's Food Store** (above), where you can buy fresh, locally grown herbs and rare, wild mushrooms. You'll taste his products in restaurants around town. Spicer's passion for organic produce is reflected in the 11,000-square-foot garden he keeps behind the store.

Two Sisters Catering To-Go, 2633 Gaston Ave., Dallas 75226; (214) 823-3075; twosisterscatering.com. Opened by siblings in 1989, this catering outfit also supplies you with take-home meals to fit nearly any appetite. Ready-made goodies you can pick up include roasted corn–black bean salad, wild rice–artichoke salad, herb-roasted sweet potato wedges, spinach-mushroom lasagna, beef tenderloin, King Ranch casserole, and stuffed chicken. Second location: 3111-C Monticello Ave., Dallas 75205.

Uptown

Easily one of the largest eating areas in Dallas in terms of density, Uptown is—in some ways—one of the newest. The main thoroughfares cutting paths through the Uptown district, however, have long been populated by desirable restaurants, cafes, and bistros. But as a neighborhood, Uptown as a collective area is relatively fresh on the scene.

The name came from a need to connect the downtown and Arts District part of Dallas with the Park Cities, the latter not really far from the city center at all. The roads that connect those two areas, running along a north–south path, are McKinney Avenue and Oak Lawn. Since the 1930s, those streets have been lined by retail businesses, but the eating establishments were, for the most part, far from celebrated hot spots we patronize today. Overall, coffee shops, delis, and the like have been replaced by trendy watering holes serving pretty good food.

But that's not to say that the Uptown dining destinations are of a frivolous nature. Many, in fact, have displayed staying power that we find admirable in a city that can have a fickle palate. The Uptown district, it should be noted, is home to restaurants belonging to some of the most important names on the Dallas culinary scene, including Dean Fearing, Stephan Pyles, Kent Rathbun, Avner Samuel, and other star chefs.

Nearly every food genre is represented in Uptown, from Middle Eastern and Greek, Japanese and Indian, to all-night dining and a century-old pharmacy. If you want to make a day of it, hop the McKinney Avenue trolley and graze your way up and down the street.

Baboush Restaurant & Bar, 3636 McKinney Ave., Ste. 160, Dallas 75204; (214) 599-0707; baboushdallas.com; Middle Eastern; $$. Dropping into this lovely enclave in the West Village area feels much like stepping into a sultan's tent somewhere in the Sahara. Immediately you're taken with the beautiful tile work, solicitous service, exotic aromas, multilayering of colors and textures in decor, and—ultimately—the food. Marketed as a place for a girlfriends' night out or dates wanting to canoodle on banquettes, this is perfectly delightful for a business lunch or dinner as well as a mother-daughter outing, too. We like to start with spreads, such as the combination platters that let you sample olives marinated in harissa, preserved lemon, cilantro, and parsley; sweet Moroccan tomato spread flavored with cinnamon, garlic, orange water, sesame seeds, and almonds; a tart eggplant spread; hummus; and grilled pita bread. A simple entree is the chicken breast that's marinated in olive oil, garlic, ginger, turmeric, and lemon, then grilled; and the skewers of grilled salmon, marinated in lime, coriander, and harissa oil, served over couscous. Traditional Middle Eastern dishes, such as falafel, dolma, kibbe, and *shawarma,* are abundant; delightful departures include the vegetarian-friendly "cigars," particularly flaky phyllo cylinders stuffed with spinach, goat cheese, olives, garlic, and preserved lemon. If you're feeling festive, enjoy something from the Sexy Drinks menu, featuring goodies like pine-cardamom martini; the rum, blackberry, lime, and mint cocktail; and the Marrakesh Express, blending gin, apricot, lemon juice, and cinnamon.

Belly & Trumpet, 3407 McKinney Ave., Dallas 75204; (214) 855-5551; bellyandtrumpet.com; American; $$. What a culinary pedigree you find in this charming little cottage alongside the brick street of

McKinney Avenue: The executive chef, Brian Zenner, is chef de cuisine at the lauded **Oak** (p. 36); and Rudy Mendoza, sous chef, comes from the **Mansion Restaurant** on Turtle Creek (p. 103). Calling their place "a celebration of food and drink," this concept manages to be chic and comfortable at the same time, giving guests a place to share plates, cocktails, and wine. While some diners are calling it a tapas place, it's not really Spanish per se, though the dishes are meant to provide small bites and to be shared. Some of the early favorites (it just opened in February 2013) include chickpea fries with eggplant dip; grilled shishito peppers with Marcona almonds, and picholine olives; Portuguese green soup; rapini salad with cauliflower, poached egg, and white anchovy; and yellowfin tuna with chayote squash and green beans. Handcrafted cocktails with fresh ingredients are a big draw. Valet parking is essential in this crowded stretch of the avenue.

Bob's Steak & Chop House, 4300 Lemmon Ave., Dallas 75219; (214) 528-9446; bobs-steakandchop.com; Steak House; $$$$. If you want a flashy, super-fancy steak house, keep looking. But if you want a place with excellent beef, superb service, and a long-standing reputation for a solid dining experience, you should be happy here. Originally, this was the first **Del Frisco's** (p. 178), but that was in the late 1980s. For more than two decades, this cozy collection of dining rooms with a collection of horse art on the walls has been a place for a great martini and a heck of a great rib eye. In particular, the bone-in rib eye and the Kansas City strip are the cuts of choice (but they're prime beef), with signature glazed carrots and potatoes on the side. If you love sumptuous food get the skillet potatoes with peppery gravy. Excellent starters include lobster bisque and bacon-wrapped shrimp stuffed with mozzarella. Crab cakes and broiled shrimp scampi are nice alternatives to steak, too. Other locations in Dallas, Plano, Grapevine, and Fort Worth.

Buzzbrews Kitchen, 4334 Lemmon Ave., Dallas 75219; (214) 521-4334; buzzbrews.com; American; $$. When you think of places that are open 24 hours, your mind goes right to the middle-of-the-night diner that will suffice when it's truly the only option or when the bars have closed and perhaps the quality of food isn't a priority. Well, forget that when thinking of Buzzbrews, which is named for the coffee selection that's guaranteed to give you the high you need. Truthfully, this is good food that we enjoy any time of day or night. Breakfast, which is always offered, includes the signature griddle toast, a thick slice of rustic bread that's spread with butter and real Vermont maple syrup. Then there's one that's covered with fresh berries. Or the one over which two eggs are placed with bacon or veggie sausage. The list goes on. Banana-nut pancakes are superb, as is the Mr. C, a plate of scrambled eggs with house-made chorizo and

sautéed onion and red bell pepper, topped with various cheeses. The lunch menu features the Flying Chicken Crepe, filled with fresh spinach, tomato, onion, and portobello mushroom with marinated grilled chicken, a topping of mozzarella cheese, and a blanket of poblano cream sauce. At dinner, our pick is the Wave Crasher, crispy taco shells filled with grilled fish, jalapeño, cilantro, tomato, and avocado. If you seek a buzz the coffee doesn't give, there's beer and wine, too. Other locations in Dallas at 2801 Commerce St., Dallas 75226; and 4154 N. Central Expy., Dallas 75204.

Café Brazil, 3847 Cedar Springs Rd., Dallas 75219; (214) 461-8762; cafebrazil.com; American; $-$$. It's our guess that the success of Café Brazil inspired others to open a coffee-and-breakfast-driven place that's open all night—like the Buzzbrews folks described above. Makes sense, because Café Brazil started doing just that more than two decades ago. Initially a small, comfy place to drink a global selection of coffee, eat inventive food, and not be subjected to cigarette smoke, this smart concept has turned into a booming local business all over town. Our favorite is this Oak Lawn / Uptown–area joint, a hippie-dippy place that hums with energy at all hours, day and night. We love the Brazilian, a plate of two eggs done sunny side up with a chorizo empanada topped in a chile-fired cream sauce, cheddar cheese, and tomato, with grilled homemade bread. The breakfast relleno, however, always tempts with a roasted poblano chile stuffed with scrambled eggs, chorizo, and cheese. For something sweeter, the signature "pancrepes" take a treatment of fresh fruit, crème anglaise, raspberry sauce, and walnuts. The special house homemade grilled bread shows up also on sandwiches that can be filled with seasoned beef fajitas, chicken salad, or a combination of cheeses with avocado. Slightly lighter, the spinach salad with bacon, feta, tomato, cucumber, and mushrooms can be topped with blackened or grilled chicken or fish. Other locations in Dallas, Carrollton, Addison, Plano, Richardson, and Fort Worth.

Cafe Madrid, 4501 Travis St., Dallas 75205; (214) 528-1731; **cafemadrid-dallas.com; Spanish; $$.** Dallas's first tapas restaurant doesn't lurk around the top of trendy people's go-to list, but that doesn't matter. It remains a good place to go for authentic Spanish food with family, friends, or a special date. The setting seems typical for an old-school tapas bar, with wooden tables and chairs, and there's usually live music, such as classical or flamenco guitar. When the weather's fine, pick a patio table. From the tapas menu, we like the potato omelet, shrimp in garlic, oxtail stew, grilled salmon with hearts of palm, and grilled white asparagus. The list of Spanish cheeses stuns even the pickiest cheese snob, and the staff is great with the proper wine pairing suggestions. When you have a party of four or more, call ahead and book the paella dinner. Cooked over a wood fire, the pan comes brimming with saffron rice, chicken, pork, clams, mussels, shrimp, scallops, and veggies. Check out happy hour, when house wines are $4.50 per glass.

The Capital Grille, 500 Crescent Ct., Dallas 75201; (214) 303-0500; thecapitalgrille.com; Steak House; $$$$. Yes, it's a national chain, but this steak house made itself right at home in Uptown, and Dallas has claimed it as its very own possession. Spreading along one side of the magnificent Crescent Court, next to the same-named Rosewood Crescent Hotel at the intersection of Maple, Cedar Springs, and McKinney, this restaurant couldn't have a better location for the shopping crowd (Stanley Korshack is next door) and the art gallery fans. Convenience to the Arts District is also a giant plus. Nevertheless, stellar, very personalized service, and exceptional steaks keep patrons coming back. At lunch, the French onion soup and pan-fried calamari with hot cherry peppers keeps us happy, but the Maine lobster salad in Champagne vinaigrette and the cheeseburger, made with chopped sirloin and smoked bacon and served with truffle fries, leaves lasting memories. In the evening, we enjoy starting with lobster–crab cakes and spinach salad with warm bacon dressing, followed by the bone-in Kona-coffee-crusted dry-aged tenderloin with shallot butter or the sesame-seared tuna with gingered rice. Coconut cream pie for dessert is dreamy.

Chuy's, 4544 McKinney Ave., Dallas 75205; (214) 559-2489; chuys .com; Mexican; $$. Exported initially from Austin before it began spreading all over the country, this Mexican-food gem unfolds within a vintage spread of buildings at one of the most desirable corners in town. Like at all Chuy's, the look gives the impression that a piñata stuffed with Elvis memorabilia exploded inside the store. Even if the extreme kitsch doesn't charm you, the food is good enough that you can overlook the gimmicks. True to its original appeal, Chuy's brings flavors of New Mexico and South Texas together to deliver a distinctive Mexican food experience, and it still turns out dishes we don't find elsewhere. The Chuychanga, a fried flour tortilla stuffed with oven-roasted chicken, cilantro, green chiles, and cheese, comes topped with a choice of sauces, and we like the South Texas–style ranchero best. The Elvis Green Chile Fried Chicken—a chicken breast coated with a potato-chip breading, then fried and blanketed in a New Mexico green chile sauce—is hard to beat. Stacked blue corn tortilla enchiladas, layered with chicken, cheese, and tomatillo sauce, make us a little weak in the knees. Be sure to order a margarita made with fresh lime juice—not a mix.

Cosmic Cafe, 2912 Oak Lawn Ave., Dallas 75219; (214) 521-6157; cosmiccafedallas.com; Indian/Vegetarian; $–$$. In a city that can be ever-so-fickle about its trends and fashionable dining, it's so good to see a quality, focused restaurant endure for what seems like ages. The bonus is that this long-standing favorite makes eating vegetarian a true pleasure, even if you're a dedicated carnivore. The flavors and textures are fresh and vibrant, so you don't mind one bit eating so healthfully. Appetizers include potato-pea samosas, served with mint and tamarind chutney; hummus, served with pappadum and naan; and soups like tomato with ginger, garlic, and basil. Entrees to investigate include curried veggies with samosa; veggie tacos with a side of black beans; spinach enchiladas in red corn tortillas; spicy portobello mushrooms over basmati rice; and the black bean burger. For something especially light, there are fruit smoothies and shakes, as well as fresh fruit and veggie juices. Beer and wine are offered, as well. What's more, you can enjoy—before or after your meal—assorted diversions, such as meditation, yoga, and poetry sessions, all meant to bring you peace and vitality. Check the website for these activity schedules.

Del Frisco's Grille, 3232 McKinney Ave., Dallas 75204; (972) 807-6152; delfriscosgrille.com; American; $$–$$$. This is the casual but fashionable version of the big-daddy steak house **Del Frisco's** (p. 178). At DF Grille, the menu is a little more relaxed, and the setting isn't as clubby as the power meat palaces. You'll see girlfriend groups out for lunch and dinner here, but it's also a good place for business and—thanks to a vibrant bar scene—meeting people of the opposite sex. Shared plates we particularly like include pimento cheese fritters with chipotle ranch sauce for dipping; steamed edamame with Korean barbecue spice and lime salt; ahi tuna tacos; and deviled 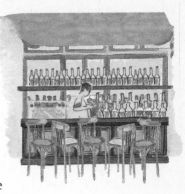 eggs with truffle-chive vinaigrette. Flatbreads include wild mushroom with fontina cheese and caramelized onion; and garlic shrimp with chorizo and mozzarella. Entrees tend toward the comfort food zone, with lamb burger, grilled cheese and roasted tomato bisque, veal meat loaf, and chicken schnitzel among good picks. For something lighter, the menu offers a seared Asian tuna salad and rock shrimp tacos. In nice weather, book a table on the sidewalk patio and watch the street theater passing by.

Dragonfly, 2332 Leonard St, Dallas 75201; (214) 550-9500; hotelzaza.com/#dallas/dragonfly; American; $$$. Down the hall from the lobby inside the enigmatic Hotel ZaZa, this stylish and sexy restaurant never ceases to amaze. Chef Dan Landsberg keeps things interesting with a changing menu that manages a balance of innovation and accessibility. His passion for comfort food shows readily, but his knack for doing things with imagination turns out plates you wouldn't have expected yet are delighted to find. His lamb lollipops, for instance, come atop a bed of greens with horseradish and a sort of brilliant sweet-hot jalapeño accompaniment; and his crispy pork belly gets soothing treatment from parsnip puree and snap from Spanish chorizo oil. And those are just the starters. Ginger-glazed beef tenderloin, braised pork osso bucco with butternut squash grits; and

Those Bodacious
Texas Gulf Coast Oysters

Everyone who eats oysters has become familiar with seeing Prince Edward Island oysters on menus. But until recently, you wouldn't have noticed place-names on menus bearing Texas Gulf Coast oysters.

It started down in Galveston, just a couple of years ago, when restaurants finally began to indicate where local oysters originated. It's become fashionable for chefs to note where oysters are derived, whether from the Gulf waters off Florida, Alabama, Louisiana, or Texas. For instance, Ladies Pass Oysters are fished in East Galveston Bay; the sources for Aransas Bay Oysters, Lavaca Bay Oysters; Mad Island Oysters, and Pepper Grove Oysters are obvious; Possum Pass Oysters come from Central Galveston Bay.

The point of origin gives a clue as their characteristics. Some are a tiny bit brinier than others, some a tad sweeter. All have one magnificent common element—they're fat, juicy, meaty, and almost too big to manage in one bite. Until Gulf oyster lovers begin to request these specially sourced jewels, however, this remains a novelty.

But some seafood-smart folks believe such selections may someday be as common as ordering Indian Creek oysters from Prince Edward Island and James River oysters from Virginia.

"Really, it's like offering varieties of fish or wine. You just give people the opportunity to pick what they want," says Jim Gossen, president Louisiana Foods Global Seafood Source of Houston. "It's branding—you put a name on it. Certain consumers want what is hand selected, whatever is the best available. I know I do."

house-made fettuccine with cremini mushrooms are among mains. The bar, a rocking gathering spot—especially at poolside in nicer weather—serves a tantalizing selection of goodies, such as The Big

Gossen, whose company supplies restaurants in all metro areas in Texas as well as **Central Market** (pp. 72 and 221) stores, figures if an oyster producer is pulling in 20,000 oysters a day, the boat crew can pick out the best 1,000 and charge a little more for the effort. The bottom line, he says, lies in restaurants promoting the oysters that way in order to create interest among chefs and, in turn, dining guests. When the demand is made, the supply has to follow.

"It's a smart marketing idea, which must have a lot to do with the success of branded oysters from the Northeast and the Pacific," says John Carver, executive chef for **Eddie V's Prime Seafood** (p. 86) restaurants in Fort Worth, Dallas, Austin, and Houston. Carver also notes that the downtown Austin store—where Eddie V's began—sells 1,500 Texas oysters on a busy night. The chain also has locations in Arizona, California, and Florida.

"But I'm not sure it's fair to charge a higher price just because they're branded from a special area. If it's just a little more, that's OK, as long as everyone benefits, from the oyster fisherman to the consumer."

In Fort Worth, Blaine Staniford, executive chef at **Grace** (p. 189), loves a Texas oyster if it's the best tasting oyster his customers can order. "I'd rather serve that than something I've had to bring in from New York or Boston."

Gossen realizes that the "branded oyster isn't necessarily for everyone, maybe not for the oyster bar that goes through a whole lot of oysters. Maybe it's really for the bistro guy who offers three or four kinds of specially picked oysters. But then again, maybe the oyster bar guy may realize, 'OK, maybe I can charge a couple of dollars more. . . .'"

Flirt, made with Absolut Mandarin, passion fruit puree, pineapple juice, and fresh berries; and the Honey Badger, made with house-infused honey, lavender vodka, lemon juice, and gummy candy. You'll hardly need dessert, but if you do, sundried cherry–white chocolate bread pudding is the way to go.

Eddie V's Prime Seafood, 4023 Oak Lawn Ave., Dallas 75219; (214) 890-1500; eddiev.com; Seafood; $$$$. There are two ways to approach this rather exceptional seafood restaurant that began in Austin—either as a place to have a crazy-fabulous fish dinner that will set you back a few bucks, or as a bar where you'll enjoy good music and some good, lighter food. If you decide to do the full-on dinner experience, be assured that the selection is as fresh and diverse as any you can find in almost any high-end restaurant in major cities. Good options include Louisiana oysters with lovely mignonette, and charred prime steak carpaccio for starters, Maine lobster and shrimp bisque or wild mushroom salad with hot goat cheese and arugula for a second course, and North Atlantic lemon sole, Florida grouper, or sautéed Georges Bank scallops for the main course. On evenings when we feel like something a little simpler, but still fairly swanky, we take a table in the bar, where live jazz plays nightly in a cozy setting with low lighting. We enjoy pot stickers filled with spicy shrimp and pork; lump crab cake; calamari fried kung pao style with roasted cashews; and fried oysters with Vietnamese curry flavors and pickled Asian cucumber. From 4 p.m. until 7 p.m., drinks and appetizers are discounted.

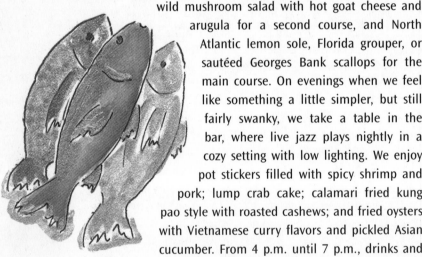

Forty Five Ten's T Room, 4510 McKinney Ave., Dallas 75205; (214) 559-2332; fortyfiveten.com; American; $–$$. Upon entering, you're thinking—wait, this is a clothing boutique with some pretty fancy price tags. Yes, it is. But keep going. In the back, the T Room is one of the better lunch spots in Dallas, bringing in a hip clientele for special eats. Start with the Asiago-Parmesan spread to smear over **Empire Baking Company** (p. 105) bread. Then choose between Thai noodle chicken salad, pecan-crusted chicken salad with cranberries, Asian pear salad with spicy pecan goat cheese, roasted tomato-basil soup, a seasonal vegetarian quiche, an artichoke panini, or tuna melt, made yummier with avocado and cheddar. For dessert, look no further than the lemon pistachio tart. Well, maybe look at the flourless chocolate cake. Unless you're trying on clothes after lunch.

Highland Park Pharmacy's Soda Fountain, 3229 Knox St., Dallas 75205; (214) 521-2126; highlandparksodafountain.com; American; $.

Possibly the oldest lunch spot in the city, this 1912 pharmacy still has a real, old-fashioned soda fountain. Belly up to the counter, hop on a stool (you can spin around, nobody minds), and get ready to take a huge step back in time. In the morning hours, enjoy eggs, bacon, and waffles. At lunch, tuck into a grilled cheese sandwich, grilled pimento cheese sandwich, chicken salad sandwich on toasted bread, Frito chili pie, or vegetable soup. You absolutely, positively want to get a handmade milk shake or malt, or an ice cream float or an ice cream sundae. If you want to linger, go at off-peak hours, when nobody waits for a seat, and you can have the leisure to visit with the staff who will tell you stories about the old-timers who come in every single day. There are even heart-warming tales about folks who have come in for lunch daily for years but were laid up with illness—in which case, the pharmacy folks delivered lunch.

JoJo Eating House & Bar, 2626 Howell St., Dallas 75204; (214) 754-4949; jojodallas.com; Mediterranean; $$.

Alsace native Laurent Poupart, whose resume includes work at L'Etoile in San Antoino and La Palme d'Or in Cannes, unveiled his Quadrangle-area Euro eatery in late 2012. Focusing on the foods of Spain, Morocco, France, and Italy, while applying classic French technique, Chef Laurent's JoJo Eating House

& Bar feels like an ultramodern residence done in clean lines, with a wraparound chef bar facing the open kitchen. There are communal tables, as well as customary dining tables and round booths. The bar has windows that can open onto the patio and street-side seating in pretty weather. Plates for sharing include an artisan cheese board with figs and olives; a charcuterie tray; and platters of iced shellfish. Classic items range from Margherita pizza and mussels and frites to osso bucco with polenta. For a finish, try one of the 40-minute soufflés or the Valrhona chocolate cake.

The Landmark Restaurant, 3051 Oak Lawn Ave., Dallas 75219; (214) 224-3152; landmarkrestodallas.com; American; $$$$. Inside the historic Melrose Hotel, at a primo address on the corner of Oak Lawn and Cedar Springs, is one of the most popular bars in the city. The Library has been a terrific piano bar for decades, and its appeal and popularity never wane, thanks to continuing praise from the likes of *Maxim* and *Playboy* magazines and the *Wall Street Journal*. But just down the hall, the hotel's restaurant shouldn't be overlooked. The Landmark provides edibles for the Library, include shrimp cocktail gazpacho; fried pork pot stickers; flatbread with prosciutto, figs, goat cheese, and lavender honey; and lamb T-bones. Inside the Landmark itself, pleasures include shrimp-crab Louie salad, escargot and pork belly, pan-seared foie gras, oven-roasted bone marrow with grilled naan and cherry marmalade, grilled octopus with Asian greens, pan-roasted halibut with bok choy, prime "baseball cut" sirloin with béarnaise sauce, a veggie noodle bowl, and myriad salads. At brunch, the embarrassment of riches runs from smoked vegetable soup, seared scallops, and steak and eggs to smoked salmon omelet, silver dollar pancakes, and orange-scented french toast. You'll want to have a room booked for your after-meal nap.

Malai Kitchen, 3699 McKinney Ave., Dallas 75204; (972) 591-3387; malaikitchen.com; Thai/Vietnamese; $$. A newish addition to the West Village ends the question of whether to go out for Thai or Vietnamese. Both find ample room on the menu, and both get the proper attention from an inventive kitchen. You can start with a glass of Napa Sauvignon Blanc, a dry Riesling, or a Gewürztraminer, all excellent pairings with Southeast Asian cuisine. Or let yourself indulge in a Kaffir Collins, a fizzy drink combing gin infused with kaffir lime, lemon, and soda, or, if you're in a sweeter mood, the Vang, a blend of Thai-spiced rum, ginger beer, lime, and green papaya. A light dinner would include a bowl of Prince Edward Island mussels in a broth of lemongrass, Sauvignon Blanc, and coconut with grilled French bread planks and a side of spring rolls, cool wraps holding seasoned shrimp, rice noodles, pickled bean sprouts, and herbs. Other light options include a bowl of pho, traditional beef Vietnamese soup garnished with raw vegetables, herbs, and chiles; and the spicy minced chicken salad called *larb*. For something bigger, start with Vietnamese meatballs of minced pork, ginger, and herbs in a tamarind glaze, then head on to the drunken noodles, flat jasmine-rice noodles with spicy chopped beef tenderloin and thai basil. Don't pass on the dessert of coconut cream pie topped with tamarind caramel, well worth that extra time in the gym to atone. Choose a patio table at this casual place, or take a seat at the friendly bar.

Max's Wine Dive, 3600 McKinney Ave., Dallas 75204; (214) 559-3483; maxswinedive.com; American; $$. From Houston comes a bar and grill that knows how to have a whole lot of fun. Its motto is "Fried chicken and Champagne? Why the hell not?" Inspired by enjoyable dive bars, this shabby-chic joint offers an excellent list of wines by the glass (and bottle), along with upscale comfort food and great tunes on the juke box. Date nights here are fun, but it's just as enjoyable to go with the girlfriends—and possibly meet someone, though that's not what brings people to Max's. Sharable small plates include bison sliders and fried chicken sliders, piquillo peppers stuffed with pulled pork, fried Gulf Coast oysters on crisp wontons with habanero salsa, and a cheese plate from nearby **Scardello Artisan Cheese** (p. 106). Big plates include Max's famous fried chicken, served with mashed potatoes, collard greens, and Texas toast; shrimp and grits; fried egg sandwich with truffle oil, bacon, gruyère, lettuce, and tomato on sourdough; and the "haute" dog, a Kobe beef frank on an artisan bun with fried onion rings, chili, jalapeños, and cotija cheese. At brunch, the cinnamon rolls come slathered in royal icing, three red velvet pancakes come topped with lemon cream cheese, and fried chicken comes with Belgian waffles. At happy hour (4 p.m. until 7 p.m. and late-night on weekdays), specials include sampler plates of wings, chicken-fried brussels sprouts, and mac and cheese. You'll need it to soak up all that wine.

Mia's, 4332 Lemmon Ave., Dallas 75219; (214) 526-1020; miastexmex.com; Mexican; $$. Brightly colored and bustling, this especially friendly Tex-Mex favorite feels like the interior of someone's warm and inviting home. Among starters to consider, the nachos locos are a pile of crispy tortilla chips covered with your choice of 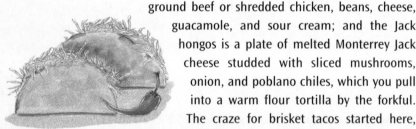 ground beef or shredded chicken, beans, cheese, guacamole, and sour cream; and the Jack hongos is a plate of melted Monterrey Jack cheese studded with sliced mushrooms, onion, and poblano chiles, which you pull into a warm flour tortilla by the forkful. The craze for brisket tacos started here, and other enduring specialties include chiles rellenos stuffed with beef, *carne asada,* shrimp in a garlic-butter sauce, and shrimp tacos. If some dishes seem kind of familiar here, it's because you may have seen very similar editions at **Mi Cocina** (p. 147), which is from the same family. A bit of trivia for sports fans: Jerry Jones met here with Jimmy Johnson, way back when Jones first bought the Dallas Cowboys, to convince his old college buddy to come coach the team and win some Super Bowls. There's a photo on the wall capturing the moment.

Mr. Mesero, 4444 McKinney Ave., Dallas 75205; (214) 780-1991; mrmesero.com; Mexican; $$. There's a lot of substance to go with the style you find oozing from every corner at this enjoyable Mexican newcomer. That's because its owner, Mico Rodriguez, knows what people want. He proved that time and again at his MCrowd Restaurants across the Dallas area, including **Taco Diner** (p. 147); **Mi Cocina** (p. 147), a descendant of **Mia's** (above); and **The Mercury** (p. 179). No longer with that group, Mico has begun reinventing himself with a smallish space that summons the spirit of San Miguel de Allende, Mexico, classy and distinguished and a good distance away from the Tex-Mex of his youth. One of the big-hit starters is the Queso Mesero, smooth white cheeses melted with roasted green chiles, spinach, and artichoke; and another is the nachos topped with black beans, cheese, brisket, and a slice of avocado. A good first-course specialty is the *fideo,* a chicken-vermicelli dish. Recommended entrees include anything with mole, one of the signatures from Mexico's interior, while a burly dish is the Mexican strip steak, grilled with serrano chiles. An enchilada combination not to be missed, the Six is a pork-cheese enchilada and a tomatillo-chicken enchilada. Alongside with any dish, you can order an assortment of specialty salsas, mixtures of various roasted chiles, and vegetables that result in a cornucopia of flavors. The specialty cocktails will wow you, particularly the La Doña, blending reposado tequila, Cointreau, and citrus juices.

Nick & Sam's, 3008 Maple Ave., Dallas 75201; (214) 871-7444; nick-sams.com; Steak House; $$$$. One of the bigger, very upscale beef palaces in town, this one comes from Phil Romano, whose contributions to the food world have ranged from Macaroni Grill to the fabulous **eatZi's** (p. 104). Opened in 1999, this beautiful showplace for beautiful diners works hard to maintain its sterling reputation and to earn the big bucks it charges for its food. Caviar is on the menu, but if your tastes are a bit more mainstream, you can start with something as approachable as oysters, crab cocktail, mussels in lobster-saffron broth, a fresh mozzarella salad with sliced beefsteak tomato and fresh basil leaves, or a field green salad with honey vinaigrette, roasted pear, and crisp goat cheese. An extraordinary steak is the dry-aged, long-bone cowboy rib eye, a monster portion of meltingly tender steak dressed in black truffle butter, with a side of lobster mac and cheese. Other meaty goodness is found in plates of maple-brined pork chop and Colorado lamb chops. Divine desserts range from chocolate chip cheesecake to pineapple upside-down bread pudding. If you're into wine, this is the place to indulge—the wine list is not something you'll forget for a long time.

Nick & Sam's Grill, 2816 Fairmount St., Dallas 75201; (214) 303-1880; nick-samsgrill.com; American; $$$. If Nick & Sam's (above) is a drop-dead handsome type of restaurant, this is the hot and dashing little brother. It's more casual, with a side of whimsy and pop music, as opposed to the dressy steak place. Regulars love it for brunch, when Cap'n Crunch french toast is the rage, as are bottomless mimosas and build-your-own omelets. For lunch and dinner, go for mussels in coconut milk with kaffir lime and ginger, the kung pao calamari, and the fried oysters. Main course musts include the flat iron steak with loaded mashers, scallops in Champagne-Dijon sauce, and pecan-crusted trout over wilted spinach. The burger has its share of devotees, probably because it comes with a side of Damn Good Fries, which are just that. Grown-Up Grilled Cheese packs in smoked ham, sliced pear, and gruyère cheese with a side of tomato-basil soup. Bring friends and sit on the patio in nice weather—you're sure to meet a few folks doing the same.

Parigi, 3311 Oak Lawn Ave., Dallas 75219; (214) 521-0295; parigidallas.com; French/American; $$–$$$. Cozy and exceptionally comfortable, this lovely bistro stays friendly and accessible, though it's in a trendy part of town. Owner Janice Provost, who is also a chef, keeps the tone here light but sophisticated, and she makes it possible for you to be indulgent or conscientious, whichever you prefer. From a menu that changes weekly, there are things like oven-roasted fish of the day with artichoke-potato puree and tarragon; escargot with garlic, butter, and toasted baguette; beef tenderloin with whole-grain mustard sauce; and a vegetable dish of acorn squash with quinoa, peas, carrots, parsnips, and spinach. Note on the menu that Janice likes to give props to local producers whose goods show up on her menu, including area farms, cheesemakers, meat markets, and vintners. The restaurant also exhibits work by local artists.

Perry's Steakhouse & Grille, 2001 McKinney Ave., Dallas 75201; (214) 855-5151; perryssteakhouse.com; Steak House; $$$$. Grown from a Houston-area butcher shop that opened in 1979, this Texas standout has become a destination in its own right, whether in Houston, Dallas, Austin, or San Antonio. In Big D, its location right by the Crescent Court and close to the Arts District has made it a must-eat establishment for the executive entertaining clients and the couple wanting lavish treatment. The interior feels like yesteryear elegance, and the service makes even the everyday Joe feel special. The Friday lunchtime pork chop—carved tableside—has become a bit of a legend, but it's intended for someone with a big appetite (maybe after a big Thursday night party?), as it's enough to feed a small village. At dinner, the iced seafood tower makes a fabulous start, followed by signature fried asparagus, topped with jump lump crabmeat. Turtle soup, in a nod to New Orleans, is a nice second, as is warm spinach salad. The prime bone-in New York strip is our favorite steak, but the chateaubriand for two, carved tableside, is especially good. Sides of roasted sherried mushrooms and lyonnaise potatoes round out the meal beautifully.

The Place at Perry's, 2680 Cedar Springs, Dallas 75201; (214) 871-9991; placeatperrys.com; Steak House; $$$$. Yes, things get a bit confusing here. Not only are there two steak houses with Perry's in the name but the two sit in the same neighborhood. The Place at Perry's was a Dallas hot spot when **Perry's Steakhouse** (above) arrived from Houston, with a longer history and the muscle to insist the Dallas upstart change its name. So The Place survived the drama, with aplomb. One of the few female-owned restaurants in the manly genre, this edition utilizes blown glass from a local artist and lighter choices in decor to soften the burly effect of the meat-eaters haven. Plentiful use of local suppliers puts fresh, seasonal items on the menu, too. We like starting the evening with a Mexican martini, made with aged tequila, sweet and sour, agave nectar, and a bit of Gran Marnier. Next, we think the barbecued Gulf shrimp with grits and the mango crab tower are the right starters, followed by tomato-artichoke bisque and then hand-cut prime rib eye in a guajillo chile rub and pan-seared Scottish salmon with quinoa and green lentils. At brunch, the crab

cake Benedict; Southern fried steak with eggs, gravy, and mashed potatoes; and bread pudding with pecans, strawberries, and green apple is the perfect way to wrap up the weekend.

Primo's, 3309 McKinney Ave., Dallas 75204; (214) 220-0510; primosdallas.com; Tex-Mex; $$. A long-time hangout in Uptown, this wonderful spot only gets better with age. Brought into fame some 20 years ago when chefs from the high-end restaurants nearby would come relax here after their work shifts, Primo's became the go-to place for everyone in the Park Cities and Uptown. The Sunday brunch is hugely satisfying, but any day of the week is perfect for top-rate margaritas and a plate of the delicious tacos camperos filled with beef fajita meat. Pile on jalapeño, cilantro, avocado slices, and a spoonful of the tomato salsa on the table. It's a good spot to take a break from shopping and gallery browsing; relax on the patio or in one of the rooms inside the 100-year-old building with creaky wooden floors. There's often a party on the patio, sports on TV, and perhaps even a karaoke session in progress.

Sangria Mediterranean Tapas and Bar, 4524 Cole Ave., Dallas 75204; sangriatapasybar.com; Mediterranean; $$–$$$. Rather than dub itself a straight-up Spanish restaurant, this effort from the Lombardi restaurant group describes itself as Mediterranean. So be it—that just means there's more to eat! Start with tomato gazpacho topped with avocado relish and basil, then dig into the Sangria salad, a work in organic greens topped by strawberries, goat cheese, spicy walnuts and sherry vinaigrette. Shared table goodies include pan con tomate with Serrano ham and manchego cheese, blisterered shishito peppers, spanakopita, fried calamari, escargot and empanada stuffed with rock shrimp spinach, pine nuts and currants. Larger plates ranged from butternut squash ravioli, diver scallops with pork belly, Greek lamb chops and gnocchi with oxtail ragù to shrimp skewers and pasta with ham, garlic, shallots and mushrooms. There's paella, too, made in classic preparation. Brunch is a delightful affair at Sangria, with an omelet that can include goodies from a list of asparagus, chorizo, ham, mushrooms, Manchego, piquillo peppers, and more. Beef picadillo in the Cuban style comes with poached eggs and hollandaise over rustic country bread. For dessert, be sure to enjoy churros with hot chocolate sauce. And don't miss those $1 mimosas.

Sfuzzi, 2533 McKinney Ave., Dallas 75204; (214) 953-0300; sfuzziuptown.com; Italian; $$–$$$. In the late 1980s, a restaurant called Sfuzzi opened on McKinney Avenue when just a few bistros and cafes dared launch businesses on the long-abandoned street. Nobody called the district Uptown yet. Sfuzzi brought a lighter, fresher approach to Italian food and introduced a frozen Champagne-peach concoction called a Bellini, and everyone went wild. It was the busiest place in town, and soon Sfuzzi spread to cities across the nation. One day, however, it was gone—*fini*. But 20 years later, another Sfuzzi arrived, in a different but wonderfully historic building along McKinney. The style of the new edition summons up ideas of a vintage New York City pizzeria, but one with a lively patio scene. Among instant hits at the new Sfuzzi, the portobello fries with tomato-basil aioli are sensational, and the Italian wedge salad, with smoked bacon and Gorgonzola dressing, is fabulous. Our favorite pizza is the one topped with poached eggs and prosciutto, but the artichoke, blue cheese, and spinach version is excellent as well. Spaghetti and meatballs pleases, and if you need your pasta gluten-free, just ask. Those frozen Bellinis are still on the menu, as are lots of specialty cocktails. The music you'll hear piped in ranges from '80s dance hits to jazz and blues to Johnny Cash. It adds up to a good time.

Stampede 66, 1717 McKinney Ave., Dallas 75201; (214) 550-6966; stampede66.com; American/Southern; $$$. Star chef Stephan Pyles opened this homage to his humble West Texas roots in late 2012. Here he puts contemporary updates on the foods many Texans grew up loving, from honey-fried chicken to Frito pie. There are fancy tamales and tacos, too, as well as smoked chicken and dumplings, barbecued beef brisket with potato salad, venison meat loaf with mac and cheese, shrimp étouffée with dirty rice, and fried oysters. For folks who simply can't live without Pyles's signature bone-in cowboy rib eye steak, it's here on the menu, too. Among several worthwhile desserts, there's the lemon tart, butterscotch pudding, and pecan pie. Ask for a Molecular Margarita and enjoy the mad-scientist tableside preparation. Be sure to check out the sexy cowgirl and cowboy artwork in the bathrooms, as well as the famous Texans' names burned onto Western belts on the bathroom doors. See Chef Stephan Pyles's recipe for **Ecuadorian Shrimp Ceviche with Orange & Popcorn** on p. 228.

Stoneleigh P, 2926 Maple Ave., Dallas 75201; (817) 871-2346; American; $–$$. Long ago, this was the neighborhood pharmacy that served residents living just north of downtown proper. In the 1970s, its function as a soda fountain expanded into a restaurant and bar, and so it remains. People in search of fashionable, fancy places to eat do not come here. This hangout appeals to the come-as-you-are crowd in search of friendly service, simple food, an excellent craft beer selection, a place to read and shoot pool, and occasionally a venue for hearing live music. The burger topped with chipotle mayo is good, but we're partial to the tuna sandwich on pumpernickel, as well as a barbecue sandwich that's sometimes a special. Out front, there's a big patio, too, where locals bring their (leashed) dogs along.

Taverna Pizzeria and Risotteria, 3312 Knox St., Dallas 75205; (214) 520-9933; tavernabylombardi.com; Italian; $$. The Caprese salad of fresh buffalo mozzarella from Puglia with cherry tomatoes and basil oil pairs well with the crisp rosemary focaccia, but more substantial is the risotto with asparagus, prosciutto, and shaved pecorino. And if you've been to Rome, you'll get why this pizza has become such a hit. Crisp as a cracker, this featherlight crust seems to have wings. It also serves as a vehicle for transporting your palate to a happy encounter with lovely, distinctive toppings. Favorites include the one with fresh, rich mozzarella, earthy Gorgonzola, pieces of pear, walnuts, and arugula, and the one spread with basil pesto, shreds of sun-dried tomato, whole shrimp, and mozzarella.

Among other good finds, there's Parmesan-crusted shrimp scampi with polenta; a rustic lasagna made with spinach pasta, wild mushrooms, and Bolognese sauce; and pan-seared beef tenderloin with arugula and roasted potatoes. For dessert, the panna cotta with strawberries, honey, and lemon sauce will satisfy. You'll find this little hideout an especially cozy place for squandering a leisurely lunch or dinner hour or two.

Texas de Brazil, 2727 Cedar Springs Rd., Dallas 75201; (214) 720-1414; texasdebrazil.com; Steak House; $$$$. Ah, the carnivore's dream come true—a place where meat is on parade and you eat until you're ready to die. When the Brazilian steak-house craze hit Texas in the 1990s, Texas de Brazil was at the forefront of the trend, opening these *churrascarias* in Dallas, Fort Worth, Addison, Houston, and San Antonio. And though the trend isn't the subject of great buzz anymore, the places remain busy. They're opulent in design, with soaring ceilings and glitzy design detail, from big chandeliers to heavy ornamental iron accents everywhere. But yet it's not a dressy place; people come in their golf attire if they like. Here's how it works: You help yourself to a giant buffet of salads and sides, the best of which include marinated asparagus and roasted red bell peppers, grilled portobello mushrooms, Greek olives, shrimp salad, numerous imported cheeses, fresh buffalo mozzarella, sushi, black bean soup, and much, much more. Then the gauchos, or servers, start roaming past your table with huge swords spearing any of 18 fire-grilled meats. You'll have a choice of different cuts of beef, pork, and lamb, as well as Brazilian sausage and marinated chicken—as much as you want. Servers also bring side dishes of mashed potatoes and roasted banana to the table, as well. Note that if you don't want to eat the meats, nobody says you have to; the salad and soup offerings will suit you just fine. There's a good wine list available, too. Other locations in Addison and Fort Worth.

Toulouse Cafe and Bar, 3314 Knox St., Dallas 75205; (214) 520-8999; toulousecafeandbar.com; French; $$–$$$. A good reproduction of the French sidewalk cafe is found in this offering from the Lombardi restaurant group. At brunch, a favorite dish is the Katy Trail Omelette, so named for the running/walking path just outside the restaurant's front door, an egg-white omelet filled with fontina cheese, spinach, and mushrooms. The crab Florentine puts poached eggs atop English muffins with sautéed spinach, jumbo lump crabmeat, and a lush cream sauce. Lunch favorites include the selection of mussels, which can be Provençal, with tomato, olive, white wine, garlic, and herbs; Thai, with coconut milk, yellow curry, lemongrass, and ginger; or saffron with kaffir lime, saffron broth, tomatoes, leeks, and herbs. Our dinner pick is the steak frites, a prime New York strip with fries and a béarnaise sauce, but for something light, we're apt to go for the puff pastry baked with goat cheese, with a niçoise salad. A lovely wine list and an artisan cheese platter are also worth noting.

T/X Restaurant & Bar, 2927 Maple Ave., Dallas 75201; (214) 871-7111; lemeridiendallasstoneleigh.com/dallas-restaurant; American; $$$. Inside the exceptionally posh Stoneleigh Hotel, this newish restaurant puts a Texas twist on its offerings. For example, the breakfast dish called the T/X Benedict puts a chipotle hollandaise

on its poached eggs, and the grapefruit halves are caramelized under a broiler. At lunch, hanger-steak sliders hold chicken-fried steak and grilled jalapeños, while the Southwest salad includes grilled hanger steak with a spicy salsa vinaigrette. A good dinner starter is the chowder filled with poblano chiles, chicken, and corn hash relish. The duck entree, including duck breast and leg confit, comes with a spicy guajillo chile sauce and crepes teased with a Mexican chocolate-orange sauce. For dessert, choices include sweet potato sopaipillas, little pastry pillows dusted with spicy Mexican sugar and laced with a cinnamon sauce.

Urban Taco, 3411 McKinney Ave., Dallas 75204; (214) 272-7619; urban-taco.com; Mexican; $$. With a list of 10 salsa options, you could spend a lot of time just nibbling on chips and dips. Jalapeño-zucchini and *pico de piña,* as well as the more dense and fiery poblano-pepita pesto and the sweet-and-three-alarm roasted-peanut habanero all deserve special praise, and they're good on the delicate, handmade corn tortillas, too. From the menu's taqueria list, the leading choice is red snapper slathered with tomatillo-serrano salsa and avocado crema. *Arrachera* (or steak) tacos reveal small adobo-marinated beef pieces tossed with diced avocado, roasted red onion, and avocado-jalapeño salsa, while a meatless potato-roasted zucchini taco with strips of roasted poblano and *queso fresco* definitely satisfies. For plenty of protein and lots of flavor, hit the ceviche list, starring a sensational *crudo,*

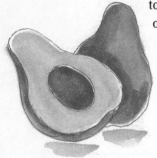

combining silken ahi tuna with bits of mango, pineapple, toasted garlic pieces, avocado, and a drizzle of chile oil, a concoction from which crisp yuca chips shoot skyward. Guacamole choices abound; the best may be the reforma, a combination of mashed avocado with roasted red onion, grilled serranos, roasted zucchini, oven-dried tomatoes, toasted garlic, and a salsa blending guajillo and chile pequin. Casual but still very chic, this spot draws a hip crowd to its stylish Mexico City–influenced space.

Yutaka Sushi Bistro, 2633 McKinney Ave., Dallas 75204; (214) 969-5533; yutakasushibistro.com; Japanese; $$$. A smash-hit upon its opening in 2006, this little but earnest Japanese cafe keeps turning out impressive, impeccable food. Owner-chef Yutaka Yamato produces lovely dishes that surprise even the jaded diner, because you find things here that aren't dumbed down for the bland American palate. Among sushi dishes, you want to take the off-menu Sushi Tour of Japan and let the sushi chefs charm you. Be bold and enjoy not just the fancy rolls but the more pure, unadorned fish pieces for their sheer flavor and texture. The *katsuo,* or Japanese bonito, is sublime; so is the *kanburim,* or wild yellowtail, as well as the *majina,* or black snapper.

For something a little fun there are sushi tacos, including jumbo lump crabmeat and guacamole. Cold dishes we love include the yellowtail sashimi with jalapeño and yuzu–soy sauce; Kobe beef *tataki* with micro greens and white truffle oil; and seaweed salad, for something cleansing. Among hot dishes, we like the seared foie gras with braised daikon radish and yuzu marmalade, and the sake-steamed clam with sansho pepper. Look on a side street for the restaurant's front door; in spite of the address, the bistro does not face McKinney Avenue.

Zaguán Bakery, 2604 Oak Lawn Ave., Dallas 75219; (214) 219-8393; zaguanbakery.com; Latin American / Bakery; $–$$. This petite Latin American bakery and cafe does a delightful *arepa,* a savory cornmeal turnover from Venezuela and Colombia, which we had stuffed with tender chicken and cheese. Our favorite remains the *cachapa,* more like a thick crepe, a larger, sweet corn turnover we had stuffed with shredded beef and cheese. The *ropa vieja* is a plate of hand-shredded beef with steamed rice, black beans, and fried sweet plantains. If you want an over-easy egg on top, just ask. The shredded chicken soup with potatoes, corn on the cob, peas, and carrots is delightful peasant food. A simple salad of greens, tomato, onion, bell pepper, and mushrooms in a balsamic vinaigrette becomes an easy lunch when topped with chicken, beef, or tuna. From the pastry list, the chocolate croissant is ridiculously sinful, and the dulce de leche, a vanilla cake filled with and topped by caramel milk and whipped cream, will put you into a swoon.

Ziziki's, 4514 Travis St., Dallas 75205; (214) 521-2233; zizikis .com; Greek; $$. Open for nearly 20 years, this pleasant, inviting Greek restaurant in Travis Walk makes you feel at home in its airy interior and on the pretty patio. Named for the yogurt sauce you see on so many of the dishes, especially those with lamb, Ziziki's is a good place to go with a group of friends who like to graze. Good sharing dishes include the plate of hummus made with artichokes, lemon, and garlic; the Mediterranean bread topped with feta, tomatoes, olive oil, and basil; and the platter loaded with spanakopita, hummus, dolmades, and grilled pita. Among salads, the marinated, grilled salmon and the Greek salad topped with feta and kalamata olives are both addictive. Specialty entrees include the Greek burger, leg of lamb, moussaka, and the Greek paella made with curried orzo, chicken, shrimp, chicken sausage, and lamb. At happy hour, the specialty drinks—such as the Grecian Sidecar and the Sunkiss—are just $7. Other locations in Dallas and Plano.

Landmarks

Abacus, 4511 McKinney Ave., Dallas 75205; (214) 559-3111; kentrathbun.com/abacus/dallas; American/Asian; $$$$. The deft touch of Executive Chef Kent Rathbun—a true Dallas culinary celebrity—and his stunning wine list have earned glorious praise from national press, thanks to such pleasures as lager-braised veal breast with English pea pierogi; grilled duck with leg confit and black pepper–ricotta cavatelli; and fascinating sushi rolls, such as the Picasso, combining spicy tuna, roasted pineapple, avocado, and salmon. For an extra treat, guests should try the chef's selection of five or eight small courses, with wine pairings, and luxuriate in the palate pampering and the soothing, sumptuous interiors. See Chef Kent Rathbun's recipe for **Lobster Macaroni & Cheese with Truffle Oil** on p. 229.

Fearing's at the Ritz-Carlton, 2121 McKinney Ave., Dallas 75201; (214) 922-4848; fearingsrestaurant.com; American/ Southwestern; $$$$. After making the **Mansion Restaurant** on Turtle Creek (below) the leading dining destination in Texas for two decades, superstar chef Dean Fearing opened a place of his own at the prestigious Ritz-Carlton. In each of seven distinct settings under one roof, the popular Southerner does much to please his ever-ardent fans, with lobster-coconut bisque, apricot-barbecue-glazed Texas quail, Dean's renowned tortilla soup, maple-black peppercorn buffalo tenderloin, pecan-crusted halibut, crab tacos, and—at brunch— stunningly good fried chicken. Drinks in his Rattlesnake Bar include El Diablo, a mixture of Patron Silver Tequila, black currant liqueur, fresh lime juice, and ginger ale. If you see Dean—he's often making rounds through the dining room—be sure to say hello. You haven't met a friendlier guy. See Chef Dean Fearing's recipe for **Dean's Tortilla Soup with South of the Border Flavors** on p. 231.

The Mansion Restaurant, 2821 Turtle Creek Blvd., Dallas 75219; (214) 559-2100; mansiononturtlecreek.com; Upscale/French; $$$$. A destination dining spot in Dallas of the first order, the Mansion Restaurant on Turtle Creek—attached to the flagship Rosewood hotel—entered a new era when French-born Bruno Davaillon came aboard from one of Alain Ducasse's restaurants. Typical food-and-wine pairings might include hamachi sashimi with green apple mustard, cucumber, daikon, and jalapeño oil, coupled with a Berroia Chacoli de Vizcaya from the Basque Country. Each week brings surprises in a new tasting menu, so repeat visits may be justifiable, even at the highest prices around. Don't overlook brunch, which stars Nutella-stuffed french toast as well as grilled prawns with ancho chile grits, chorizo Bolognese, and a poached egg.

S&D Oyster Company, 2701 McKinney Ave., Dallas 75204; (214) 880-0111; sdoyster.com; Seafood; $$. Since 1976, this standby on McKinney was a regular haunt of thousands of Dallasites long before Uptown was called Uptown. Very New Orleans in style and personality, this oyster bar has been consistent with its food, service, and loyal crowds always. The raw menu simply consists of oysters on the half shell (these are the big Gulf daddies, typically) and peeled, deveined shrimp that you eat with cocktail sauce or Southern-style remoulade. Seafood gumbo is good, but don't overlook the fried oysters, broiled trout (warning—there's lots of butter going on here), and fried grouper. Speaking of butter, the New Orleans–style barbecued shrimp, served with a loaf of French bread for sopping up the spicy butter sauce, is divine—and the closest we've found to that in the Crescent City outside of Louisiana. French fries and hush puppies are the popular sides here. Keep an eye out for local celebrities; the Wilson Brothers (Owen and Luke, in particular) have been coming here since they were little kids.

Specialty Stores, Markets & Producers

Chocolate Secrets, 3926 Oak Lawn Ave., Dallas 75219; (214) 252-9801; chocolatesecrets.net. Don't think for a second that this is any chocolate shop. In fact, it's a lot of chocolate wonderfulness of myriad descriptions. Yes there are glass cases filled with truffles and other exquisite goodies that are made by hand to look like works of art. Chocolates are made with everything from sunflower seeds to balsamic vinegar to sea salt and caramel to bacon. But there's also a cafe side to the business, where you sit and enjoy crepes, wine, live jazz, and the company of someone who loves chocolate as much as you do. In addition to wine, there are coffee drinks and—oh, be still my heart—drinking chocolate. On your way out, be sure to take home some bourbon chocolate popcorn.

eatZi's Market & Bakery, 3403 Oak Lawn Ave., Dallas 75219; (214) 526-1515; eatzis.com. An homage to the exquisite corner stores found all over Europe, this small gourmet grocery brings joy to a foodie's day. Upon walking in, you're surrounded by opera music and enveloped by the smell of freshly baking bread. To the right, those breads and a multitude of just-made pastries await. Beyond that, cheeses by the hundreds. Past that, you'll see a refrigerated case of ready-made meals that can include mac and cheese and lasagna, crème brûlée, and lovely salads. There's a sandwich counter, where chefs will prepare something on fresh breads with any number of artisan meats and cheeses. A central food deli dispenses everything from sushi to fresh beef tenderloin for you to take home and prepare. On the far wall, a hot cooking station keeps foccacia, grilled salmon, and much more ready to take home. The market also stocks a broad range of wines, packaged things like imported crackers and fine mustards, and a pretty selection of fresh-cut flowers. You can feel good about shopping here, too: The company donates a great deal to Hunger Busters, a mission to feed hungry children in Dallas.

Empire Baking Company, 5450 Lovers Lane, Dallas 75209; (214) 350-0007; www.empirebaking.com. Begun in 1994, Empire has been the name most associated with fine artisan breads in Dallas. More often than not, this is the name you'll see touted on restaurant menus, as Empire supplies a good many chefs with their baked goods. Best of all, however, you can buy the Empire breads right at the source. Popular choices include apple-walnut, kalamata, braided challah, jalapeño cheese, walnut-scallion, and raisin pecan. In addition, there are numerous bagel varieties made on-site, as well as cinnamon rolls, cream cheese Danish, scones, brownies, banana bread, rugulach, and muffins. Cookies include M&M, trail mix, and ginger-molasses. The store also

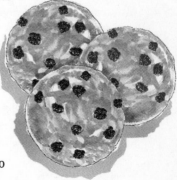

sells Zip Code Honey (good for allergies); In a Pickle jams, jellies, and pickles; and **Dude, Sweet Chocolate** (p. 124) sweets.

Paciugo Gelato, 3699 McKinney Ave., Dallas 75204; (214) 219-2665; paciugo.com. The gelato shops you see nearly everywhere grew from this West Village shop in Dallas. Dallas resident Cristiana Ginatta, a native of Italy, began the place in 2000 out of yearning for the gelato she grew up on and so dearly missed in her new country. A culinary school graduate, Cristiana set about making gelato as fine as that of her homeland, and it's now enjoyed by people all over America. You'll find a few dozen flavors available at any one time; among the most intriguing and rewarding are almond praline, banana chocolate chip, dulce de leche, ginger vanilla, toasted coconut, and vanilla lavender. The shop also offers a number of sorbet flavors, such as raspberry pomegranate and orange basil. Soy-based gelato is offered, as well.

Scardello Artisan Cheese, 3511 Oak Lawn Ave., Dallas 75219; (214) 219-1300; scardellocheese.com. Cheese lovers rejoiced when this shop opened just a few years ago. The focus here is on 150 (give or take) artisan cheeses from American and European farmsteads, with a very good number of Texas farms represented. Customers are given samples so they can know what cheeses to buy, and, inevitably, you wind up ordering a board of cheeses with a bottle of wine so you can sit and enjoy the goodness on the spot. Among sandwiches to order, there's the Sweet Italian, made with thinly sliced prosciutto, burrata cheese, and fig confit on a freshly baked bagette. Stuart's Cheddar Press melts Royal Cheddar from Veldhuizen Farmstead at Dublin, Texas, on a sandwich with garlic dill pickles—and it's to die for. Owner Rich Scardello so loves the cheese business, and so enjoys educating people, that he creates a number of special events for customers to enjoy, including cheese and wine or cheese and beer-pairing classes.

Oak Cliff

Once a township on the south bank of the Trinity River just 2 miles south of downtown Dallas, Oak Cliff was originally called Hord's Ridge when a community was initially founded in 1845. The community grew when the railroad came through, and developers in the late 19th century began creating an impressive residential area that would come to boast beautiful homes. Eventually, Oak Cliff became loved for its Marsalis Park and Zoo, now the very popular Dallas Zoo.

But much of Oak Cliff fell on very hard times through the years. Other than the lovelier residential areas of Kessler Park and Stevens Park and a handful of others in North Oak Cliff, this southwestern part of Dallas was one generally to be avoided by the 1960s. Most unfortunately, Oak Cliff became forever associated with one of the darkest days in American history, when Lee Harvey Oswald was arrested in an Oak Cliff movie theater for the assassination of President John F. Kennedy on November 22, 1963.

Even as recently as 15 years ago, if you'd told most Dallasites that the hippest place to eat, work, shop, and live in their city would one day be in Oak Cliff, they'd have sent you to have your head examined. Yet, community-minded individuals with a passion for history, architecture, and restoration saw great promise in an area of Oak Cliff called the Bishop Arts District—and that's where you'll find a vast majority of Oak Cliff's most desirable dining destinations offering everything from Mexican-Salvadoran cuisine, Thai and Japanese cooking, pizza, and Southern specialties to French bistro fare and killer burgers.

That's not to say that you shouldn't wander around to enjoy other places to eat and imbibe nearby Bishop Arts, as there are immensely worthwhile flavors to be consumed outside the historic district, of course. Even if some of the exteriors look like a face-lift is in order, don't worry—that's part of the well-loved character of Oak Cliff. Chances are a restoration is coming to that block, sooner rather than later.

Foodie Faves

Boulevardíer, 408 N. Bishop Ave., Dallas 75208; (214) 942-1828; dallasboulevardier.com; French; $$–$$$. A smash hit upon opening in late summer 2012, this laid-back but hip bistro made Bishop Arts an even hotter dining destination. Instant signature dishes include crawfish beignets; the killer charcuterie platter with country pork pâté, tongue pastrami, and salmon gravlax; steak frites; grilled Lockhart quail with field pea succotash; and duck sausage cassoulet. And that barely scratches the surface of divine works at this place. Oysters plucked out of chilly waters from the Pacific Northwest to Maine and the Texas Gulf coast (in winter) make the ideal starter, as does the tender, juicy shreds of pork cheek over firm, sweet grits cakes. Among entrees, it's impossible to do better than the bouillabaisse, a gorgeous bowl piled with mussels, clams, jumbo shrimp, and baby octopus in a lobster-saffron broth hinting of white wine, with grilled planks of bread piled on top. A carnivorous orgy breaks out when the massive lamb neck is served, and it's the size of a small roast; you pull forkfuls of the silken meat away, stab a piece of fingerling potato and a tiny carrot, swish that around in the wine reduction, and eat. Then swoon. Reservations aren't taken, so without them you take your chances. There's a friendly bar up front where you can cool your heels. See Chef Nathan Tate's recipe for **Beef Burgundy** on p. 227.

Chan Thai, 312 W. 7th St., Dallas 75208; (214) 948-9956; chanthai.net; Thai/Asian; $$. Among the earlier arrivals in the first wave of hip restaurants to bring Bishop Arts into the world of trendy dining, Chan Thai strikes a nice balance between stylish and delicious. Yes, it's a pretty place, but it doesn't sacrifice substance in the process. At lunch, the special $7.99 deals include everything from *pad khing,* ginger stir-fried with jalapeños and mixed vegetables with your choice of chicken, beef, pork, or tofu, to *pad tak khai,* Japanese eggplant with lemongrass basil, bell peppers, and your choice of those proteins. At lunch or dinner, lighter options may include grilled salmon salad with ginger or peanut dressing; fresh summer rolls stuffed with noodles, shrimp, crab, mango, lettuce, and bean sprouts; or spicy beef salad, thinly sliced marinated steak tossed with cucumber, tomato, lime, baby greens, cilantro, and mint. Among soups, the best is *tom ka gai,* blending coconut milk, chicken, mushrooms, hot chiles, and herbs with tart lemongrass. The most elaborate dishes include the Phi Phi Island, mixing scallops, calamari, shrimp, mussels, and egg with noodles in a sweet yellow curry sauce. If you still have room, check out fried ice cream for dessert.

Chicken Scratch, 2303 Pittman St., Dallas 75208; (214) 749-1112; cs-tf.com; American/Southern; $. From the creators of the profoundly wonderful **Smoke** (p. 122) comes an even more casual dining spot, sort of around the corner from the sister restaurant. As the name would indicate, there's plentiful fried chicken, pan-fried in a cast-iron skillet, as good fried chicken should be, as well as chicken roasted on a pecan-wood-fired rotisserie. The chicken, naturally, is hormone-free and never frozen, plus it's raised on area farms, so you're eating really good stuff here. If you want to be "bad," you can have biscuits and fried chicken gravy, but you can be good, too, and enjoy spicy chunky veggie–quinoa salad.

Other offerings include spicy tacos with salsa verde, chicken-vegetable soup, wraps of lettuce and hummus, and all sorts of side dishes, including mac and cheese with green chiles and charred tomato-roasted eggplant. Attached to Chicken Scratch is one of the better bars in Dallas, a place called The Foundry, with excellent, straightforward cocktails and a sensational selection of microbrews. You can sit inside or out in the sprawling courtyard, decorated with storage containers, wooden palettes, and pieces of heavy machinery. Dogs are welcome in the outside seating area, too.

Driftwood, 642 W. Davis St., Dallas 75208; (214) 942-2530; driftwood-dallas.com; Seafood; $$$. Newer among the most popular destinations in Bishop Arts, this seafood upstart makes our heads swim with pleasure. Done in blues and shades of sand, with wood and other natural materials, Driftwood's rather petite size adds to the exclusivity factor, and everyone wants to dine here. Weekend reservations are snapped up several days in advance, so you'll be stuck with a 5:30 or 9:30 p.m. booking on Friday unless you plan carefully. But all the planning is well worth your trouble, because this charming hipster delivers the goods. The runaway hit on chef Omar Flores's menu is the chargrilled octopus, which is nirvana to those already in love with this delicacy, and a fabulous surprise to all the doubters who are brave enough to go for it. It comes with a potato confit, manzanilla olives, watercress, and pickled onions in a smoked tomato vinaigrette, so the whole dish tantalizes. A good non-fish option, the crispy duck confit leg and seared duck breast sits atop swiss chard with ricotta gnocchi and huckleberry jus, just for fun. The *crudo* and shellfish options make the palate sing, starting with Kumamoto oysters in white shoyu with Asian pear and *sudachi* mignonette; Florida rock shrimp ceviche with Rio Star grapefruit from South Texas, shaved fennel, and avocado-jalapeño mousse; and smoked Japanese hamachi with a mandarin-fennel puree and mint. Cocktails are plenty of fun at Driftwood, too: Our favorites are the spicy R'evolution, blending peach vodka with tequila, Grand Marnier, Tabasco, and lime; and the OC 75, vodka spiked with pear liqueur, bubbly, and lime.

El Jordan Cafe, 416 N. Bishop Ave., Dallas 75208; (214) 941-4451; Mexican; $. Rather an anomaly among so many trendy, stylish Bishop Arts eating establishments, El Jordan shines for its unapologetic, unsophisticated plainness. Booths are old, some are ripped; chairs and tables don't match, and no one cares; the decor, notable most for an old mural of a pastoral Mexican scene on one wall, is ages old. Oh, and it's small, crowded, and the servers may or may not speak a language you do. That's just the way the regulars like it, so understand that if you like the dive vibe, you'll be in heaven. You'll also be thrilled if you like cheap, plentiful, homey Mexican food, by the way. We're especially fond of the generous breakfast plates, particularly the *huevos con papas,* or soft-scrambled eggs mixed with chunks of potatoes; and the giant breakfast burrito stuffed with eggs, jalapeños, chorizo, and onion. At lunch, the *carne asada* and *tacos al carbon* are hard to beat. The homemade salsa and big basket of warm chips that precede your meal—sometimes forgettable at other establishments—are solid at El Jordan. And where else can three people eat for less than $25, total?

Eno's Pizza Tavern, 407 N. Bishop Ave., Dallas 75208; (214) 943-9200; enospizza.com; Pizza; $$. Typically crowded most times of day and night, Eno's is two places in one—a place for excellent pizza and a hangout for fans of microbrews. For starters, we're likely to dive into a bowl of the special soups, always friendly for vegetarians, such as corn chowder, tomato-basil, or baked potato. The Italian beef sandwich keeps palates pleased, as does the chicken salad wrap that includes artichoke hearts, fresh tarragon, and dried cherries. Among salads, the Streetside combines assorted olives, bell peppers, shallots, tomatoes, sport peppers, feta, and cucumber-dill-oregano vinaigrette over mixed greens. The pasta dish we keep coming back to is the one with orzo, cherry tomatoes, fresh basil, and spicy sausage in a fennel broth. But, oh yeah, we remembered that the point was to come eat pizza, so we're likely to dig into Eno's Original, with mushroom, garlic, freshly sliced tomatoes, sport peppers, and salami. Unless, of course, we're going for the Yard Pie, combining fennel, basil, mushroom, garlic, onion, charred tomatoes, olive oil, ricotta, and fresh mozzarella. The beverage choices include Texas-made Fireman's #4 Ale, Four Corners Palatero, and Revolver Blood and Honey; cocktails that mix together goodies like cranberry, mint, sugarcane, and tequila; and wines from a list that offers Cortijo, a Tempranillo from Spain, and Block Nine, a Pinot Noir from St. Helena, California. Happy hour daily special includes discounts on microbrews from 2 p.m. to 6 p.m., and on weekends Eno's is open until midnight.

Gonzalez Restaurant, 367 W. Jefferson Blvd., Dallas 75208; (214) 946-5333; gonzalezrestaurant.com; Mexican; $–$$. Closer to downtown than the trendier neighborhood of Bishop Arts, this Tex-Mex classic has endured the tougher times of Oak Cliff. In business since 1973, Gonzalez won us over first of all with its handmade tortillas, crafted on-site. These are perfect for spreading with guacamole and salsa and for sopping up the lovely liquids in the bowl of pozole. You can choose between chicken, beef, or chicken mole enchiladas, and you can go somewhat lighter with seafood options, too: shrimp can be fried, sautéed with chiles, or served in a Mexican cocktail salad. Circling back to those fabulous tortillas, they're the wrapping for a burrito that you can get stuffed with *carne guisada* (stewed beef), pork, beef and bean, *lengua,* or *barbacoa.* Breakfast dishes to check out include eggs and potatoes, huevos rancheros, and eggs with pork chop. Want a cold one? Our favorite Mexican beer, Carta Blanca, is here. In warmer weather, lighten up with the *michelada,* a beer poured over ice and tarted up with lime and a little Tabasco or other spicy sauce.

Greek Cafe & Bakery, 334 W. Davis St., Dallas 75208; (214) 943-1887; **Greek; $–$$.** Here's another small, no-frills family operation that does great food. Spanakopita tops the list of our favorite dishes, but the gyros are very solid as well. Dolmades come in a dish with lemon, which we love with accompanying appetizer dishes of falafel, hummus, and baba ghanoush, with lots of warm pita for dredging in all the good juices and smears. For a big meal, the combo platter puts gyro and chicken together with grilled red onion, tomato, and bell peppers, alongside a village salad (love the chunky feta here) and more pita. If you're not after meat, have the grilled salmon with grilled veggies, rice,  Greek salad, and pita bread. From the bakery side of the operation, the *tsoureki,* or Greek Easter sweet bread, is simply lovely. Much like brioche, it's braided and buttery, and it's topped with sliced almonds. We like to take it home to eat at breakfast as french toast or buttered and spread with apricot preserves. The staff is unfailingly friendly, but if there's a complaint, it's that there's not a lot of organization apparent in the service side of the operation.

Hattie's, 418 N. Bishop Ave., Dallas 75208; (214) 942-7400; **hatties .com; American/Southern; $$–$$$.** One of the first restaurants in Bishop Arts to take the risk of opening a higher-end restaurant in an area where almost nothing of the sort existed, Hattie's proved in 2002 not only that the neighborhood was hungry for finely crafted food but also that people would come from other parts of the DFW area just to eat here. The popularity of shabby-chic Hattie's shows absolutely no signs of slowing down, either, probably because the food continues to be fresh and exciting. The owners come from the Carolinas, Virginia, and Georgia; therefore, the food they're sharing with you is inspired by their coastal region, called Low Country cuisine. That shows up as slow-roasted pulled pork over grits with braised greens and onion marmalade; shrimp and grits made with goat cheese and Tabasco-bacon pan sauce; New Zealand lamb chops with savory spoon bread; and bacon-wrapped meat loaf with wild mushroom gravy. At brunch, the fried green tomato sandwich, pecan-crusted fried catfish, and poached eggs on crab cakes ends your week just right. There's a wonderful wine list at Hattie's, as well as cool cocktails, including a Lucky Limeade, made with acai vodka, fresh lime, sage, and cucumber.

Hunky's Hamburgers, 321 N. Bishop Ave., Dallas 75208; (214) 941-3322; hunkys.com; Burgers; $–$$. The name sort of sums up the point of this Bishop Arts spot—it's all about hunka-hunka good burger eating here. The double-meat burger tends to be the best choice, but you can get all crazy with cheese (American, swiss, cheddar, Jack, or mozzarella), bacon, chili, ham and swiss, mushroom, or hickory sauce.

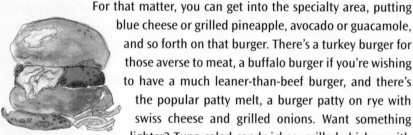

For that matter, you can get into the specialty area, putting blue cheese or grilled pineapple, avocado or guacamole, and so forth on that burger. There's a turkey burger for those averse to meat, a buffalo burger if you're wishing to have a much leaner-than-beef burger, and there's the popular patty melt, a burger patty on rye with swiss cheese and grilled onions. Want something lighter? Tuna salad sandwiches, grilled chicken with all sorts of treatments, and a veggie patty and black bean patty give you options, as do a number of salads. The favorite side remains the sweet potato fries, although Tater Tots, fried mushrooms, fried zucchini, and spicy fried pickles are hard to resist. Milk shakes are made with Texas's own Blue Bell ice cream. Service is always friendly, too. Other location: 3940 Cedar Springs Rd., Dallas 75219.

Jonathon's, 1111 N. Beckley Ave., Dallas 75203; (214) 946-2221; jonathonsoakcliff.com; American; $$. Home-cooking is not in short supply in Oak Cliff, and Jonathon's is easily among the more popular options. At breakfast and brunch, there's almost no way to order anything other than the chicken and waffles, a certain Southern staple, or the signature peanut butter waffles. Unless, of course, you want the biscuits with link sausage and the killer peppery cream gravy. Oh but there's the Huevos Juanitos, a mixture of eggs with bacon, roasted green chiles, and caramelized onions in a tortilla cup. Did we mention that breakfast is served all day? At brunch, enjoy the do-it-yourself Bloody Mary bar, with a boatload of mixing options. The rest of the menu covers lunch and dinner, when you can choose from steak and eggs; chicken salad over greens with blueberries and toasted almonds; and chicken potpie. Bring the family; it's casual and friendly here.

Kitchen LTO, 3011 Gulden Lane, Suite 108, Dallas 75212; (214) 317-0757; kitchenlto.com; American and International; $$–$$$. One of the most intriguing ideas ever seen on the Dallas culinary scene, this permanent pop-up restaurant made its debut in the fall of 2013. Spreading out within the very new Trinity Groves area—a development immediately west of downtown and skirting the northern edge of Oak Cliff, at the foot of the magnificent Calatrava Bridge over the Trinity River—Kitchen LTO serves as a restaurant business model. A new restaurant opens and operates in the space every four months, giving the chef, front-of-house team, design firm, and other involved parties a chance to try on new concepts, cuisines, and operations. It's a proving ground, of sorts, and the participants are chosen via an involved process. Applicants undergo an extensive interview with local industry leaders, who select finalists. The public votes for favorite finalists to choose each new season's winner. The first such winner was Chef Norman Grimm (Dallasites may remember him from York Street, Nosh, and Mercury), whose Modern French-American cuisine was served from September through December 2013. The look came courtesy of winning designer Coeval Studio, whose credits include Belly and Trumpet (Dallas) and Hacienda San Miguel (Fort Worth). This delightful changing presentation should provide fun for years to come, while giving creatives a chance to shine.

La Calle Doce, 415 W. 12th St., Dallas 75208; (214) 941-4304; lacalledoce-dallas.com; Mexican; $$. Ceviche scores as the right appetizer, with white fish and shrimp deeply marinated in lime, served as a chilled fish cocktail or atop a tostada. Other worthy starters include calamari Mexicana, served in fried strips, with chipotle cream for dipping; or nachos topped with lump crabmeat and melted cheese. The classic seafood soup, filled with shrimp, clams, mussels, and sliced octopus, continues to be a top pick, while the right salad choice is the Ensalada Calle Doce, filled with fresh spinach leaves, avocado slices, firm shrimp, sliced mushrooms, and a Caesar dressing. Blackened salmon tacos with black bean-corn relish and crispy tacos stuffed with shrimp and served with cucumber salad are both good lighter entree choices. If you're not loving fish, chick out the shredded beef tacos; tenderloin steak Tampiqueña, topped with grilled white cheese, or the *guisao de res,* a traditional beef tip stew. A popular stop very near the Bishop Arts District, this old house has been serving hungry patrons for more than 20 years. Second location: 1925 Skillman Ave. in Lakewood.

Lockhart Smokehouse, 400 W. Davis St., Dallas 75208; (214) 944-5521; lockhartsmokehouse.com; Barbecue; $$. If you've been to Central Texas and you're savvy to the brand of barbecue for which that region is so rightfully famous, you'll be in (pardon the pun) hog heaven at this Bishop Arts hangout. Owned by descendants of the families that launched Kreuz Market and Smitty's, two of Texas's renowned smokehouses, both in Lockhart, not far from Austin, Lockhart Smokehouse brings the rich flavors of meats long smoked over wood cut from post oak trees. In particular, the flavors discovered in the black-edged beef brisket, the jalapeño beef sausage, the pork chops, and the deviled eggs, stuffed with a different smoked meat each day, will give you an entirely new perspective on barbecue and why people in Texas feel so strongly about the kind that comes from the heart of the Lone Star State. Pitmaster Will Fleischman, with a long red beard, looking a little like a modernized version of a ZZ Top band member, can entertain you with stories of smokehouse lore. Among his wisdoms learned in his craft, there's one that isn't easy to learn: "Success depends on how many mistakes you're willing to make," as he told writer Hanna Riskin in her story for *Southern Living*. True to the old Central Texas smokehouses, the use of forks and barbecue sauce is discouraged—but in Dallas, they couldn't get away with not offering those, so you can find them if you ask really nicely. But plates? Forget it—the style of eating right off the butcher paper is firmly in place. Plan to spend some time enjoying the bar here, too; specialty drinks using Texas-made liquors include the Texas 2 Step, mixing Deep Eddy Sweet Tea Vodka with lemonade and ice tea, and Whiskey Creek, blending Rebecca Creek Whiskey with bitters, sweet vermouth, and orange sour. Lots of good beer is poured at Lockhart, as well, including a rotation of Texas-made draft choices.

Lucia, 408 W. 8th St., Dallas 75208; (214) 948-4998; luciadallas .com; Italian; $$–$$$. For most of 2011, this was the hardest table to book in Dallas, and the popularity hardly eased up in 2012. Since opening, the 36-seat dining room has stayed wildly busy, thanks in no small part to the exquisite dishes put forth by David Uygur, former chef at Lola in Dallas, and the front-of-house hospitality extended by his wife, Jennifer, who managed the wine department at **Central Market** (p. 72) before the couple pursued their dream of owning their own place. This isn't a place for heavy red-sauced plates. Instead, you'll find handcrafted pastas that may change daily, along with the house-made *salumi*. From the Antipasti section of the menu, I love the crostini with

chicken liver and Black Mission figs, and the eggplant soup. Among Primi picks, the elegant tagliatelle with chanterelles, thyme, and bread crumbs tickles me pink; and the braised rabbit with polenta is my Secondi choice, although the veal chop with potato puree and hen-of-the-woods mushrooms works well, too. For Dolci, David had me at toasted brioche with chocolate mousse, sweet ricotta, and orange confit, though the lighter Meyer lemon panna cotta with caramelized pineapple deserves strong consideration, as well.

Mesa, 118 W. Jefferson Blvd., Ste. A, Dallas 75208; (214) 941-4246; mesadallas.com; Mexican; $$. When you're ready to skip the Tex-Mex but go into Mexico's interior, here's another good option. The signature chicken mole finds a quarter of a chicken in a dark mole that's plenty deep and not too sweet. Mole dishes also include those made with lamb or duck. Ceviche is a solid appetizer, made with shrimp or red fish, or both. Margaritas are nearly as popular as the food here, made in that perfect balance of sweet and tart. For dessert, the top choice is the orange flan, hands down. At brunch, pancakes are fluffy, and the egg dishes bring together texture and spice in happy ways. The decor tends to be a bit industrial but still just stylish enough to be appealing. There's a terrific patio that's even heated in cooler weather.

Norma's Cafe, 1123 W. Davis St., Dallas 75208; (214) 946-4711; normascafe.com; American/Southern; $. A favorite for years and years, Norma's is home-cooking heaven of the old-school sort. At breakfast, your best bet is two eggs over easy with your choice of bacon, ham, or sausage, with hash browns and homemade biscuits. But you can get those eggs, any style, with chicken-fried steak, rib eye steak, or pork chops, too, and you can sub grits for the hash browns, if you like. Pancakes, waffles, and french toast also are exceedingly popular, and there are more than a half-dozen omelet choices, too. For something spicy, the *migas* is Mexican breakfast glory, a plate of eggs scrambled with tortilla chips, jalapeño peppers, tomato, onions, and a blend of yellow and white cheeses. And, oh, my, there's that boffo cinnamon roll that should be outlawed. For lunch and dinner, consider the fried pickles or giant hand-battered onion rings for an appetizer before rib-sticking entrees, such as Texas Frito pie, steak finger basket, chicken-fried steak, meat loaf, chicken and dressing, pot roast, or fried catfish. For dessert, think about banana pudding, German chocolate cake, cherry pie, blackberry cobbler, and pies with mile-high meringue and fillings like lemon, coconut, and chocolate-peanut butter.

Oddfellows, 316 W. 7th St., Dallas 75208; (214) 944-5958; oddfellowsdallas.com; American; $–$$. Breakfast seems to be the gateway meal at this Bishop Arts hangout, and why not? It's easily among the best morning meal options in all of North Texas. House-made honey ham stars on the Oddfellows Benedict, along with baby mustard greens, hollandaise, and hot-house tomato slices, on ciabatta bread. Fried chicken accompanied by ricotta waffles and the pancake sampler—that's a trio of gingerbread, red velvet, and berry-chocolate chip—count among the stick-to-your rib options. On weekends, those go oh-so-well with the Phillips Head, an eye-opener made with Tito's Vodka from Austin and freshly squeezed OJ. For lunchtime, there are deviled eggs and garbanzo fritters for sharing, as well as cool little Buffalo Mac Cups, smallish portions of fried chicken with a house-made buffalo sauce topped with blue cheese and scallions. You can find a skinny dish, such as a salad of quinoa, arugula and strawberries with grilled salmon. Or you can throw caution to the wind and just dig into the burger made of local Burgundy Pasture Beef topped with a balsamic tomato slice, sweet and sour pickles, and shaved onions. At supper, consider the lamb-mint sausage Bolognese or the chile relleno stuffed with butternut squash, goat cheese, and chickpeas and topped with salsa verde. Just be sure to arrive relaxed—this 1920s storefront space feels as homey as Uncle Joe's farmhouse kitchen.

Veracruz Cafe, 408 N. Bishop Ave., Dallas 75208; (214) 948-4746; veracruzcafedallas.com; Mexican; $$–$$$. Dig into the desert soup, a veggie-heaven blend of diced cactus, hominy, zucchini, chayote, carrots, corn, and epazote leaves in a tomato-based broth, sprinkled with a little *queso fresco* and served with rice and lime wedges on the side. Red snapper Veracruz presents a pan-seared filet in a bath of tomato, onion, bay leaves, and olives, served over a large piece of romaine with sautéed zucchini, broccoli, and fresh corn alongside. The grilled chicken breast is lavished with mole Xiqueño, made dark rust in color thanks to chiles such as mulato and pasilla, and speckled with toasted sesame seeds on top. The chile relleno comes breaded and stuffed with marinated jalapeños layered with brisket shreds and topped with *queso fundido,* sour cream, raisins, and toasted pecans, with a slurry of smooth black beans alongside. Meat fans can't resist fork-tender carne asada beneath a blanket of ranchero sauce, served at brunch with *chilaquiles* and more black beans. A distinctive favorite in the Bishop Arts District, Veracruz's walls are painted deep purple and hung with oversized paintings by local artists. Popular for date nights, it's OK for well-behaved kids, too.

Zen Sushi, 380 W. 7th St., Dallas 75208; (214) 946-9699; zensushidallas.com; Japanese; $$–$$$. This Bishop Arts charmer uses "thoughtfully crafted modern Japanese cuisine" as its tagline, and that's as accurate as you can get. Executive chef and creator of the restaurant Michelle Carpenter worked for a dozen years at the much-loved Yamaguchi in North Dallas. There, she built a clientele and reputation that made this transition to Oak Cliff doable, enough so that her new patrons feel comfortable calling ahead to book her omakase menu, one that allows her to choose the 10-course tasting menu for the booking guests. Showing her brilliance are dishes like the curry kabocha squash soup, carnitas in steamed buns, brandy-and-soy-glazed duck breast with mashed yams, and grilled prime New York strip with asparagus tempura. From the specialty sushi list, the sakura roll combines clam with shrimp and crab in a soy wrapper; the jalapeño roll incorporates octopus, avocado, and flying fish roe; and the zen roll includes tuna and albacore inside a cucumber wrapping. From the Green Menu, especially appealing to vegetarians and vegans, there are rolls incorporating combinations of avocado, shiitake, tofu, asparagus, beets, pickled daikon, and sweet potato, along with entrees like vegetarian ramen and grilled vegetable chef's salad. Ask about the Secret Sushi Society, a Dallas group of elite diners for whom Chef Michelle designs prix-fixe dinners of seven to ten courses on the last Wednesday of each month.

Landmarks

Bolsa, 614 W. Davis St., Dallas 75208; (214) 367-9367; bolsadallas .com; American; $$. One of the local pioneers in the farm-to-table movement, Bolsa is a Bishop Arts hot spot that utilizes as many local, fresh, seasonal products as possible. The kitchen thrills your palate with things like house-cured meats, wild boar pâté, and Red Waddle pork *rillettes,* all stars on the charcuterie plate. His Prince Edward Islands mussels delight with a country-ham broth laced with leeks, mustard greens, and tomato jam, and his veal sweetbreads—oh-so-tender to the bite—are heavenly with green tomato chutney, bacon, and onion. Those are just the starters. Entrees like the ricotta gnocchi with Tom Spicer's mushrooms (he's a local farmer), sweet peppers, and pecorino; and bone-in pork chops with fennel and apple-braised cabbage are typical dishes that never fail. Brunch winners include the roasted beet, orange, and radicchio salad with pistachio brittle; house-made *kolaches* (a Central Texas pastry from Czech settlers) filled with wild boar and fontina cheese; an egg sandwich piled with piquillo peppers, mixed greens, and bacon; and sunny-side-up eggs served with local duck breast sausage and biscuits made with duck fat. Though the place is very casual, the chic crowd keeps the tables—inside and out—packed at almost all hours.

Gloria's, 600 N. Bishop Ave., Dallas 75208; (214) 942-1831; gloriasrestaurants.com; Latin American; $$. Although originally known for its Salvadoran food, Gloria's Mexican qualities speak to the purist. Up front there's the fresh, simple guacamole that begs only for a squirt of lemon and perhaps a dab of salsa; then there's the creamy black bean dip that comes alongside the salsa. The ceviche tostada consists of a crisp corn tostada topped with a layer of guacamole then coarsely chopped orange roughy, marinated with just a little lime, tossed with chopped onion and tomato. Tamales here are the variety found in the Yucatán and Central America. Wrapped and steamed within a banana leaf, the tamale's pudding-like masa is filled with chicken shreds and bits of potato and bell pepper. A big dish is the *carne de res asada,* a flank steak, served with a tart chimichurri of parsley, peppers, onion, and vinegar with oil. An accompanying chicken enchilada crowns the plate with its satiny red chile sauce and layering of Chihuahua cheese. Enjoy the surroundings of a beautifully renovated vintage (circa 1920s) firehouse. Other locations in Addison, Arlington, Colleyville, Uptown, East Dallas, Fort Worth, Frisco, Garland, Rockwall, and Fairview.

Smoke, 901 Fort Worth Ave., Dallas 75208; (214) 393-4141; smokerestaurant.com; Farm-to-Table; $$. Nobody deserves the good fortune more than hard-working chef Tim Byres, who earned stripes at the **Mansion Restaurant** on Turtle Creek (p. 103) and at Stephan Pyles's namesake restaurant (p. 46). His mainstay now is a funky and immensely comfortable restaurant attached to the hip Belmont Hotel in Dallas's reemerging Oak Cliff neighborhood, where Byres truly came into his own. Not only do he and his staff break down all the meats on-site but they also cook everything by smoking, braising, roasting, and grilling over hardwoods, thus fashioning a whole new idea about cooking from scratch, a concept he calls heritage-inspired cuisine. Brunch especially takes the breath away, with smoked brisket cornbread hash with poached egg, green chili rajas, and pearl onions; pulled whole hog barbecue eggs Benedict with goat cheese potato cakes; and "heavy-handed" blueberry and house-made ricotta cheese pancakes with vanilla poached apricots and cream.

Tillman's Roadhouse, 324 W. 7th St., Dallas 75208; (214) 942-0988; tillmansroadhouse.com; American; $$–$$$. This "roadhouse" pretty much launched today's Bishop Arts excitement. Opening originally as Tillman's Corner and offering good food and drink at reasonable prices, a fashionable redo turned the hangout into an even more stylish place for quaffing and noshing. This is where you go for stick-to-your-ribs food that's made with panache. Everyone's favorite snack is the trio of fries served in a wooden box. You get Parmesan-and-black-pepper-dusted Kennebec potatoes; chile-flecked purple potatoes; and sweet potato fries coated in sea salt. Alongside, there are dipping sauces, including a house-made ketchup and a horseradish pickle mayo. The crispy, cornmeal-jacketed fried pickles come with a spicy ranch dressing, so you may as well go all the way. From the menu of plates, I'm partial to the smoked Cornish game hen with Dr Pepper BBQ sauce and the coffee-crusted prime rib. Decor is far more fashionable than any roadhouse you've ever experienced, with banquettes made cushy by throw pillows, and artwork reflecting a very hip boho vibe.

Specialty Stores, Markets & Producers

Bolsa Mercado, 634 W. Davis St., Dallas 75208; (214) 942-0451; bolsadallas.com. Walk out of the door of Bolsa (p. 121) and down

THE QUEEN OF CHOCOLATE

To visit Dude, Sweet Chocolate is to understand how beautifully a Bohemian interpretation of lush chocolate creations can work.

First of all, this petite shop in Dallas's booming Bishop Arts district serves as a magnificent reflection of the neighborhood's renaissance, and Dude, Sweet Chocolate, likewise, embraces the zeitgeist as if scripted by Hollywood. The vintage, century-old storefront immediately suggests an old-fashioned Mayberry spirit, with giant panes of glass and brass fittings on the front door.

And inside, the setting stays simple with period furnishings that don't detract from the soaring ceilings. One wall is covered with shelving laden with brilliant chocolate creations, made from all-natural ingredients. You're eager to investigate details on the brown-and-white labels, but your attention swings to the open workspace. And you can't look anywhere else.

There, you see the congenial mad-scientist chocolatier and her masterful crew at work. Curly hair pulled back into a ponytail, delicate wire-rim glasses perched on her nose, Katherine Clapner works quickly and efficiently, breaking one of her chocolate concoctions into pieces to stash into tan-colored cardboard gift boxes. As she reaches and moves about her worktable, your eyes are riveted on her lean arms, prettily roped with muscles and covered in colorful, delicate skin art.

The Texas native looks up and flashes a smile that lights up the room, welcoming you as she talks about the goodies she is packaging at the moment. Her energy is contagious, and you're instantly trying to decide whether you want to try her Orange Soda Pop chocolate bar, crafted with 85 percent African chocolate and orange Pop Rocks; the bark-style Crack in a Box, made with salted and candied whole hazelnuts, almonds, macadamia, and soy nuts submerged into a perfect blend of South American 73 percent dark chocolate and pure cocoa beans; or the box of artisan chocolates, with selections that include Black Gold chocolate, incorporating black garlic and sweet wild mushrooms; Miso Happy chocolate, with red miso, tahini, and black sesame seeds; and Tahitian chocolate, made with passion fruit and ginger salt.

Katherine's ideas may be out-of-left-field new, but she balances her work with time-tested, grassroots simplicity in using pure, real ingredients. As often as possible, she's sourcing goods from within 100 miles of Dallas, including Lucky Layla Farms and Zip Code Honey.

She loves sharing her journey, the path she took from pastry chef to dominant chocolate force in North Texas. In working as pastry chef for the beloved Dallas chef and restaurateur Stephan Pyles, Katherine found with Stephan the joy in pairing sweet and savory items. When she was making truffles, she decided to toss in a handful of Maldon salt one day—and found it was "awesome!" Soon she was pairing beets with dark chocolate when making a Venezuelan Steamed Chocolate Cake with Roasted Beet Sorbet. And so on.

Her passion for working with chocolate started early; she loves to recall the time when, as an elementary school student, she made crepes filled with chocolate mousse for a class project. For more than 20 years, her clever ideas won her pastry chef jobs at places like Charlie Trotter's in Chicago, The Windsor Court Hotel in New Orleans, Hotel Cipriani in Venice, and The Savoy Hotel in London before she went to work for several years for Stephan Pyles at several of his Dallas restaurants.

Now in finding a jubilant clientele clamoring for more exciting creations from her delightful factory and store in Dallas's Bishop Arts district, Katherine and a talented staff are busy making Dude, Sweet Chocolate goodies for sale at dozens of outlets, including **Whole Foods** (p. 181), **Central Market** (p. 72), **Scardello Artisan Cheese** (p. 106), **Avoca Coffee** (p. 205), and other food destinations in the Dallas–Fort Worth area. In 2012, she began opening additional shops across DFW. Find the original at *408 W. 8th St., Dallas 75208, (214) 943-5943*; find new locations at dudesweetchocolate.com.

Davis not even 1 block, and you'll come to the sister business of the exceptional restaurant. Here, you can find provisions for exceptional dining to take home. There is a small but superb wine selection, as well as a deli offering locally procured meats and cheeses of all descriptions. On the shelves, an abundance of fine packaged goods—cookies, crackers, condiments, and such, most of them locally crafted—give you options when you're dashing in to find some kind of hostess gift to take to a friend's soiree. And each day, you'll find a blackboard advertising the daily changing Dinner for Two: It may be roasted chicken with cauliflower and broccoli, roasted dill potatoes, Caesar salad, and banana tile (a popular Bolsa dessert); meatballs with fettuccine, green beans, and mixed greens salad with walnuts, dried cherries, and balsamic vinaigrette; or roasted pork loin with butternut squash and braised endive. At lunchtime, stop in for a sandwich or salad from a changing menu that may include meatball sub with plum tomato sauce and provolone or duck confit on spinach.

Emporium Pies, 314 N. Bishop Ave., Dallas 75208; (469) 502-6469; emporiumpies.com. Baking partners and enormously talented, Mary Sparks and Megan Wilkes grew their little pop-up pie business into a force of nature in 2012. When demand for their pies exploded, they took over and renovated the cutest cottage you've ever seen, right in Bishop Arts. Their business continues to boom, as apparently there are still plenty of people in the world eating sugar and flour. Even the most virtuous person can't resist the confections coming from this duo, whose signature Drunken Nut, a bourbon pecan pie with a shortbread cookie crust, is the stuff surely served in heaven. We've been a number of times, and cannot figure out what's better—that Drunken Nut, Dr. Love, which is a red velvet chess pie; Lord of the Pies, the deep-dish apple with cinnamon streusel; or the Smooth Operator, a French silk chocolate pie with pretzel crust. We're pretty sure we need to research and investigate further. Please join us.

Espumoso Caffe, 408 N. Bishop Ave., Dallas 75208; (214) 948-2055; espumosocaffe.com. There's a Latino vibe in this Bishop Arts coffeehouse, where you can enjoy a number of coffee drinks, as well as teas, juices crafted from exotic fruits, sandwiches, and desserts. There's South American music, such as bossa nova and such, on the stereo, and room to chill on couches and in window seats. The healthy breakfast of choice is the Amazonian Acai Bowl, a combination of acai berries, blueberries, raspberries, strawberries, and cranberry juice over granola, topped with sliced banana and honey. The rest of the day, you can nibble on beef, chicken, or veggie empanadas, a grilled veggie panini, or—if you really owe yourself a serious treat—the banana-Nutella panini. Flan and tres leches cake rank high among most popular sweets, but for our money, you cannot do better than the *affogato,* a dish of ice cream drowned in espresso. Other coffee drinks include cafe mocha, cafe con leche, cortado, and caffe Americano.

La Original Michoacana, 415 W. Davis St., Dallas 75208; (469) 867-3092. Across Texas you can find little Latino ice cream shops like this one, and this particular edition could be our favorite. These shops specialize in *paletas,* or ice pops crafted from fresh fruit and fresh juices. Flavors include everything from strawberry, lime, and banana to spicy mango. This locale, like many of its brethren, also sells ice creams—and if you haven't had the kind of ice cream that originated in Mexico, you owe yourself this distinct treat. You'll find genius in the pure creations, which can include flavors like pine nut, avocado, rum raisin, peanut butter, and coffee. On some visits, we've encountered 25 to 30 flavors. They're all made on-site, with real ingredients. And they're all very inexpensive.

Taqueria El Si Hay, 601 W. Davis St., Dallas 75208; (214) 941-4042. Taco stands can hardly be considered unusual in the greater Dallas–Fort Worth area anymore. They're everywhere, in market areas, in front of Fiesta Marts (the big Latino grocery chain), in convenience stores. And there are probably hundreds of freestanding shacks around the metropolitan area. So why is one more special than another? El Si Hay—roughly translated as, "Yes, we have it"—has been popular in a cross-cultural sense for longer than many. It was here before Bishop

Arts became the "it" place to eat in Dallas, and it's only become more popular with its legions of new fans. The old faithful still love the standby, too, coming two or three times a week for a fix of *bistek* (steak), *lengua* (tender tongue), *al pastor* (pork), and *barbacoa* (barbecue) tacos, made with smallish, very fresh and delicate corn tortillas and garnished with finely chopped white onion and cilantro. You can get salsa, too, but the vibrant flavors ask for no assistance, other than perhaps a squeeze of fresh lime. Bonus: You can get Mexican Coca-Cola here, as well—that's the important kind made with pure cane sugar, not corn syrup. Be prepared to eat in your car; there's no seating at this tiny shop.

Park Cities

Just 4 short miles north of downtown Dallas, a pair of tiny, picture-perfect cities sit alongside a lovely, tiny waterway called Turtle Creek. Highland Park, the slightly older of the two, rests between what is now called Uptown (to the south) and its sister city, University Park (to the north). The city of Dallas surrounds the duo, with North Central Expressway as the eastern border and the Dallas North Tollway as the western boundary. Together, they're called the Park Cities.

Highland Park, or HP, originated as a development by Philadelphia investors who spent a half-million dollars in the 1890s. It was the early 1900s, however, before Highland Park got its name, one that's always been synonymous with exquisite living and a multitude of green spaces. The city of Dallas refused HP's annexation request, so the small community incorporated. Later, the big city wanted to annex the little one, and the small but mighty HP said "No, thanks."

University Park grew up around Southern Methodist University (SMU), incorporating in 1924. What distinguishes this twosome from all others in Dallas? Two things: the school district and the real estate. The Highland Park Independent School District ranks among the nation's leading systems in academics, and it's common to see the high school graduates heading off to matriculate at Ivy League schools. Because the schools are exceptional, school taxes are high, as is the cost of homes. And they are extraordinary homes, some of them mansions from the city's earliest days, some constructed only recently and resembling Tudor estates or French chateaus.

Along Mockingbird Lane, Highland Park's boundary from University Park, there's the Highland Park Village, a 1931 shopping center with Moorish design, thought to be the first shopping center of its kind in the nation. Within HP Village, you'll find a good many of the best dining places in Dallas. In pockets throughout the Park Cities, cafes and bistros feature a magnificent mélange of menus. Eat your way through them all, knowing you'll be joined by residents with the best taste in Dallas.

Foodie Faves

Bistro 31, 87 Highland Park Village, Dallas 75205; (214) 420-3900; bistro31dallas.com; French/International; $$–$$$. Named for the year this renowned shopping center was opened—1931—this bistro from the Lombardi's group aims to take you to the French Riviera's salons and sidewalk cafes. The menu brims with classic French-influenced cuisine and a huge wine selection. At brunch, try the Basque omelet with Spanish chorizo; the *tortilla espanola;* or the steak and eggs, with a pain au chocolate on the side. At dinner, steamed mussels from Prince Edward Island and tuna tartare are ideal starters, with lobster salad sandwich or grilled pork T-bone fine main courses. Upstairs, Lounge 31 gives you a place for drinks and lighter dining, with cozy corners for canoodling or gossiping with the BFF. An outdoor patio and terrace villa feature unique lighting and a Spanish-style Carrera marble bar, while the indoor Champagne lounge begs you to bring a celebration with you.

Carbone's Fine Food and Wine, 4208 Oak Lawn Ave., Dallas 75219; (214) 522-4208; carbonesdallas.com; Italian; $$. Half dining spot, half grocery, this newcomer boasts its mission to "celebrate

Italian-American food traditions" and "make as many products as possible in house." Mission accomplished at lunch and dinner, when antipasti includes ricotta with garlic bread and St. Louis–style toasted ravioli; salad choices include escarole hearts with red onion, walnuts, and pecorino, and marinated baby beets with Maytag blue cheese and apples; sandwich options are meatball, chicken Parmesan, and an Italian combo; and specialty pasta dishes include baked penne, linguine with shrimp scampi, and eggplant Parmesan. Favorites include the four-course Sunday dinner for $40 (call for a reservation!), in which you get antipasti, pasta, secondi (such as spezzatino of Berkshire pork with braised corona beans), and a sweet to finish. And speaking of sweets, if you crave homemade cannoli or lemon semifreddo, this is your place. If you're shopping, pick up freshly baked bread, wine, and pasta to take home for dinner. Note that parking can be a challenge here.

Digg's Taco Shop, 6309 Hillcrest Ave., Dallas 75205; (214) 520-0155; diggstacoshop.com; Tex-Mex; $. You get just what the sign says—tacos. And they're good ones, too. Have your tortillas filled with chicken (the healthy, free-range kind), beef brisket, grilled shrimp, shredded pork, or just grilled vegetables. Ask for guacamole on it, too. The tortillas are soft white corn, not the tough, thick variety. Other goodies include burritos made with flour or spinach tortillas, nachos, salad bowls, quesadillas, and burgers. There's a pretty good beer selection, as well as margarita popsicles for dessert. This is a college hangout (it's right across from SMU), so expect a crowd and parking issues. Second location: 445 S. Pecan St., Arlington 76010.

Dive Coastal Cuisine, 3404 Rankin St., Dallas 75205; (214) 891-1700; dive-dallas.com; Seafood; $$. Following the growing trend, this is another fast-casual place that offers counter ordering and then self-seating and dining. The runaway favorite in this Snider Plaza locale is the ahi tuna wrap, followed closely by the ahi tuna sliders. Ceviche features striped bass in a mango-citrus-jalapeño marinade, served with plantain chips. A trio of crab cakes tops a salad with charred tomato vinaigrette. Salmon never had it so good, grilled and served with cauliflower truffle hash and sautéed spinach. Vegetarians are happy with the kale salad, quinoa salad, and black beans, by the way. Kid food (the menu calls this The Kiddie Pool) includes a peanut butter and banana sandwich, baby barbecue sandwich, crudités with peanut butter and cream cheese dip, and panko-fried fish sticks.

East Hampton Sandwich Co., 6912 Snider Plaza, Dallas 75205; (214) 363-2888; ehsandwich.com; American; $. Another upstart in Snider Plaza, a shopping center in University Park, within shouting distance of SMU, this "elevated sandwich concept" gives you everything from the advertised sandwich to soups, sides, and desserts—and every tiny thing is made in-house. Again, the fast-casual setup lets you order at the counter, then take your food away, or sit and eat on-site. Within moments of opening, the lobster roll, hot cheese–short rib, and the roast beef and spinach sandwiches were winning new fans. And the burger's no ordinary effort, either: With the ground beef patty, you get aged cheddar, marinated lettuce shreds, pickles, onion, jalapeño, tomato, avocado, and bacon with Sriracha dijonnaise swiped on the bun. Only looking for a salad? Try the one with arugula, spinach, roasted pear, chopped pancetta, basil, and blue cheese in Champagne vinaigrette. If you love locally made **Empire Baking Company**'s bread (p. 105), you'll be pleased with this sandwich spot. Beer and wine are served, as well.

Flying Fish, 6126 Luther Ln., Dallas 75225; (214) 696-3474; flyingfishinthe.net; Seafood; $–$$. Designed to resemble the most laid-back lakeside fish shack you can imagine, this come-as-you-are joint does a lot of things well. At first glance, you think it's all fried, all the time—but take a closer look. Yes, the menu groans under the weight of fried catfish, fried shrimp, fried oysters, and fried chicken, all of which are served on sandwiches, in baskets with fries and hush puppies, or even atop a bed of greens for a salad. But there are also ways to be virtuous here, such as by choosing a grilled fish plate, with picks including catfish, rainbow trout, salmon, tilapia, shrimp kebab, snapper, grouper, and chicken. Fish tacos can include either fried or grilled fish. And boiled platters include shrimp, crab legs, and—in season— crawfish. In the morning hours, Flying Fish offers breakfast dishes like pancakes, french toast, granola with yogurt, avocado- egg sandwich, grits and gumbo, omelets, and—for those of us loving a Mexican kick in the early hours—*migas,* a plate of eggs scrambled with tortillas and served with hash browns or beans. The Fish also does very cold beer, wine, and frozen margaritas. Other locations in Addison, Arlington, Fort Worth, and Garland.

The Front Room at The Lumen Hotel, 6101 Hillcrest Ave., Dallas 75205; (214) 219-8282; thefrontroomdallas.com; American; $$–$$$. The ultracontemporary Lumen Hotel (it's a Kimpton, which are always stylish) opened a new restaurant across the front of its ground floor in the fall of 2012. To soften the very modern edges, the menu is one that's meant to bring comfort but in fashionable doses. An all-day menu features spaghetti and meatballs with spicy ricotta; shrimp and grits prepared with cream cheese, green tomatoes, pickled onions, and jalapeño; and baskets laden with selections like fried chicken, BBQ ribs, and fish tacos. Nibbles to share while enjoying cocktails include french fries (triple fried!) dressed in sea salt and malt vinegar; fried pickles; and root vegetable chips with pumpkin seed aioli for dipping. At breakfast, there's everything from an egg-white omelet to Belgian waffles with ham biscuits. The cocktail program is impressive, with lots of fresh ingredients. Among interests is the Garden Variety, a tequila drink mixed with blood orange liqueur, lime juice, simple syrup, jalapeños, cucumber slices, cilantro leaves, and a little smoked sea salt.

Hillstone, 8300 Preston Rd., Dallas 75225; (214) 691-8991; hillstone.com; American; $$–$$$. Formerly known as Houston's, this is the name of the parent company that also has locations in Manhattan, Boston, Santa Monica, and plenty of other swishy locales. The setting hasn't changed; it's still chic and modern, with lots of stone and wood in the decor. Lighting is low, service is smooth, and the food suits people with demanding palates. Our favorite starter is the grilled artichoke, served with a tart dipping sauce. Parmesan cheese toast is a good nosh to share, as are oysters St. Charles. Caramelized onion soup and Newport Beach clam chowder are excellent soups, and the salad topped with steak and thai noodles in a mango-avocado treatment always pleases. Among entrees, the jumbo lump crab cakes with Pommery mustard sauce and the lamb sirloin steak cooked over a wood fire and served with mashers and sautéed spinach bring plentiful comfort. A lovely wine list is offered, too.

Kuby's Sausage House, 6601 Snider Plaza, Dallas 75205; (214) 363-2231; kubys.com; German; $$. Nothing in Dallas can be considered more authentic than Kuby's, which traces its meat market heritage back to Kaiserslautern, Germany, where Friedrich Kuby opened his store in 1728. Descendent Karl Kuby opened this place in 1961, and his family continues to run the place with care. Under one roof, there's a restaurant that serves breakfast, lunch, Sunday brunch, and dinner (the latter on Friday and Saturday only); as well as a meat market and deli; grocery store; bakery; wild game processing plant; and shop where you can order custom European-style gift baskets. When you visit at lunch, be sure to enjoy the sausage plate with hot German potato salad and red cabbage, and then return another time for the potato pancakes, schnitzel, Reuben, and other specialties. Be ready to wait for tables at prime lunch time and at breakfast on the weekend.

La Duni, 4264 Oak Lawn Ave., Dallas 75219; (214) 520-6888; laduni.com; Latin American; $$. Charged by the Luna Negra, a double-shot espresso, you're ready for a serving of baked salsa eggs, a Spanish specialty served in a ramekin filled with poached eggs topped by a bubbling blanket of roasted tomato salsa and a combination of cheddar and gruyère cheeses, with warm flour tortillas on the side. The ham-gruyère scramble also scores big points, as does a side of fennel-laced Argentine sausage. At lunch, bring someone with whom to share the iron skillet filled with seared shrimp, topped with chipotle mojo, then proceed with the Brazilian-style pulled roasted chicken salad with a creamy lime dressing. Evening specialties include the *carne asada arrachera,* a prime skirt steak marinated in lime and garlic, grilled, and served with basmati rice, sweet plantains, black beans, and roasted poblano chiles, which pairs nicely with the best mojito in all of Dallas or with the Lemon 43, a Spanish cocktail made with rum, muddled lemons, cane sugar, and crushed ice. Tart and lush, the *pollo aljibe* is a roasted half chicken in a Champagne–green orange treatment. Don't dare resist one of owner–pastry chef Dunia Borga's renowned desserts, such as her legendary quatros leches cake and her Venezuelan triple chocolate truffle cake. Other locations: 4620 McKinney Ave., Dallas 75205; North Park Center, 8687 N. Central Expy., Dallas 75225; and 233 Town Place, Fairview 75069.

Nonna, 4115 Lomo Alto Dr., Dallas 75219; (214) 521-1800; nonnadallas.com; Italian; $$$. Chef Julian Barsotti struck gold when he opened this smallish, lovely bistro at the edge of the Park Cities.

Learning to cook under Paul Bertolli in Oakland, California, and traveling to Italy to learn the craft of pizza making, Barsotti brings a level of sure authenticity to the Dallas dining landscape. His production of *salumi* and pasta, all from scratch, creating everything from raw ingredients, renders sublime results. One of our favorite antipasti picks is the *salumi* plate with spicy sopressata, duck prosciutto, and chicken liver *spuma* (a whipped spread), followed closely by the burrata with sunchoke caponata. The tagliolini pasta with Nantucket scallops, house-made sausage, and white wine–tomato sauce is delicate and fulfilling, while the pizza topped with littleneck clams, sweet onion, and fresh herbs brings on happy sighs around the table. Pancetta-wrapped quail with mushrooms and polenta spells a dozen kinds of comfort, particularly when paired with one of the carefully chosen wines on the list. The only complaint ever heard about Nonna: It can be loud when fully crowded.

Nosh Euro Bistro, 4216 Oak Lawn Ave., Dallas 75219; (214) 528-9400; nosheurobistro.com; International; $$–$$$. Owner-chef Avner Samuel could be the city's most itinerate chef, but no matter how many times he moves around the city, his food is quite beloved. He's been in one spot for a while now, so perhaps Nosh will be around for a good long time, too. Chances are good, as Samuel's business partner, Jon Stevens, is chef here and keeping a loyal clientele very happy in a causal but sophisticated setting. That's done with appetizers such as shared plates filled with falafel, hummus, olives, and marinated peppers; ahi tuna tartare; lobster-chicken shooters in sake, thai red curry and coconut broth; and roasted beef bone marrow with red onion marmalade. Entrees include caramelized diver scallops, barbecue-dusted tiger shrimp, and crispy duck confit. A lovely wine program is in place, too. Second location: 4701 W. Park Blvd., Plano 75093.

Olivella's, 3406 McFarlin Blvd., Dallas 75205; (214) 528-7070; olivellas.com; Pizza; $$. Just a couple of blocks from the SMU campus in Snider Plaza, this favorite among the Park Cities crowd specializes in Neapolitan-style pizza with cracker-crisp crust. *Pulcino e porco*, also known as The Dream Pizza, features house-made mozzarella, Gorgonzola, tomato sauce, chicken, pancetta, and jalapeño. Note that it's not a pizza joint but a real restaurant, though a very small one. Seating can be a little cozy, but there's a patio, too. Check out salads, such as the Caesar and one with pear, walnuts,  and Gorgonzola, and another with arugula and prosciutto. Among pastas, lasagna and cannelloni are popular. If you're tailgating with a big crowd, call in advance and get some of this heavenly Italian fare.

Patrizio, 25 Highland Park Village, Dallas 75205; (214) 522-7878; patrizios.net; Italian; $$. Truly one of the enduring, wildly popular places for the well-heeled patrons in this part of town, Patrizio has been around for more than 20 years. This cornerstone at the Highland Park Village has been pleasing customers with salads, pizza, fish, and chicken dishes, as well as frozen concoctions such as the Bellini, with simple style. Menu picks we've liked include the featherlight fried calamari, crispy goat cheese with mixed greens and sun-dried tomato, open-faced ravioli with artichoke hearts, and veal piccata. For dessert, the Italian cream cake with fresh strawberries satisfies. Be forewarned that this place stays crowded, so booking ahead is advised. Parking can be tricky at the Village, but there's ample valet parking availability. Other locations: Plano, Fairview, Highland Village, Southlake, and Fort Worth.

Peggy Sue BBQ, 6600 Snider Plaza, Dallas 75205; (214) 987-9188; peggysuebbq.com; Barbecue; $–$$. Originally opened in the early 1940s, this barbecue joint was Howard & Peggy's and, later, Peggy's Beef Bar, for a total of 40 years. A consummate SMU/Highland Park hangout, the little corner shop at Snider Plaza closed in the late

1980s before finding new life as Peggy Sue. Though it still has a look that strikes a balance between humble and kitschy, the menu reaches far beyond the everyday barbecue place: Shared starters, for instance, include a trio of sliders with brisket, turkey, and

pulled pork fillings; griddled **Empire Baking Company** (p. 105) bread is studded with cheese and jalapeños; and quesadillas are stuffed with smoked brisket or chicken. One-dish meal options include Frito chili pie, packed with brisket chili, and Hoppin' John, a Southern specialty that combines black-eyed peas, rice, and pulled pork. Barbecue plates range from pork spare ribs or baby back ribs, smoked brisket, turkey, ham, sausage, pulled pork, and rib combos. But wait, there's more: Sides include the usual coleslaw, potato salad, and fried okra, but there are other picks, like squash casserole, steamed broccoli and spinach, sweet potatoes, and pinto beans. Be sure to order an apricot, chocolate, coconut, cherry, or apple fried pie.

Penne Pomodoro, 6815 Snider Plaza, Dallas 75205; (214) 373-9911; pennepomodoro.com; Italian; $$. Another long-standing neighborhood favorite near SMU, this mainstay continues to score extra points for $1 mimosa, Bloody Mary, and Bellini drinks. At brunch, there's a savory waffle with jalapeño, bacon, and cheese that changes your mind about waffles altogether. On lunch and dinner menus, you can find everything from grilled chicken in lemon, garlic, and rosemary to pan-seared beef tenderloin with arugula and roasted potatoes to risotto with assorted shellfish. There's also pasta—you pick the variety—with goodies like wild mushroom ragout or garden vegetables. Of particular interest is the sizable gluten-free menu: Pizza, pasta, and focaccia can be crafted with gluten-free ingredients, and they're really good. A gluten-free kids' menu includes mac and cheese and pizza. Other locations in Dallas.

R+D Kitchen, 8300 Preston Center Plaza, Dallas 75225; (214) 890-7900; hillstone.com; American; $$–$$$. Chic enough for the more demanding Park Cities palate, this duplicate of a Newport Beach, California, favorite (with a Santa Monica sister) looks to be a casual place but actually feels rather elegant. Mediterranean seared-tuna salad with goat cheese is a good bet, as is the coconut shrimp sushi and the beef short ribs. For comfort food, the mushroom meat loaf is filling, as are the fried fish with dill tartar sauce, roasted chicken in the French country style, and *carnitas* sandwich. The burgers inspire much happy eye rolling, as do skinny fries and their dipping sauce. A good wine list includes plentiful selections by the glass, including Kung Fu Girl Riesling from Washington, Vionta Albarino from Spain, Becker Iconoclast Cabernet from the Texas Hill Country, and Hook & Ladder Pinot Noir from the Russian River Valley.

Rathbun's Blue Plate Kitchen, 6130 Luther Ln., Dallas 75225; (214) 890-1103; kentrathbun.com/blueplate/dallas/; Southern; $$. Here's yet another restaurant from Dallas celeb chef Kent Rathbun, whose **Abacus** (p. 102) helped put Dallas on the national cuisine map. Here the chef settles into some of his favorite comfort foods, culled through an illustrious career that began in his native Kansas City and has grown during his decades in Dallas. At lunch, we're drawn to his slow-smoked pork shoulder sandwich, the polenta-crusted fried green tomatoes, black-eyed pea and sausage soup, and his wood-grilled salmon. At dinner, duck cassoulet or roasted lemon chicken and a side of short rib mac and cheese give good vibes. For kids, you can choose between cheeseburger sliders, fried or grilled chicken strips, or grilled cheddar on Texas toast. Dress casually, even if there's valet parking outside.

Sevy's Grill, 8201 Preston Rd., Dallas 75225; sevys.com; American; $$$. For nearly 20 years, this upscale enclave near Preston Center has kept a particular public very happy. Some patrons choose it for business lunches, others like it for date night. Women consider it the ideal place for a girlfriend gathering, but it's not a feminine place at all. Monday-evening wine-pairing dinners are extremely successful, giving you a lot of food and drink variety at a good price. Starts to consider include local goat cheese topped with tomato, roasted garlic, and basil over crostini; smoked shrimp cakes; and spinach–five grain salad with pancetta vinaigrette and feta cheese. Entree salads like hickory-grilled chicken salad and warm crab-cake salad let you feel you're behaving yourself. Almond-crusted sole and a mixed grill featuring venison medallions and grilled quail show you the range of kitchen talent here. Valet parking is free here—bonus!

Spoon Bar & Kitchen, 8220 Westchester Dr., Dallas 75225; spoonbarandkitchen.com; Seafood; $$$–$$$$. It took some time, but Chef John Tesar finally landed in the place he was meant to run in Dallas. Owner-chef of a jewel that opened late in 2012, Tesar— recently a *Top Chef* contestant—arrived in town several years before to be the executive chef at the **Mansion Restaurant** on Turtle Creek (p. 103), a spot vacated when long-loved Dean Fearing went over to the Ritz-Carlton to open his own place. So why does his new place, Spoon, fit Tesar so perfectly? Because we first recognized his genius when he was in Las Vegas at Rick Moonen's RM Seafood— one of the nation's extraordinary places to eat fish. Since coming to Dallas, however, his focus was on a number of other genres, as he moved about town to different kitchens. Finally he's opened his own shop, and it's swell, to say the least. Sleek, understated, and mellow in a study of white and gray, with a multitude of spoons in design details, his smash-hit new venue is dedicated to foods from fresh- and saltwaters. Starters come in the form of raw bar options, as well as *crudos*—the latter offering things like a spiny lobster with onion, orange, and mint oil; or geoduck (a large, saltwater clam) with chile oil and pink salt from the Himalayas. First courses run the gamut from oyster with black truffle stew and Singapore-style chile lobster with Texas toast to grilled octopus with crispy pork belly. Mains include butter-poached Maine lobster and roasted monkfish, each with intriguing treatments. For people really not into fish, there are usually two beef options and a pasta. Do reserve, or take a seat and eat at the pretty bar up front. If you're a real foodie, book a seat and the kitchen bar where you watch Tesar and his staff at work.

Village Kitchen, 32 Highland Park Village, Dallas 75205; (214) 522-6035; hpvillagekitchen.com; American; $$$. Replacing Village Marquee Grill & Bar, next door to the venerable movie theater, this upstart immediately won a feverish clientele. Chef Andre Natera wins us over with his high-end neighborhood cafe menu, keeping away from overly fancy preparations. The roasted chicken over quinoa pilaf comforts after a busy workday, as does fried chicken with waffles punctuated with bacon and chives. Barbecue fans are happy to see Pecan Lodge's smoked brisket on flatbread, too. The dining room feels unfussy, thanks to wooden floors and tables and butcher paper instead of tablecloths. If you just want a drink before taking in a movie, there are craft beers on tap and sangria by the pitcher.

Landmarks

Al Biernat's, 4217 Oak Lawn Ave., Dallas 75219; (214) 219-2201; albiernats.com; Steak House; $$$–$$$$. The Park Cities crowd has long considered this their playground when it comes to meeting for cocktails, then enjoying exceptional steaks and selections from a fine wine list. It's a prestigious place but not stuffy. The setting is pretty but yet not formal; for instance, the room dividers are tall wooden panels that have a rather Moroccan look, offering a bit of noise buffering—this place gets crazy crowded nightly—and a certain warmth. Service is unfailingly professional, and the staff shows its proficiency in answering all questions and making spot-on recommendations. At lunch, a lighter way to go is with chilled jumbo prawns with remoulade sauce or a salad of warm goat cheese with a sun-dried tomato vinaigrette. The signature salad, Al's, features hearts of palm, avocado, shrimp, and crab with Russian dressing. That's our pick for the dinner starter, followed by beef tenderloin with roasted red potatoes and a Port wine–foie gras sauce. Grilled sea scallops and prawns come with coconut rice and ginger butter. For dessert, try peanut butter–chocolate-banana cream pie. Keep an eye out for local sports celebrities as well as TV stars, like hometown girl Angie Harmon.

Bubba's, 6617 **Hillcrest, Dallas** 75205; (214) 373-6527; **bubbas catering.com; Southern; $–$$.** This converted 1927 Texaco station has been an exceptionally popular place since opening in 1981. When you find out that it's owned by the folks who own Babe's Fried Chicken—popular across North Texas—you understand why the fried chicken at Bubba's makes you want to weep tears of joy. Yes, it is that good, all hot, crunchy crust outside, juicy and plump inside. Get the two-piece (all white) dinner with a huge, yeasty roll, a side of mashers—smooth with a nice, peppery gravy—and pintos, which were unadulterated, as God intended. Other entrees range from chicken-fried steak and chicken and dumplings to fried catfish. Assorted sides include squash casserole, black-eyed peas, lima beans, okra and tomatoes, candied yams, and other great Southern specialties. For dessert, there's apricot fried pies, cherry cobbler, and banana pudding.

Burger House, 6913 **Hillcrest Ave., Dallas** 75205; (214) 361-0370; **burgerhouse.com; Burgers; $.** Yes, another great burger place sits right across from SMU, and it's another one with a local history since the 1950s. Always in this location, the original owner was named

Jack, and everyone talked about going to "Jack's Burger House" to eat. The patties were coated in a seasoning salt, then cooked on a flat griddle and served hot on a toasty bun, all wrapped in a tissue paper jacket. The recipe is still the same, though the ownership has changed, and the Burger House has become a franchise. You can still sit at one of the original counter stools or outside at a sidewalk table. The fries continue to be seductive, coated also in that seasoning salt, and the malts and shakes and vanilla Coke still taste wonderful. In addition to burgers, the place now makes grilled chicken breast sandwiches, which you can have topped with bacon, grilled onion, and jalapeño slices. Hot dogs are on the menu, as well. Three other locations are in Dallas.

Cafe Pacific, 24 Highland Park Village, Dallas 75205; (214) 526-1170; cafepacificdallas.com; Seafood; $$$–$$$$. For more than 25 years, this go-to destination for fine dining in the 'hood never fails to please. Some folks not from the Park Cities tend to be intimidated at Cafe Pacific, but that's just silly—the staff is welcoming, and you don't have to be attired in Chanel to feel worthy of dining here. At lunch, when business is brokered and ladies lunch with aplomb, you should seriously consider the lobster roll—it's one of the best in the city. Seafood crepes are lovely, as is the niçoise salad, but some regulars refuse to ever order anything but the superb burger, of all things. At dinner, try the fresh oysters from far-flung cold waters, as well as Atlantic sole amandine, lobster tail with white truffle risotto, or the pepper steak in cognac sauce. At mid-day, you can sit at the bar and enjoy Caesar salad, calamari, ceviche, and crab cakes. On Sunday, the brunch menu is loved for its eggs Benedict with smoked salmon, shrimp and grits, and huevos rancheros with beef tenderloin.

Our Favorite Margaritas

Blue Mesa Grill, *locations across DFW; bluemesagrill.com.* Quite possibly the largest selection of tequilas in any Dallas–Fort Worth restaurant, Blue Mesa's tequila bar features Tequila Tuesday happy hour each week. A different tequila is featured during a given month, with a different top-shelf margarita and tequila flights at special prices and a complimentary taco bar noshing offered. Every day, there's the Classic Blue Signature margarita, frozen or rocks, as well as a top-shelf margarita or a fresh fruit feature, with goodies like Meyer lemon and mint as the starring addition.

Hacienda San Miguel, *2948 Crockett St., Fort Worth 76107; (817) 386-9923; hsmw7.com.* You step deep into the interior of Mexico, alighting in a handsomely appointed home, when you visit Hacienda. Settle in with a pomegranate margarita, or sip one of the frozen versions made with fresh lime, tamarind, mango, kiwi, or papaya. The signature drink is the margarita made with Don Julio Silver, agave nectar, and fresh lime juice. The way it's enjoyed in Mexico.

Lonesome Dove Western Bistro, *2406 N. Main St., Fort Worth 76164; (817) 740-8810; lonesomedovebistro.com.* What goes with garlic-stuffed tenderloin or elk nachos? One of chef Tim Love's cucumber-jalapeño margaritas. The cook cuke tempers the fiery chile, and the silver tequila, fresh lime juice, and Cointreau make it all go down so very easy.

Mi Cocina, *locations all over DFW; micocinarestaurants.com.* The Dallas-based chain crafts legendary drinks with tequila. First, there's the Mambo Taxi, a frozen confection made with Sauza Blanco Tequila and swirled with house-made sangria. The Mambo Limousine puts a Chambord meltdown atop the Taxi. The Dilemma is a three-layered work, with strawberry margarita, topped with a Taxi, finished on top with a mango margarita. And the Anniversario Margarita is a rocks creation, blending Sauza Blue Reposado with Cointreau Noir, agave nectar, and lime juice. Mmmm. Take two aspirin and call us tomorrow.

Mi Dia from Scratch, *1295 S. Main St., Grapevine 76051; (817) 421-4747; midiafromscratch.com.* This Grapevine destination for super-fresh Mexican food has a margarita menu to make your head spin. We like the Upsell, a top-shelf version made with El Jimador Reposado, Cointreau, lemon juice, and agave nectar; The Stars at Night, made with Republic Tequila (from Austin) plus Cointreau, lemon juice, and agave nectar; I Can't Drive 55, made with Sammy Hagar's tequila, called Cabo Wabo, plus Grand Marnier, lemon juice, and agave syrup; and the Once in a Blue Moon, made with Lunazul Reposado, Blue Curacao, lemon juice, and agave nectar.

Rattlesnake Bar, *2121 McKinney Ave., Dallas, 75201; (214) 922-4848; fearingsrestaurant.com.* Dean Fearing's self-named restaurant inside the Ritz-Carlton (p. 102) in Dallas features a tasty temptation called El Diablo. Made with Patron Silver Tequila, it also mixes in Mathilde Blackcurrant Liqueur, freshly squeezed lime juice, and ginger ale. Watch it—too many, and you'll feel like the devil!

Stampede 66, *1717 McKinney Ave., Dallas 75201; (214) 550-6966; stampede66.com.* Just to make every night a party, Stephan Pyles's newest restaurant features a roving margarita cart that goes table to table to make your cocktails. The Molecular Margarita is a big deal here, with clouds of cool smoke from liquid nitrogen billowing up from the server's tools as she crafts the drink. It's purplish and sweet and lots of fun. But the passion-chile margarita is good, too, made with just a bit of spice and passion fruit. You can't go wrong.

Goff's Hamburgers, 6401 Hillcrest Ave., Dallas 75205; (214) 520-9133; goffshamburgers.com; Burgers; $-$$. A legend in the Park Cities since the 1950s, the original location on Lovers Lane is long gone, but new owners acquired the old charcoal grill, encased in brick, and moved it to the new location. The flavors remain absolutely the same in this sunnier locale facing SMU. But what baffles newcomers is the longtime fans' addiction to this burger: Deeply charcoaled in flavor, these burgers tend to be smaller than the monster burgers younger generations have come to expect. Regulars, along with their parents and grandparents, will argue whether the #2 (with hickory sauce) or the #9 (with a Thousand Island dressing) is better. Others still will claim that nothing beats the chili cheeseburger. If you want to get crazy, try the #12, which combines a #2 burger and the #6 "puppy" (that's a hot dog) with chili, cheese, and onions. You just have to figure it out for yourself. The fries tend to be thicker than some, and they're addictive, as are the handmade fried pies (the apricot is superb). Take time to examine the memorabilia on the walls: It's a history walk through Highland Park High School sports.

Javier's Gourmet Mexicano, 4912 Cole Ave., Dallas 75205; (214) 521-4211; javiers.net; Mexican; $$$. The staff hustles to refill bowls of warm, thin, golden corn tortilla chips and dishes of accompanying tart green salsa and mild red salsa. Typical of northern Mexico's hacienda region, the menu gets weight from steak options, many of which come with chile or brandy treatments. The exceptional filet pimiento consists of thick beef tenderloin slathered in a black peppercorn sauce, with buttery carrot slices and a slurry of black beans alongside, the latter covered in salty, white cheese. Fish choices, such as the Chilean sea bass, pan grilled and swept with a fragrant Veracruzana blend of tomatoes, olives, onions, and mild green peppers, are worthy options. A smooth, lush mole poblano hinting of dark chiles graces a juicy broiled chicken half. Expect solicitous service in this ramble of dining rooms that bring the Mexican heartland to Big D with heavy wooden furniture, hunting trophies, and skins of exotic beasts.

Mi Cocina, 77 Highland Park Village, Dallas 75205; (214) 521-6426; micocinarestaurants.com; Mexican; $$. Enduring traditions in the Park Cities include eating once a week at this stylish Tex-Mex favorite. Some families make it a Sunday-evening tradition. Some girlfriends meet there every Monday at 6 p.m. That's just how it is. But you don't have to be an insider to get the pleasures of eating here. All you need to know is that the lunch special #4, one beef taco, one cheese enchilada, and rice and beans, is the go-to standard, and that Tacos Habana, a pair of tortillas stuffed with chile-adobo-marinated chicken breast with rice, salad, and sliced avocado on the side, is Tex-Mex done a little on the lighter side. Bigger offerings, such as bacon-wrapped grilled shrimp, tilapia grilled with garlic and lime, and tacos stuffed with beef brisket, will all treat you right. Signature drinks at Mi Cocina include the Mambo Taxi, a potent elixir combining a frozen margarita with sangria; and the Dilemma, a Mambo Taxi plus strawberry and mango margarita mixed in. Other locations in Dallas, Irving, Plano, Richardson, Flower Mound, Southlake, and Fort Worth.

Taco Diner, 4011 Villanova St., Dallas 75225; (214) 363-3111; tacodinerrestaurants.com; Mexican; $$. A sister restaurant to Mi Cocina (above), the Diner goes deeper into Mexico, bringing to the plate a taste of Mexico City. The effect is a somewhat lighter menu, with more ingredients from Mexico's interior but with a distinctly contemporary application. The Diner itself is all clean lines with bursts of bold color here and there. The food is executed with precision and an eye toward prettiness. We love the Los Cabos salad, a tidy production of lettuce, avocado, tomato, bacon, and grilled chicken, and we are fond of the classic tortilla soup. The Estilo Diner tacos finds pan-seared tilapia treated with guajillo chiles and wrapped inside tiny, tender corn tortillas. A signature, the Mico's Shrimp Roll brings together sautéed shrimp, carrots, peas, cabbage, and white cheese inside a flour tortilla with rice and beans alongside. Some of the same Mi Cocina cocktails are found here, along with a fabulous banana-pineapple drink and a great mojito.

Specialty Stores, Markets & Producers

Crème de la Cookie, 6706 Snider Plaza, Dallas 75205; (214) 265-5572; cremedelacookie.com. A particularly pleasing place for the sweet tooth, this place with the rather cutesy name has become a magnet for moms, girlfriends, babysitters, grandparents, party-planners, and anyone in search of clever baked items. The simple chocolate chip cookie—called the OMG, because that's what everyone exclaims upon biting into one—is divine, and the red-velvet brownie is nirvana. Cake pops—that's a cake ball on a stick—are pretty darn adorable. Macaroons? Why, yes. In flavors like chocolate, pistachio, lemon, hazelnut, and more. How about pie? There's apple, berry, buttermilk chess, chocolate silk, and so forth. But the coffee is excellent, too, as is the chai latte. You'll want one to go along with a cinnamon roll, slice of quiche Lorraine, or a muffin. Other locations in Dallas and Frisco.

Drip Coffee Company, 4343 Lovers Ln., Dallas 75225; (214) 599-7800; dripcoffeeco.com. Owner Steve Thatcher first opened Roasters Coffee & Tea Company in his hometown of Amarillo, and he later opened a coffee place in Boston. What's special about Steve's coffee today is that chefs such as Dean Fearing at his namesake restaurant in the Ritz-Carlton (p. 102) in Dallas's Uptown serve Drip Coffee to guests. Drip's coffees are all 100 percent Arabica beans, sourced from South

America, Africa, the Pacific, and the Middle East. His brokers are finding coffees on estate plantations and small family-owned farms. In the shop, you can get any number of coffee drinks, as well as other beverages, including the Fort Worth–based Holy Kombucha.

Food Co., 4115 Lomo Alto Dr., Dallas 75219; (214) 521-7193; foodcompanytx.com. One of the leading caterers in Dallas for 20 years, this creative business make your party for 10 or 100-plus something to remember always. Bring your ideas or let the food wizards run wild. It can be a spring fling with lots of green vegetables and fish, a decadent chocolate orgy, or a feast combining Indian and Moroccan cuisine.

Molto Formaggio, 66 Highland Park Village, Dallas 75205; (214) 526-0700; moltoformaggio.com. Don't go here unless you really love cheese, chocolates, wine, and other stuff like that. And great customer service. The proprietors—who decided to create this place while in culinary studies in Florence, Italy—work hard to source some very interesting, very appealing cheeses, made from cow, sheep, and goat milk, most of which you probably have never heard of—and that makes it a lot of fun. Inventory in this boutique, tucked into the vintage spaces at the Highland Park Village, include also meats, fish, and other gourmet goodies, such as honey, tapenade, crackers, and more. They'll put together trays for you to take to a party, as well as cool gift baskets, with or without wines.

Plaza Health Foods, 6717 Snider Plaza, Dallas 75205; (214) 363-2661; plazahealthfoods.com. A longtime business in a shopping center that's seen numerous incarnations in more than 70 years, this health food store is most loved for its frozen yogurt. Open since 1949, and considered the oldest health food store in the city, it's remained a place where clients come for nutritional guidance and vitamin and herbal supplements. In addition, the staff offers lifestyle coaching that begins with proper nutrition.

Tu-Lu Gluten Free Bakery, 6055 Sherry Ln., Dallas 75225; (214) 730-0049; tu-lusbakery.com. Baking with nutritional consciousness has come into its own—finally. Arrived in 2012 from New York, this charming bakery does cookies, cupcakes, breads, panini sandwiches, and much more without gluten. What's more, there are vegan and dairy-free products available, as well. In addition to brownies, doughnuts, granola, croutons, cakes, muffins, and quiche, there is cookie dough to take home and bake, too, in flavors such as chocolate chip, snickerdoodle, and oatmeal. Best of all, everything's really pretty—you will never, ever think this isn't the baked wonderfulness your grandma made. Second location: 3699 McKinney Ave., Dallas 75204.

Village Baking Co., 5531 E. University Blvd, Dallas 75206; (214) 951-9077; villagebakingco.com. Originally opened in Colleyville, this bakery could be the single greatest example of fine European baking technique ever to come to Texas. For years, you could only find these breads and pastries at farmers' markets around the Dallas area. But the arrival of this brick-and-mortar shop just east of SMU brought joy to people passionate about exquisite baked goods. The almond croissant will bring tears of joy to your eyes. The pear croissant is a little taste of heaven. The baguette and sourdough are treasures. The scones will have you rethinking everything you only thought you knew about scones.

Wild About Harry's, 3113 Knox St., Dallas 75205; (214) 520-3113; wildaboutharrys.com. Yes, so the hot dogs (The Junkyard Dog, a spicy Polish with jalapeños is TDF) here are well worth a taste. But it's the frozen custard that will bring you back, time and again. Harry's Favorite, the vanilla custard plus hot fudge and peanuts, is a killer. But you can do as you please with additions, including caramel, butterscotch, Magic Shell, and Hershey's, along with Nilla Wafers, Waffle Bits, M&Ms, Reese's, and various fruits. It's a really special place.

North Dallas

The way Dallas gives into a desire to sprawl makes you think it took lessons from Houston. The landmass that's now loosely referred to as Dallas reaches from DFW Airport on the west to points east that touch Mesquite and other former farmlands that eventually turn into the Piney Woods of East Texas. Sometimes people around here joke when heading up to McKinney and Frisco that they're traveling to Oklahoma. The area we've come to call North Dallas extends from Dallas County northward into Collin County and even a corner of Denton County.

This chapter covers an area that begins with neighborhoods just outside of the Park Cities to the north. These are Bluffview, just northwest of University Park, and Preston Hollow, due north of University Park. Northwest of that there's Irving, home to Las Colinas and the Four Seasons Resort, where the Byron Nelson golf tournament is played. North of Preston Hollow is what's collectively called "far" North Dallas, and that often flows into Addison, Plano, and Richardson. Up north of those, you'll find Frisco, Allen, and McKinney.

Much of the dining in these areas lies in retail districts, such as shopping centers. Even if a restaurant doesn't exist in a freestanding building, it may still be a really good, deservedly popular restaurant. In North Dallas Plus, it's important not to judge a place from its exterior. Just point your car and go—but be aware that traffic can be tangled at any time of day. Allow yourself plenty of time to arrive. While you're at it, budget in extra time to do some shopping.

HOW DALLAS GOT ITS
DINING GROOVE ON

Dallas's modern cuisine era began when the Texas legislature saw fit to bring the state into the 20th century of dining by allowing restaurants to sell liquor by the drink, including beer and wine. Until 1972 Texas was a cultural backwater that required diners to "brownbag" their liquor and purchase setups.

This change in law opened a new world of sophisticated hospitality. The economic boom of the '80s, and the coming of age of Dallas as a business destination, created consumer demand for sophisticated hotels and restaurants and shone an international spotlight on the city. All this occurred at the beginning of the era of chefs as celebrities and cooking competitions as game shows, contributing significantly to the zeitgeist that has made food an entertainment medium, as well as an expression of hospitality and means of nourishment. Since then, the city has become recognized for venues, along with rock star chefs, such as Dean Fearing and Stephan Pyles.

But before them came Helen Corbitt, head of food service for the legendary Neiman Marcus department store, and NM's visionary leader, Stanley Marcus.

Texas Monthly dubbed Corbitt "tastemaker of the century" as the 20th came to a close. In that tribute to Corbitt, Prudence Mackintosh wrote: "In a career that spanned nearly forty years in Texas, she delivered us from canned fruit cocktail, plates of fried brown food, and too much bourbon and branch into a world of airy soufflés, poached fish, chanterelle mushrooms, fresh salsify, Major Grey's Chutney, crisp steamed vegetables, and fine wine. She was a creative pioneer who came here reluctantly and learned to love us. She taught us, she fed us, she entertained us, and best of all, before she left us in 1978, she wrote down the how-to of Corbitt hospitality in five cookbooks, giving us confidence that the civilizing pleasures of the table were within our reach. Superstar chefs Dean Fearing, Stephan Pyles, and Robert Del Grande may pay homage to Julia Child and Simone Beck, but long before they learned to clarify butter, there was Corbitt."

Helen Corbitt succumbed to Stanley Marcus's siren song in 1955, taking over food service at Neiman's, the flagship of refined taste for the moneyed of big banks, insurance, and oil during the period.

Besides running the famed Zodiac restaurant, she taught Dallasites cooking and entertaining classes. Mr. Stanley, as he was known, made sure that those who wanted it, and could afford it, could buy the finest wines in the world. The continental cuisine period followed this awakening with names like Ewald's, Patry's, Mr. Peppe, and the Old Warsaw, familiarizing Dallas diners with fried parsley and rack of lamb. Building toward what became known as the Southwestern cuisine movement, Callaud and Jean Claude's caught the nouvelle cuisine wave. The Grape, going strong today after 40 years, was Dallas's first wine bar and bistro.

With the rise of American regional cuisine, chefs Fearing and Pyles ushered in Southwestern cuisine, a style applying classic French techniques to sophisticated regional ingredients like chile peppers, Texas wild game, and grits.

The Mansion Restaurant on Turtle Creek made tortilla soup and the lobster taco internationally known dishes that have become as familiar today as hummus and fried calamari.

Following that golden age, the '90s recession made a steak house out of every restaurant because that's the only thing chefs and restaurateurs were confident consumers would spend big bucks on.

Happily, despite the more recent economic downturn, Dallas restaurants and chefs are resurgent with original concepts, neighborhood feel, and a consuming dedication to local and sustainable ingredients that characterize Dallas in a way that we've never seen before. Dallas is redefining itself as a culinary destination with confidence in who we are and what we want to be. *The Food Lovers' Guide to® Dallas & Fort Worth* truly updates the current state of Dallas cuisine and informs the reader about today's important players.

Dotty Griffith is a longtime observer of the Dallas restaurant scene, from both sides of the fence. She is the current executive director of the Greater Dallas Restaurant Association. She is a former food editor and restaurant critic for the Dallas Morning News *and the author of eight cookbooks.*

Arthur's Prime Steaks and Seafood, 15175 Quorum Dr., Addison 75001; (972) 385-0800; arthursdallas.com; Steak House and Seafood; $$$$. In the 1970s, the Arthur's that sat within a stone's throw of NorthPark was absolutely the be-all, end-all in Dallas dining. That's when continental fare was your quest when you set out for very special-occasion evenings. Today it's relocated up north in Addison, and it's a swanky place again, one that's still popular for the opulent evening out. There's a bar for enjoying cocktails before dinner and a lounge singer and dancing after dinner. In between, the dining room offers the old-school circular booths that lend themselves to quiet business dinners or close conversations between lovebirds. Most guests dress to the nines and bring their finest accessories; for some, that's a trophy wife. Dinner should begin with the signature lobster cocktail with remoulade or cocktail sauce, pâté, smoked salmon or oysters on the half shell—and there's caviar, if you so desire. Champagne-brie soup wows guests, as does the sea bass, crusted in onion and seared; cioppino; Australian lobster tail; tournedos with seared foie gras and black truffles; and steak au poivre with green peppercorn–brandy sauce.

Bistro B, 9780 Walnut St. at Audelia, Dallas 75243; (214) 575-9885; bistrob.com; Vietnamese; $. Almost every evening it seems as though a Chinese New Year celebration is taking place—that's how busy and bustling this huge restaurant typically is. It's where you find patrons of every description, whether Asian or otherwise. We love settling in for a big bowl of pho, the traditional soup filled with sliced rare steak, brisket, and flank steak and rice noodles, hugely aromatic with subtle layerings of anise and coriander; we add in some fresh jalapeño and purple basil with a few bean sprouts for crunch. Another favorite is grilled pork over superfine vermicelli, a knock-out with sliced green papaya on top and a boat alongside filled with mint, two kinds of basil, shredded carrot salad, cilantro, and crunchy fried onion. It's BYOB, so be sure to take along your favorite New Zealand Sauvignon Blanc to complement those spicy flavors.

Blue Mesa Grill, 5100 Belt Line Rd., Addison 75254; (972) 934-0165; bluemesagrill.com; Mexican; $$. Not only does Blue Mesa bring a strong degree of New Mexican and interior-of-Mexico flavors to the party, but it's a restaurant with a sense of integrity. Owners Jim and Liz Baron have grown their mini-chain from this original in Addison with food and drink that makes customers really happy, but they've also been giving back to their communities since the beginning. Each month, they have programs in their restaurants that give a certain percentage from their sales to charity; one of the most popular such programs is Tacos for a Cause. Another program is their Community Night, in which local organizations near their locations can stage fund-raisers at the restaurants. So in eating at Blue Mesa, you can feel extra good about tucking into a dish of guacamole, crafted tableside; quesadillas made with avocado, sun-dried tomato pesto, and jalapeño relish; Painted Desert Soup, a combo of black bean and corn chowder sharing space artfully in the bowl; and virtuous menu choices like the spa chicken-spinach enchiladas and spa grilled fish of the day with pineapple-habanero salsa. At the renowned Sunday brunch, you can go crazy, loading up your plate with blue corn enchiladas, salads, carved meats, fruit, and the signature Adobe Pie, a corn masa dome filled with spicy chicken, cheese, and roasted chiles.

Bonnie Ruth's Café Trottoir et Patisserie, 6959 Lebanon Rd., Frisco 75034; (214) 705-7775; bonnieruthsfrisco.com; French; $$–$$$. Borrowing a page or two from a bakery-brasserie in the Sixth Arrondissement, Bonnie Ruth's brims at lunch, brunch, and dinner with loyal locals who make regular visits to this corner sport in the Shops at Starwood. Begun in 2007 as a bistro and patio for dining and libations, Bonnie Ruth's has evolved to include a dedicated bakery—and one that grabs your undivided attention as soon as you arrive inside the front door. Jewels there inside the bakery case include chocolate praline cake, red velvet cake, and carrot cake, enjoyed either with a very strong cup of French roast or after a sumptuous meal of chicken paillard, duck confit with a honey-lavender sauce, prime rib sandwich, mussels served in a cast-iron skillet, or steak frites. Brunch, in particular, is an event at Bonnie Ruth's, with a bountiful buffet as one option and a brunch menu that includes caramel french toast, omelet Provençal, and shirred egg casserole as another. If you enjoy a cocktail, you've come to the right place: Bonnie Ruth's offers a $3 Bloody Mary at brunch and $3 Martini Madness at happy hour. Just don't let the staff catch you trying to swipe the Frank Sinatra photo in the ladies' room; many have tried, all are doomed to be caught.

Café on the Green, Four Seasons Dallas, 4150 N. MacArthur Blvd., Irving 75038; (972) 717-0700; fourseasons.com/dallas/; American; $$$$. A destination unto itself, this restaurant inside the Four Seasons Resort in Las Colinas lives up to every inch of a luxury hotel's reputation—and then some. We love taking out-of-towners here who have long layovers at DFW Airport, and we like going here on weekend getaways when we go for serious me-time at the Four Seasons's fabulous spa. That's because we love the food at Café on the Green, along with stunning wine service from sommelier James Tidwell. Always requesting a window-side table so we can gaze out on the exquisitely manicured grounds, we start typically with a salad of green apples, goat cheese, and pecans with a cider vinaigrette, followed by a flight of Texas cheeses served on a board with grapes, balsamic figs, local honey, and apple-walnut bread crisps. Crispy oysters in a truffle sauce of frisée greens and grilled quail over jalapeño grits is a great second course, and for a main course, we like the striped bass bouillabaisse with leeks and potatoes, as well as the Texas Akaushi (like Kobe beef, only raised in South Texas) short ribs with smoky cheddar mac and cheese. James always picks the best wines to pair with whatever we're having.

Canary by Gorji, 5100 Belt Line Rd., Addison 75254; (972) 503-7080; canarybygorji.com; Mediterranean / Middle Eastern; $$$. Intimate dining at this 10-table retreat means a relaxed evening of inspired food. Chef-owner Gorji has won legions of devout fans who are utterly bewitched by his food and his honest, warm smile. His barbecued veal ribs in a pomegranate reduction sauce, quail over kale with honey and berries, and lamb brain with green garbanzos and butter will transform you, even if you think you don't like those items. His proficiency in cooking a steak better than any you've ever tasted has been proven at the cooking competitions he wins, and he shows you that skill in his lamb T-bone steak and his prime, bone-in pork chop. If you're into fish, his rainbow trout with artichoke and Chablis will woo you. Vegetarians rejoice at such finds as baked eggplant with pomodoro sauce and mozzarella. Watch for seasonal, prix-fixe menus, when a $39 menu that changes every few days or so will include three courses that feature things like red Bartlett pear, arugula, and almond salad, pan-seared striped bass with dill and fava bean Provençal, and Medjool dates with Turkish kefir and pomegranate reduction. Note that this place is for people who want to luxuriate in the culinary experience; there are no TVs in the bar, and the owners politely ask that you not bring young children.

Cedars Woodfire Grill, 4710 Preston Rd., Frisco 75034; (972) 377-8886; cedarswoodfiregrill.com; American; $–$$. Here's a fast-casual concept, born in North Texas and opened in Frisco in summer 2012, that lives up to its boasts about healthy eating options. Freshness emanates from every corner of the menu, as the kitchen operates with no freezers, fryers, or microwaves. Each item is crafted from seasonal fruits and vegetables, all-natural chicken, choice Angus steak, fresh Atlantic salmon, whole grains, natural vegetable stock, genuine, pure cheeses—all preservative- and additive-free. By grilling everything—using aromatic cedar, mesquite, and cherry woods—the quick cooking and dry heat brings out the proper flavors without robbing the food of nutrition. With a strong working connection with nutritionists from the renowned Cooper Clinic in Dallas, guests are assured that a high degree of care goes into the recipe development. Among certified hits on the menu, the steak satay with Asian salad and ponzu sauce; grilled vegetable bruschetta, glazed in balsamic vinegar and dusted with shaved Parmesan; and the signature California bowl of wild rice, grilled veggies, and salmon have made believers out of even the most particular diners. Kids get ample attention, too, with menu choices that include noodle bowls, grilled chicken-on-a-stick, and melted cheddar on grilled bread.

Chamberlain's Fish Market Grill, 4525 Belt Line Rd., Addison 75001; (972) 503-3474; chefchamberlain.com; Seafood; $$$. The sister restaurant to **Chamberlain's Steak & Chop House** (p. 177), this seafood destination comes from owner-chef Richard Chamberlain, whose years at the prestigious Little Nell Hotel in Aspen, Hotel Bel-Air in Los Angeles, and the **Mansion Restaurant** on Turtle Creek (p. 103) in Dallas gave him the expertise to open fine-dining places anywhere. He keeps a sea of regular clientele happy with fish dishes that cross all sorts of borders, with pot stickers stuffed with lobster, shrimp, and scallops; mini crab tacos; and seafood gumbo among many examples. Lobster bisque is an excellent choice, with its inclusion of shrimp and crab; and even the humble tilapia gets exciting when done with a Parmesan crust and a sauce of lobster, scallop, and shrimp. Steelhead trout done Hong Kong style means it's cooked with ginger, garlic, shrimp, and ponzu sauce. Landlubbers can get the carnivore's fix with a variety of steaks, a prime beef meat loaf, and grilled chicken at their disposal. In the bar, appetizers are half price weekdays between 4:30 and 6:30 p.m.

Crossroads Diner, 8121 Walnut Hill Ln., Dallas 75231; (214) 346-3491; crossroads-diner.com; American; $$. While perusing the overwhelming breakfast menu, it only makes sense to pounce on a massive sticky bun as an appetizer. You'll be ready for savory choices, such as an airy frittata punctuated with South Texas chorizo, chunky goat cheese from Dallas's **Mozzarella Company** (p. 74) and roasted red bell peppers, one of a number of smart dishes conjured up by owner-chef Tom Fleming. Shredded corned beef hash, topped with two eggs, gets high marks, as does the brioche french toast. At lunch, creamy tomato-basil soup is a good preamble to the curry chicken salad sandwich or the pit-smoked ham sandwich with white cheddar on a croissant. If you're aiming to be somewhat light at lunch, check out the young baby field greens topped with apples, almonds, and goat cheese. The most popular midday meal, however, is the spinach, bacon, and goat cheese quiche, served with a salad of fresh greens. Weekends can be a bit crazy at this relatively new addition near Presbyterian Hospital, just off North Central Expressway. Weekdays are a little less busy.

Cuquita's, 13260 Josey Ln., Farmers Branch 75234; (972) 243-1491; Mexican; $–$$. A taste of Mexico's interior awaits in this unpretentious neighborhood favorite with gracious hospitality. Handmade corn tortillas, served still puffy and hot from cooking on the *comal* and featherlight to the touch, should be dredged through the rustic, rich-red tomato salsa with a hint of jalapeño. Smooth refried beans, replete with bacon flavor, are a suitable side to gorditas (corn masa pockets), plump with filling of *queso blanco* and roasted poblano chile strips or red chile shredded beef. Pozole, a bowl of chile-tinged broth filled with chunky pork and hominy, with condiments of shredded cabbage, chopped white onion, and lime wedges on the side, provides authentic flavor. A traditional chile relleno, an ample poblano coated lightly in golden-crisp egg batter, which reveals a picodillo filling bearing peas, carrots, bell pepper, and wee bits of tomato, deserves applause. Don't expect anything fancy; this strip-center space made warm and inviting with a giant Aztec-style wooden wall hanging, clusters of garlic strung on twine, and pottery and paintings decorating sunny yellow walls is pleasant guilelessness in a mix of real and fake green plants.

Densetsu, 4152 W. Spring Creek Pkwy., Ste. 176, Plano 75024; (972) 964-7874; Japanese; $$. Close to the University of Texas at Dallas, this friendly, lively spot is great for families, as well as food freaks. If you're new to sushi, this place will ease you into the process with some very approachable rolls. If you're a picky veteran, worry not—there are some lovely things for purists. Among favorites, the hamachi (yellowtail) roll comes fairly simply with scallion and cucumber. A little more jazzed up, the Summer Breeze Roll includes tuna, cooked shrimp, and avocado atop a California roll. A huge hit, the Pinky Promise is a roll of spicy tuna, spicy albacore, scallops, and roe wrapped inside reddish-pink soy paper, atop a pool of sweet-salty ponzu sauce. Texans who love their fried food go nuts for the Lone Star Roll, packed with lobster, cream cheese, and avocado, then fried. Perfect sashimi is abundant, just in case you're wanting something streamlined. Friendly staffers make you want to return soon.

Dough Pizzeria Napoletana, 11909 Preston Rd., Dallas 75230; (972) 788-4600; doughpizzeria.com; Pizza; $$. Now that it's been on *Diners, Drive-Ins and Dives,* life may not be the same at Dough again. But we have faith that the owners—whose mission it was to make us love "Pizza Forever!"—won't let fame get in the way of a great thing. And you gotta love a place whose proprietors so love cheese that they named one area of the restaurant the Burrata Bar, in honor of the mozzarella. There, you can enjoy a *spiedini,* oven-roasted mozzarella wrapped in prosciutto as well as smoked salmon rollatini. From a list of antipasti, we like the oak-roasted mushroom bruschetta with roasted garlic and Rain Drop Farms' heirloom tomatoes. Among pizzas, there's the Margherita, the pasta puttanesca, and the fontina pizza, which is topped with roasted marshmallows, fontina, and caramelized onion. Hankering for an old-fashioned soda pop? Dough makes them in flavors like cherry, peach, blackberry, and raspberry. For dessert, dig into something like polenta cake, Nutella panini, or tiramisu.

Fernando's Mexican Cuisine, 4347 W. Northwest Highway, Dallas 75220; (214) 351-9010; fernandosmexicancuisine.com; Mexican; $$. Legion are the regular customers willingly admitting to their addiction to Fernando's three house salsas, starting with the dark green salsa melding cilantro and green chiles, the pale green salsa incorporating some guacamole, and the warm red salsa with sweet tomato overtones. The favorite of all meals here is Saturday and Sunday brunch, when the mimosas are complimentary and bottomless. The best brunch dishes to consider include huevos con chorizo, scrambled eggs topped with Mexican sausage and pico de gallo; and huevos rancheros, the ages-old dish of fried eggs topped with smooth red ranchera sauce atop corn tortilla with exceptional refried beans and Mexican potatoes on the side. For lunch the spinach salad topped with sun-dried tomatoes, grilled shrimp, and a tart citrus vinaigrette and a crostini smeared with goat cheese is about as virtuous as you could hope to find. At dinner, settle in with the crab-stuffed shrimp in a white wine sauce or the tender *carne asada*. When the weather is pretty, try to snag a patio table, but know that it can be a long wait for one of these. Inside, the setting is sleek and simple—but the crowd can be a bit loud, depending on the margarita consumption. A second location is at 4512 Travis St., Dallas 75205.

Grill on the Alley, 13270 Dallas Pkwy., Dallas 75240; (214) 459-1601; thegrill.com; American; $$$–$$$$. The original's in Beverly Hills, California, if that tells you a little about the special nature of this restaurant. Nevermind that it's attached to a shopping mall—albeit one of the most luxurious such shopping destinations in North America—you shouldn't dismiss this place, just because it's at the Galleria. Understand that the things you're eating here are the same as what guests at the Hollywood location are eating. There, don't you feel more special? Concern with elegance shows up in the plush setting, as well as on the menu. Start with a fancy cocktail, such as the Red Velvet Martini, made with Ketel One Citroen, pomegranate juice, and Chambord, or the Tarragon Sling, made with Tito's Vodka, fresh tarragon, lemon, and lime juice. For an appetizer, the pan-seared scallops are lovely, but so is the lobster bisque soup. A salad of endive, spicy pecans, romaine, and Gorgonzola sets you up for the main course, whether that's a filet mignon with onions and bordelaise sauce or baked Idaho trout with jumbo lump crab on top. If you need some soothing after an arduous day of shopping, check out the Grill's chicken potpie.

Isabella's Italia Restaurant & Wine Bar, 1279 Legacy Dr., Frisco 75034; (214) 618-3384; isabellasfrisco.com; Italian; $$$. Owner Kenyon Price pours his passion for Italian food, wine, music, and art into this wildly popular destination restaurant that's a neighborhood favorite, just a short walk from the Westin Stonebriar. Taking the treasures collected from his work and adventures in Lake Garda, Rome, Siena, and throughout Italy, Kenyon fashioned a place to showcase the best of Italian culture and named it for his little girl, Isabella. A perennial winner of a multitude of local "best of" lists, Isabella's thrills the palate with traditional dishes that include a centuries-old recipe for Bolognese and modern creations such as sea bass with olive pâté atop. Obvious care goes into small details, such as the daily fresh roasting of tomatoes for crafting the pomodoro found in the pizza and atop bruschetta. The wine cellar stocks intriguing vintages, such as Barolos, Barberescos, Amarones, Chiantis, and Montepulciano, as well as those from around the world. The patio draws enthusiastic crowds in temperate weather, as does the wine bar—at any time. Be sure to note the proliferation of artwork from Italy, too.

Jasper's, 7161 Bishop Rd., Plano 75024; (469) 229-9111; kentrathbun.com/jaspers/plano/; American; $$$. Dallas celebrity chef Kent Rathbun puts a fancy spin on homey food from the heartland and the South. Signature house-made potato chips draped in a Maytag blue-cheese dressing start out the meal with a bit of gluttony, as does the focaccia topped with three cheeses, caramelized shallots, portobellos, and sweet basil. Among salads, the smoked-salmon cobb salad comes with a scattering of smoked bacon pieces, goat cheese, and avocado slices. You can easily make a meal of the side dishes, served in cast-iron skillets: bourbon-spiked creamed corn, hickory grilled asparagus, creamy baked potato salad, mac and cheese made with aged Gouda and ham, and buttermilk-battered onion rings are just a few. Smoked crab fills a chile relleno for a southwestern flavor, but the runaway favorite here is Rathbun's homage to his Kansas City upbringing, the slow-smoked baby back ribs, lauded by no less than *Bon Appétit* magazine. Though the food suggests a laid-back feel, the restaurant has a sleekness with leather, wood, and stone that lends itself to an atmosphere well-suited to business lunch and special-occasion dinners, too. See Rathbun's Lobster Macaroni & Cheese with Truffle Oil recipe on p. 229.

The Loft Restaurant & Lounge, 1001 W. Royal Ln., Irving 75039; (972) 373-8900; nylohotels.com/Irving/; American; $$$. Inside the super-sleek NYLO Hotel in Las Colinas, this warm but uber-contemporary restaurant brings in a crowd of locals for a terrific happy hour, a great sushi bar, and good lounging-and-grazing spaces at the poolside bar and at the fire pits outside. Grab some friends for sharing the pork belly with maple butter; truffled potato puffs with arugula, and a fabulous dip called Salsa Quesada, a blend of melted white cheese, spinach, and spicy white beans that you scoop up with tortilla chips. The lobster-corn chowder is worth forfeiting your diet, and the BLT with avocado can make a bad day a lot better. For dessert, the pot de crème comes with a butterscotch base and chocolate chip swirl. At breakfast, the Bird's Nest presents your egg cooked in a toast ring with meat on the side. If you need to go light, there are fruit plates and yogurt, of course.

Mama Pita Mediterranean Grill, 5800 Legacy Dr., Ste. C6, Plano 75024; (972) 403-1609; mamapita.com; Mediterranean; $. The enthusiastic fans of this place love it for its ease and simplicity, comparing it to Chipotle in terms of quick preparation of fresh food, made while you watch. The platter includes warm pita, and you build the ingredients as you go, choosing things like tzatziki sauce, tabbouleh, cucumber salad, falafel, grilled skewers, lamb, rice, and so forth. Other options are the wrap and the bowl; chose your fillings as you move down the line. Vegetarians and vegans find plenty of options here, and it's an easy place to get a big order to go, too.

Mercy Wine Bar, 5100 Belt Line Rd., Ste. 544, Addison 75254; (972) 702-9463; mercywinebar.com; American; $$$. It's hard to say whether you should consider this more of a girls' night out place or date-night option. Might as well try it for both, we decided. For starters, it's a wine shop that happens to do great food and offers warm hospitality. Most days you visit, you'll find 10 to 20 wines being tasted at the bar, so you can figure out what you'd like to enjoy here and what you want to take home with you. But for dining here, give a look at all the sharing plates, as well as the suggested wine pairings, and you'll realize you'll need several visits here to get all the great benefits. We like the Prince Edward Island mussels steamed in white wine with tomato and garlic with a Chilean Sancerre, as well as the red pepper hummus and flatbread paired with a fabulous French rosé. On days when nothing but cheese will do, we pick a goat gouda to go with Spanish white wine,  brie to pair with a California Pinot Noir, and Manchego for our reserve Chianti. Blackened salmon, with a zippy Petite Sirah, is darn good, as is the tortellini in sun-dried tomato sauce with a hearty Malbec.

My Temptation Cuisine, 4070 N. Belt Line Rd., #138, Irving 75038; (214) 492-1229; Indian; $–$$. Bar none, the best naan ever tasted is the garlic version, served steaming hot, redolent with fresh garlic and cilantro. The chicken *sekuwa* is one of the Himalayan specialties, a dish of barbecued chunks of chicken thigh, deeply marinated with garlic and ginger, baked in the clay oven and swathed in a spicy, thin sauce. On the tray with it is a serving of yellow, toasty rice puffs, a serving of crunchy soy beans in a tart chile sauce, and a fermented radish salad, all for $7.99. The Aloo Baigan from the vegetarian options offers a mixture of eggplant and potato baked in a curry-tomato sauce and served with basmati rice. I'd drive back there in a heartbeat for either dish. The place is big, clean, and bright; it's located in a typical suburban strip mall, but it's cheery. Service is exceptionally sweet and helpful.

Nazca Kitchen, 8041 Walnut Hill Ln., Dallas 75231; (214) 696-2922; nazcakitchen.com; Latin American; $$. Opened in late 2012, this new arrival draws attention for finding a niche nobody in Dallas had quite addressed—that of healthy South American comfort food done in a style we've come to expect only in Austin. Open for three meals daily, Nazca offers authentic foods from Peru, which, over the centuries, has been heavily influenced by cuisines of Africa, Asia, and Europe. The chef sources local and seasonal ingredients, which you see in dishes from roasted chicken to ceviche to acai breakfast bowls. Morning specialties include the Three Happy Cows yogurt bowl, with yogurt coming from a nearby dairy, topped with honey, granola, and fruit; and breakfast wraps, incorporating scrambled eggs, cheddar, cilantro, onion, and peppers with additions that can include spinach and bacon, chorizo and potato, or roasted kale and pepitas. At other hours of the day, choices range from aji amarillo hummus, a hummus with yellow chile-pepper drizzle; steak sandwich with jicama slaw; quinoa salad with a tahini glaze, broccoli, feta, pepitas, pecans, and olives; and fish tacos wrapped in either butter lettuce leaves or corn-and-flour-blend tortillas. To drink, choose from a list that includes South American coffees and wines.

Nosoo Hibachi-Sushi-Sake, 604 W. Bethany Dr., Allen 75013; **(214) 383-0989; Japanese; $$.** Opened by Benihana veterans, this gem in a shopping center does a lot of things well. The bento box, always a favorite at lunch, lets you try a number of goodies, from tempura to sushi to grilled chicken or beef. From a long  list of sushi options, you can go the route well-suited for the nervous newbie—for example, cooked shrimp roll with mango sauce—or you can get seriously into the simple, raw fish variety. From the hibachi table, which is always fun for a little cooking theater, the tuna is excellent, and there's a kids' menu specifically for the hibachi diner. Asian fusion options include green curry pad thai, always a good pick for the noodle lover. For the happy hour fan, specials happen daily between 4 p.m. and 7 p.m.

Nuevo Leon, 12895 Josey Ln., Farmers Branch 75234; (972) 488-1984; nuevoleonmexmex.com; **Mexican; $$.** Handcrafted Mexican specialties bearing fresh ingredients include borracho beans slow-cooked with beer, jalapeños, chorizo, bacon, tomato, and onion, as well as smooth, mild chili con carne atop the tamales that hold a filling of pork chunks in a guajillo sauce. Lush shrimp al mojo de ajo, riddled with butter and garlic and paired with spinach salad in a tangy mustard vinaigrette, is lighter than many dishes. Creamy green mole sauce surrounding a plump chicken breast is perfect for dipping the side of fresh zucchini and yellow squash, too. Brisket tacos make for a hearty lunch or dinner, and if you still crave more beef, there's *carne asada* in an Argentine chimichurri sauce, topped by a cheese enchilada ladled with chile pasilla sauce. Pains have been taken to make this space in a small strip center rise above its mundane location. Plentiful copies of classic Mexican paintings adorn two dining rooms.

Oceanaire Seafood Room, 13340 Dallas Pkwy., Dallas 75295; theoceanaire.com; Seafood; $$$$. Now ubiquitous, with locations from Baltimore to San Diego and Miami to Minneapolis, Oceanaire came to Dallas in its early years and delighted the city with an unprecedented fish selection. We were charmed at the outset with its look and feel of a vintage ocean liner from a gilded age in the past as well as its sensational menu. The Oyster Bar selections, which change daily, may offer things like bivalves from Cape Spear in New Brunswick, Rocky Bay on Prince Edward Island, Katama Bay in Massachusetts, and the James River in Virginia. While that may not mean anything to most people, the servers can tell you exactly the flavors and distinctions that go with each. Cold appetizers we like include the oak-smoked Scottish salmon and tequila shrimp ceviche. Among hot starters, there's the shrimp and grits and escargots. Entrees we keep returning for include baked stuffed lemon sole, North Carolina fluke Louie, and crab-crusted Icelandic cod. Sides get lots of attention, too: There are matchstick fries, smoked Gouda and bacon pasta, and mushrooms roasted in Chardonnay.

One2One Restaurant & Bar, 1339 Legacy Dr., Frisco 75034; (214) 618-2221; one2onerestaurant.com; American; $$$. You get two gastro gathering spaces under one roof at this rather upscale hangout: Guests can perch in the stylish bar to dine at dinner, or they can opt for the elegant dining room. Either way the dishes come from the creative hands of executive chef Tommy Simpson, a graduate of the California Culinary Academy in San Francisco and a fan of putting fancy spins on comforting foods. One bite into the Kobe beef meat loaf or the pan-seared wild salmon (the latter served over Israeli couscous, teased with cinnamon and mustard seed), you'll understand why these signatures never leave the menu. There's also a plate of wild boar ribs, served over creamed corn with a tangle of tobacco onions on top. The menu changes quarterly, according to the seasons, but the items always make smart pairings for the exceptional wine selections, which the staff is constantly familiarized with in weekly training sessions. Pizza is half price at happy hour, and cigars are complimentary on the patio on weekends.

Pizzeria Testa Napoletana, 8660 Church St., Frisco 75034; (469) 200-8015; pizzeriatesta.com; Italian; $$. A taste from the royal pizza makers' ovens landed in Collin County in late 2012, as owner and concept creator Rod Schaefer taps into family heritage. He descends on his mother's side from the Testa family, once responsible for baking pizzas for Italian royalty, and he employs a Naples native to make the pizzas on-site. Though newly opened in Frisco Square, Pizzeria Testa looks as though it's a vintage dining destination, warmed with lovely woods, reclaimed bricks from historic streets in Chicago, and two wood-burning ovens. Those ovens, also imported from Naples, weigh 7,000 pounds each and cook a pizza in 60 seconds at 1,000°F. Menu delights are simple, such as the marinara pizza topped with San Marzano tomatoes, oregano, garlic, and extra-virgin olive oil, and the pie topped with mozzarella, sausage, and broccoli rabe, as well as *panuozzi*, or bread dough stuffed with ingredients such as mozzarella, arugula, tomatoes, and prosciutto cotto, and classic antipasti. The sausage you taste is a proprietary blend made by **Jimmy's Food Store** (p. 73) in Dallas, so you know it's the best. To drink, you'll enjoy several charming boutique wines—all from Italy—and a number of imported and domestic craft beers.

Platia Greek Kouzina, 1590 Gaylord Pkwy., Frisco 75034; (972) 334-0031; platiagreek.com; Greek; $$. Co-owner and chef Sally Maglaris shares the flavors she's known intimately since her childhood in Chicago, enjoying the foods of her family's native Greece. Great care has been taken to provide you with both the food and setting that takes you to the homeland, where you're pampered as though by a doting grandmother. Start with dolmades, the rice-stuffed grape leaves, spanakopita, the crispy phyllo pie layered with feta and spinach, or saganaki, the sizzling white cheese that's flamed tableside. Your tour of Greek specialties continues with a bowl of the most traditional soup, avgolemono; the Greek favorite, a "village" salad called horiatiki; and entrees such as souvlaki, the plate of lamb or chicken medallions; moussakas, a layering of roasted eggplant, potato, ground meat, and béchamel sauce; and brizola, a flame-broiled skirt steak dusted with oregano and slathered with lemon. That's just a hint of the family recipes that trace back through generations. Be sure to remember, it's BYOB at Platia.

The Ranch, 857 W. John Carpenter Freeway, Irving 75039; (972) 506-7262; theranchlc.com; Steak House; $$$. Fully embracing the farm-to-fork philosophy, this restaurant's management takes great care to source beef from Texas ranches, fish from the Texas Gulf Coast, and produce from the North Texas area. That alone makes us feel proud to patronize this Las Colinas favorite, and the atmosphere, which is animated with live music performances by Texas artists, adds to the allure. But then, a restaurant is about the food, and this one scores big points with onion rings accented with guajillo-lime ketchup; chicken and waffles served with whipped sweet potatoes; mini tacos filled with spicy Kobe beef; blackened shrimp salad over local greens; venison chili with warm corn bread; East Texas catfish fillets crusted in cornmeal and served with hand-cut fries; and smoked fried chicken, served with warm potato salad and farmers' market veggies. From the bar, try the Texas Sunset, a mix of vodka, Texas Chardonnay, St-Germain liqueur, guava juice, and fresh lemon, or the Two-Step Mojito, made with gin, a Texas lemon liqueur, muddled fresh mint, and orange, fresh lemon, and agave nectar.

Randy's Steakhouse, 7026 Main St., Frisco 75034; (972) 335-3066; randyssteakhouse.com; Steak House; $$$–$$$$. Owner-chef Randy Burks cut his teeth as kitchen manager and chef at the Dallas legend, **Del Frisco's Double Eagle Steak House** (p. 178), before leaving the nest to open his own fine-dining refuge in the 1990s. Turning a charming 19th-century Victorian home into a steak house, Burks called it Randy's Country Kitchen before shifting the focus to an upscale beef palace. He carved seven intimate rooms out of the home, imparting warmth through the use of fireplaces and candlelight, and elegance with white tablecloths and special wine-pairing dinners. Menu winners range from the traditional staples, including crab cakes, giant onion rings, Caesar salad, and prime New York strip, to the innovative, such as panko-crusted brie with roasted garlic, beef fillet stuffed with blue cheese and topped with roasted walnuts and cognac sauce, and filet mignon in a blackberry–red wine sauce. There's a comfortable bar in one corner of the house, where the specialty is a rich dessert drink, the Randy Alexander.

Rex's Seafood Market, 5200 W. Lovers Ln., Dallas 75209; (214) 351-6363; rexsseafood.com; Seafood; $$. Originally a fish market, the shop has grown to also include a restaurant that has won a huge fan base of particular diners from the nearby Park Cities. There's not much in the way of ambience, but the food way more than makes up for that. Popular with families, there's something for every palate here. Shrimp cocktail, ceviche, and steamed shellfish are among appetizers, and salads include warm spinach, blue cheese wedge, and Caesar, all of which can be topped with lump crab, shrimp, or smoked salmon. Entree salads include the seafood cobb, as well as a shrimp salad with remoulade sauce. For big plates, choose between trout amandine, shrimp fettuccine, blackened redfish, and salt-crusted big-eye tuna.

Rise No. 1, 5360 W. Lovers Ln., Dallas 75209; (214) 366-9900; risesouffle.com; French; $$$. A bistro that feels like it's pulled straight from a Paris picture book, this is a place for elegant dining and a little shopping on the side. Women love this as a place to meet and gab, but we've taken our menfolk here plenty of times, and they're happy as clams. Starters to strongly consider include onion soup with plenty of melted cheese atop; steamed artichokes; the Rise salad with baby greens, blue cheese, roasted pecans, Granny Smith apples, and vinaigrette; and selections from the cheese cart. Soufflés to dream about include those combining ham and gruyère, creamed spinach, smoked salmon, truffle-infused mushrooms, herbs and spicy sausage, and escargot. *Salade niçoise* is also exceptional, as is the seared ahi tuna steak. For dessert, it's a certain sin to not try the blueberry, apricot, or Grand Marnier soufflé. Allow time after your meal to shop the boutique in the front of the store; goods have been hand-selected from French home-goods shops.

Seasons 52, 7300 Lone Star Dr., Plano 75024; (972) 312-8852; seasons52.com; American; $$–$$$. From the same folks who brought us **The Capital Grille** (p. 81), there's Seasons 52, a newish concept with "Fresh Grill" in its subhead. It pulls off the neat trick of not feeling like a

cookie-cutter restaurant, and there's a high degree of customer service that you'd expect in an independently owned place, and the food shows so much thought, you are assured that it's not coming from a central commissary thousands of miles away. Best of all, no dish at Seasons 52 contains more than 475 calories. We like starting with a sampler of flatbreads, including one with ripe plum tomato, basil shreds, roasted garlic, and mozzarella, and the steak and cremini mushrooms with fresh spinach and fragrant blue cheese. Cedar-plank-roasted salmon gives a mix of smoky and juicy impressions, and roasted carrots and crisp fresh asparagus alongside are the perfect pairing. Among mini desserts, the chocolate–peanut butter mousse, Key lime pie, and red velvet cake are best.

Steve Fields' Steak & Lobster Lounge, 5013 W. Park Blvd., Plano 75093; (972) 596-7100; stevefieldsrestaurant.com; Steak House and Seafood; $$$$. You know this isn't the same old steak deal when the bread that comes out early on is a great rosemary variety with an olive oil–jalapeño treatment for dipping. Little touches like this set Steve Fields apart from competitors, and that's why this place has had lasting power in a very competitive area. Appetizers we like most include seared Hawaiian tuna over mixed greens with a ginger sauce and the lobster-crab dip on crostini. The blue crab–corn chowder is a nice second course, and we're big on the filet mignon crusted with wild mushrooms or peppercorns, with a side of smoky cheddar mac and cheese and steamed broccoli. Another lovely main is the signature bone-in pork chop with a cranberry demi-glace. You don't have to reserve this place just for special occasions, either. There's happy hour on weekdays when you can sip wine or cocktails in the lounge and enjoy piano music and nightly specials that include a Maine lobster and baked potato for $23 and, on Sunday, prime rib and baked potato, also for $23.

Suze, 4345 W. Northwest Hwy., Dallas 75220; (214) 350-6135; suzedallas.com; American; $$$. Preston Hollow's long-standing place for upscale cuisine sits in a most unassuming spot, next to an Albertsons. Don't let the shopping center location fool you—this is a destination for very good food. Owner-chef Gilbert Garza keeps the menu interesting with frequent changes, and he's always looking for something new and seasonal to add. Among items we've come to love, the Kobe beef carpaccio, pheasant roll with king trumpet mushrooms, and fried green tomatoes with shaved Manchego cheese are choice starters. For the main course, ravioli filled with portobello mushrooms, beef tenderloin seared in a cast-iron pan, and almond-crusted rainbow trout typify the goods that keep us coming back. For a sweet ending, we're partial to the sticky toffee pudding and the selection of gelato.

III Forks, 17776 Dallas Pkwy., Dallas 75287; (972) 267-1776; iiiforks.com; Steak House; $$$$. Rather than the quiet, dark, and clubby steak-house experience, this is much more of a cavernous-restaurant sort of steak dinner place. Begun by the same beef experts that delivered **Bob's Steak & Chop House** (p. 78) and, later, **Del Frisco's Double Eagle Steak House** (p. 178), this place does huge business with the corporate crowd, here at the original and at other locations from Austin to Chicago to Palm Beach. Meaning, you're likely to see large groups dining here. Menu favorites range from French onion soup, huge and golden onion rings, bacon-wrapped scallops, grilled Atlantic salmon and Chilean sea bass, double-cut pork chop, chicken-fried prime rib steak, prime New York strip, prime flat iron steak, and tenderloin medallions Oscar. What appeals to the diner searching for great value: All entrees come with sides, which typically consist of whipped potatoes, sugar snap peas, corn that's cut from the cob and served in a cream base, and ripe tomato slices with spring onions.

Tipico's, 3118 W. Northwest Hwy., Dallas 75220; (214) 357-9296; Mexican; $–$$. Hooray! Both corn and flour tortillas are made on-site at this humble but colorful cafe. Order some of each to go with warm rust-colored salsa, an order of bacon-tinged refried beans, and a bountiful bowl of *caldo de res,* a beef stew combining big pieces of meat with cabbage, carrots, red potato, corn on the cob, and a side of rice with lime wedges. Other homey specialties from deep inside Mexico include simple tacos filled with spicy beef picadillo, tender calf's tongue and diced cactus with bits of tomato and onion. Disregard the fast-food look you get from the outside of the building, by the way: Inside, there's full service at both tables with mismatched chairs and at plastic booths. Though most patrons speak Spanish, and the TV is tuned to *telenovelas,* the staff is mostly bilingual.

TJ's Seafood Market, 11661 Preston Rd., #149, Dallas 75230; (214) 691-2369; tjsseafood.com; Seafood; $$. This is high-end dining quality at a super-casual setting—what's not to love about that? The Maryland jumbo lump crab cake with a field green salad is sensational, as is the miso-honey-seared tuna, Connecticut-style lobster roll, and sea bass topped with tomato confit tapenade. Best of all,

it's a fabulous market for fresh fish, selling things you cannot find elsewhere, including trigger fish, ivory salmon, and much more—along with sauces and marinades. Second location: 4212 Oak Lawn, Dallas 75219.

II Brothers Grill & Bar, 5858 Main St., #190, Frisco 75034; (214) 387-0807; iibrothers.com; American; $–$$. Yes, this is really a sports bar for everyone, even women and kids. That's because a family designed this place, owned by a pair of brothers whose folks were in the burger business for ages in North Texas and southern Oklahoma. While there's plenty of sports memorabilia strewn about the decor, the setting is clean, bright, and wholesome as can be. It's also possibly the most popular place in Frisco for breakfast—yep, breakfast. That's because culinary consultant and longtime server Heather Finney (whom the owners sent to culinary school) has dreamed up some inspired dishes, such as eggs Benedict with a roasted poblano hollandaise, and a Monster Burrito stuffed with eggs, sausage, hash browns, potatoes, tomatoes, and cheese. At lunch or dinner, you can have a prime beef filet with a wedge salad, or go lighter with a sensational seared ahi tuna salad. Whatever games are on, you'll see them on a dozen flat-screen TVs, and you're wise to watch while sipping a craft beer and munching on hand-battered fried cheese, with house-made ranch.

Via Reál, 4020 N. MacArthur Blvd., Irving 75038; (972) 650-9001; viareal.com; Mexican; $$. Situated right next to the Four Seasons in Las Colinas, this long-standing favorite in a shopping center has aged handsomely since opening in 1985. Appetizers that please include crab cakes with mango salsa, a spinach-tortilla salad, and black bean soup, topped with chipotle sour cream. Southwestern flavors sing in dishes like the beef tenderloin in a guajillo chile–Port sauce, topped with fried onions; jumbo shrimp sautéed in an orange-mojo sauce; and dry-aged pork loin teased with a chipotle–wild berry sauce. Tex-Mex offering include tacos, enchiladas, and tamales, too. At Sunday brunch, you can help yourself to waffles, french toast, Southwestern eggs Benedict, breakfast burritos, and a carving station. The bar offers a solid tequila selection, as well as an impressive menu of margaritas.

Whiskey Cake Kitchen, 3601 Dallas Pkwy., Plano 75093; (972) 993-2253; whiskey-cake.com; American; $$. With the subtitle "Kitchen and Bar," you know this joint will show you a good time. The chef and owners subscribe to the importance of serving from-scratch-only dishes and support local farmers in the process. There's no microwave oven on-site. Slow-cooking methods mean the foods come to your table from a grill, smoker, or spit. And what approachable food it is: Snacks, at the top of the menu, include fried green tomatoes, deviled eggs, chicken meatballs, lobster rolls, and mesquite-grilled mussels. Among casual entrees, you have a choice between fried portobello stacked with herbed cheese, avocado spread, and greens; hot corned beef melt; tuna burger; and barbecue bahn mi. Mains include mesquite-smoked duck breast, open pit–grilled pork tenderloin, and a spit-roasted chicken with sweet potato-fennel hash. To drink, there are wines organized by price, which is kind of brilliant: Choose bottles grouped in $25, $35, $45, and $60 categories. From the list of beers, check out all the craft offerings from near and far. There are plenty of hard-liquor options, too. You can even opt for a flight of rye whiskey, bourbon, or scotch selections.

Wicked Po'Boys, 1811 N. Greenville Ave., Richardson 75081; (972) 238-1313; wickedpoboys.com; Cajun; $–$$. With a tagline like "Crazy good food from good crazy people," you know this has to be pretty special. A young couple with New Orleans roots brought their favorite casual edibles from the Crescent City to North Texas, and they're serving most of it on a crusty French roll. But first, you must start with the Ridiculously Charred Oysters, a half- or full-dozen oysters laced with a little olive oil and Parmesan, then charbroiled and served with French bread. Cajun crab bisque, with a little corn in the mix, satisfies, too. A crispy soft-shell crab po'boy, with a lettuce-tomato-mayo dressing on the sandwich, cures a jones, especially with house-made, spicy potato chips—"wicked chips"—on the side. The Extra Wicked Po'Boy is the one piled with crawfish étouffée and fried crawfish, a mountainous sandwich that one person cannot possibly finish. If you're not into seafood dishes, there are burgers and po'boys with everything from ham and cheese to tofu, as well as roast beef and gravy. For dessert, the trio of hot beignets with

Nutella and confectioners' sugar should be illegal. The bar serves up exceptional New Orleans–style Bloody Marys and a Pimm's Cup. Live jazz sometimes breaks out here in a very small space that can get crowded quickly; patio tables are an excellent option. Second location: 6030 Luther Ln., Ste. 130, Dallas 75225.

Landmarks

Celebration, 4503 W. Lovers Ln., Dallas 75209; (214) 351-5681; celebrationrestaurant.com; American/Southern; $$. Open for more than 40 years, Celebration introduced stylish comfort food in simple, unfussy fashion long before we knew we were seeking comfort. It's the kind of food many of us grew up on, but it's not offered in the coffee-shop fashion that's common at other restaurants. This version is sort of like a farmhouse with a bar attached, because you can get a pint of Fat Tire or Newcastle Ale or a glass of Pinot Noir or Chardonnay with your big plate of meat loaf or shrimp with grits and bacon. The everyday menu includes grilled Cajun catfish, fried catfish, broiled rainbow trout, pot roast, meat loaf, chicken-fried chicken, spaghetti, and vegetable plates; on most of those, you can have as many second helpings as you'd like. Nightly specials are added and may include something like roasted chicken stuffed with apples, cranberries, and walnuts. Desserts are always an event, too: Popular picks include chocolate cream pie, coconut cream pie, banana pudding, chocolate layer cake, brownie sundae, and fruit cobbler. There's a kids' menu, as well.

Chamberlain's Steak & Chop House, 5330 Belt Line Rd., Addison 75334; (972) 934-2467; chamberlainssteakhouse.com; Steak House; $$$$. Richard Chamberlain crafted a niche for himself in the 1980s by opening the best steak house in the northern reaches of the Dallas area, and the grateful folks of Addison and points nearby have kept his series of dining rooms plenty busy. He does a wonderful job of offering something a little different than his competitors, such as fresh pea soup with applewood-smoked pork; pot stickers filled with Kobe beef; lump crab cake served with Southern pecan slaw; almond-crusted goat cheese over spinach salad; 40-day dry-aged prime rib eye; and Texas farmstead blue cheese butter. A remarkable wine list and a cigar lounge are available—and very popular.

Del Frisco's Double Eagle Steak House, 5251 Spring Valley Rd., Dallas 75254; (972) 490-9000; delfriscos.com; Steak House; $$$$. Though you will find Del Frisco's now in cities from Houston to New York, Chicago, and Charlotte, it all began right here. And though it's large—there are 8 dining rooms—this steak house manages a feeling of intimacy with fireplaces and very skilled service. We make a habit of dining here, enjoying shrimp remoulade, fried

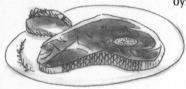

oysters, marinated shrimp, and big bangle onion rings for appetizers. The salad of sliced beefsteak tomatoes and onions sings with freshness, and the smoked chicken–andouille sausage soup gives a good taste of New Orleans. Among steaks, we love the New York strip, finished with sizzling butter, and the filet mignon with blue-cheese-mashed potatoes. For dessert, don't miss the multilayered creamy lemon Doberge cake. Second location: 812 Main St., Fort Worth 76102.

Dunston's Steak House & Bar, 5423 W. Lovers Ln., Dallas 75209; (214) 352-8320; dunstonssteakhouse.com; Steak House; $$. Campy and unadulterated since opening in the 1950s, this steak joint is nothing if not a trip back in time. Regulars take their Dunston's ritual very seriously and would rather give up Christmas than give up their weekly trip to eat at this throwback. First of all, there's the very old-school salad bar. Then there are the appetizers, such as shrimp cocktail, fried mushrooms, calf fries (from the most delicate part of the baby bull), potato skins, and baby back ribs. Steak choices include a prime tenderloin, strip, T-bone, and chicken-fried steak. Not into steak? Try fried oysters or even enchiladas. The bar makes a strong cocktail, so drink with care. Other location: 8526 Harry Hines Blvd., Dallas 75235.

The Mercury, 11909 Preston Rd., Dallas 75230; (972) 960-7774; themercurydallas.com; American; $$$$. Preston Hollow's favorite address for fine dining, The Mercury brings to the plate the inventive cuisine of chef Chris Ward. The setting is sleek and contemporary but not so chic as to be off-putting. The point here, however, is the food, starting with salmon croquettes with bacon salad, truffle sausage with warm potato salad, Texas tomato-heirloom apple salad with Marcona almonds, grilled quail with green bean–pear salad, rabbit confit with potato cakes, pan-seared Idaho trout with chilled strawberry soup, and braised oxtail with short ribs and topped by a poached egg. Wine pairing suggestions here are spot-on, as are the seasonal menus that capture the best of area producers. Note that regular patrons here are President George W. Bush and wife, Laura, among many well-heeled Dallasites.

Pappas Bros. Steakhouse, 10477 Lombardy Ln., Dallas 75220; (214) 366-2000; pappasbros.com; Steak House; $$$$. Frequently noted by area critics as serving the best steak in Texas (the other location is in Houston), this steak house works very hard to continue earning such accolades. Of the several dining spaces under one roof, we most prefer the stone-and-wood area that once housed the cigar lounge. Ask for a table by the fireplace, the best for settling into a cup of lobster bisque, followed by seared foie gras, shrimp remoulade, or bacon-wrapped scallops, then a salad of mixed greens, sliced apples, and oranges with blue cheese. For the main course, the prime bone-in rib eye is divine, but so is the prime bone-in strip. All you need on it is the dash of kosher salt, black pepper, and swipe of butter that bring the flavors to a zenith. Alongside, haricots verts and skillet potatoes are sublime. If you can handle dessert, have the New York cheesecake—the best this side of Carnegie Deli. An astounding wine cellar delivers a selection unduplicated in many places in Texas, or the world.

Specialty Stores, Markets & Producers

Celebration Farmer's Market, 4515 W. Lovers Ln., Dallas 75209; (214) 351-5681; celebrationrestaurant.com. Open daily, the market next door to the renowned restaurant (p. 177) offers a place to pick up great meals to go. You can order online, preferably 3 hours before you want to pick up. There's everything from entrees, boxed dinners, sides, salads, casseroles, desserts, party foods, holiday feasts, and more. Seasonal farmers' markets are held here, too, with vendors ranging from tea producers to gourmet gift makers to soap, jewelry, and baked goods vendors.

Double Dip Frozen Custard, 7511 Main St., Frisco 75034; (972) 377-8668; doubledipfrozencustard.com. Taking you back to the 1950s, this corner sugar shack in a renovated Dairy Queen will have you melting with nostalgia, regardless of the weather. Overhead garage doors are slung open to reveal the most popular ice cream stop in town, close to downtown Frisco, where creamy frozen custard awaits in a multitude of shapes and sizes. You're wise to do the usual and order a Caliche, a combination of vanilla or chocolate custard blended with any of 40 toppings that range from bite-size candy or fresh fruit to nuts or syrups. Hot fudge sundaes warm you up in cooler weather, but any temperature is perfect for Pie in the Sky, a layering of fudge brownie with hot fudge topping, marshmallow cream, and pecans. If you need a prelude to the sweets, check out the Super Dog, piled with green-chile relish and Texas chili, or the chicken salad sandwich on croissant.

Sigel's Fresh Market, **15003 Inwood Rd., Addison 75001; (972) 387-9873; www.sigels.com.** From the liquor store company comes a specialty foods store with 150 cheeses, olives in bulk, jams and jellies from everyone, artisan breads, elegant chocolates, specialty herbs, and selective deli meats.

Trader Joe's, **2400 Preston Rd., Plano 75093; (972) 312-9538; traderjoes.com.** North Texas shoppers now have a way to get their hands on fabulous ethnic frozen foods, inexpensive, quality cheeses and nuts, and an excellent supply of affordable wines at the first of this chain to arrive in the Dallas area. Flowers and greeting cards are a bargain here, too.

Whole Foods Market, **8190 Park Ln., Ste. 351, Dallas 75231; (214) 342-4850; wholefoodsmarket.com/stores/park-lane.** A 62,000-square-foot store with more natural and organic foods than you can imagine, this store is extra special for its enormous gluten-free foods area, a stunning bakery, an in-house smoked meats department, a huge wine department with a wine bar, and a sensational prepared foods selection with a vast selection of ethnic foods. The juice bar and raw foods area will impress. The cafe area, both inside and out, is sizable. Watch for exceptional special events.

Fort Worth

Woe to anyone who would still dismiss Fort Worth as anybody's little sister. Though it shares an airport and freeway linkage with Dallas, Fort Worth, the seat of Tarrant County, sparkles on its own—without the flashy this and plastic that. The jewels of this beloved, so-called Cowtown include world-class art museums, a vibrant downtown that's the envy of much larger cities, and a hearty spirit that continues to uphold the long-held Fort Worth motto: "Where the West begins and the East peters out."

The food scene has its distinctive characteristics, as well. Mexican food, steak houses, and burger joints have long been the staples in town, as you might expect in a city with a palpable depth of ranching in its heritage. But cuisine of higher styling has become more pronounced, with a strong increase of restaurants run by chefs whose focus is on locally sourced ingredients. The supply of restaurants featuring game seems more abundant today than ever, and the ethnic options continue to increase in number.

Restaurants loved by locals and attracting visitors are concentrated in several areas: downtown, both close to the convention center and a few blocks north, in Sundance Square; on the Near Southside, immediately south of downtown, in neighborhoods called Fairmount and around Fort Worth's cluster of hospitals; in West 7th and the Cultural District, adjacent areas immediately west of downtown; Camp Bowie, the area extending west of the Cultural District; and the North Side, to the north of downtown and home to the National Stockyards Historic District.

To honor the distinguished profile of Fort Worth's booming culinary community, the Fort Worth Food + Wine Festival highlights the city's diverse gastronomy culture by promoting what Fort Worth now calls its "Homegrown Culinary Revival." Food-and-drink-focused events are held throughout Fort Worth, with assorted happenings appealing to families and to adults celebrating a love of excellent, locally produced things to eat and drink.

Foodie Faves

Benito's, 1450 W. Magnolia Ave., Fort Worth 76104; (817) 332-8633; benitosmexican.com/; Mexican; $$. Long before Magnolia went into its massive boom stage—before you could say, "Over on Magnolia," and everyone knew what you meant—there was this colorful, friendly little Mexican joint with good food. It was kind of an insiders' thing, popular for weekend and very late-night breakfast. Benito's has endured the onslaught of fashionable new arrivals, and it keeps on trucking. Dishes from Mexico's interior include chiles rellenos stuffed with Oaxacan cheese, the Yucatcán-style tamale steamed inside a plantain leaf, and pork tips sautéed with *calabacitas,* or a stew of squash and tomato. Dishes with Tex-Mex leanings are offered, too, such as enchiladas in sour cream sauce and chalupas smothered in cheeses and beef. Breakfast is offered all the time, which is popular with the after-bar crowds that stream in on weekends. Strong margaritas and a selection of Mexican beers add to the appeal.

Bonnell's Fine Texas Cuisine, 4259 Bryant Irvin Rd., Fort Worth 76116; (817) 738-5489; bonnellstexas.com; American/Southwestern; $$$–$$$$. Owner-chef Jon Bonnell authored a pair of cookbooks, traveled to New York multiple times to do national morning TV shows and cook at the James Beard House, traveled to Napa on numerous trips to custom bottle his own label, volunteered at every chef-driven fund-raiser in town every year for the past decade, and still managed to keep running a fabulous restaurant. His energy and enthusiasm makes him beloved, and his stunning food, made with ingredients he sources from local providers, earns him respect from even the toughest foodies. Among specialties are his elk tacos, lamb chops, pecan-crusted Texas redfish, and green chile–cheddar grits. Service is usually smart and attentive, and there's a nice bar area for just sipping and nibbling. A good wine cellar is on-site, too. See Chef Jon Bonnell's recipe for **Crab Stuffed Jalapeños** on p. 234.

The Buffet Restaurant at the Kimbell Art Museum, 3333 Camp Bowie Blvd., Fort Worth 76107; (817) 332-8451; kimbellart.org; American; $–$$. Lunch is nothing short of lovely inside one of the most celebrated museums in the nation. This airy, light-filled space inside Louis Kahn's architectural masterpiece—with a stunning Renzo Piano expansion unveiled in late 2013—has become a favorite lunchtime meeting spot. On mild days, you can sit beneath the wisteria on a small patio, but you bask in sunshine almost anywhere you perch here. Manager-chef Shelby Schafer turns out a splendid selection of salads, soups (the chili is amazing, as is the gazpacho), quiche, sandwiches, and desserts each day; you pick up your choices in a self-service line, then find a table—if you're lucky enough to show up before or after the crowds. Typically a lunch-only spot, its occasional Friday evening dinners are special, too.

Buttons Restaurant, 4701 West Freeway, Fort Worth 76107; (817) 735-4900; buttonsrestaurant.com; Soul Food; $$$. Live music nightly keeps crowds happy, as does food from the smooth spirit of chef Keith Hicks. He redefined soul food with his restaurant, which carries his childhood nickname. Chicken and waffles gets deluxe treatment here, as does oxtail stew, shrimp with jalapeño grits, fried green tomatoes, and pork chops. Note that Sunday brunch is wildly popular; sometimes the wait for a table is 30 minutes or more. A martini menu is popular, too. Second location: 15207 Addison Rd., Addison 75001.

Café Modern, 3200 Darnell St., Fort Worth 76107; (817) 840-2167; themodern.org; American; $$. The world took notice when brilliant Japanese architect Tadao Ando created the magnificent building that's home to the Modern Art Museum of Fort Worth, notable for housing works by Francis Bacon, Dennis Blagg, Andy Warhol, Jackson Pollock, and Robert Rauschenberg. One of the important facets of the design holds the restaurant, whose space reaches out into a reflecting pool with smooth lines and cool slate tones invoking a serene feel. Chef Dena Peterson's food matches the setting, winning praise from national critics. Vegetarians will like plentiful offerings, including tomato-basil soup with pine nut–crusted mozzarella and eggplant napoleon, while carnivores can't resist the King Ranch chicken, Asian barbecued beef with udon noodles, a gourmet burger, and the signature Moroccan chicken salad. A small bar is on-site, too.

Carshon's Delicatessen, 3133 Cleburne Rd., Fort Worth 76110; (817) 923-1907; carshonsdeli.com; Delicatessen; $$. Here's the only true deli in town. While it's not true kosher, it's as close to the real deal as you'll find in this part of the world, and it's enormously popular—particularly at high noon. Not far from Texas Christian University, this south-side, no-frills spot has a following addicted to the Rachel, concoction of corned beef and turkey with melted swiss, coleslaw, and Russian dressing, grilled on buttery rye. Other faves include french toast stuffed with bananas, as well as the split-pea soup, chicken noodle soup, and chopped liver on rye. Don't even think of skipping the chocolate or butterscotch pie. Insiders' tip: If you're having a party, order a baked brie from Carshon's. Your guests will go crazy.

Cat City Grill, 1208 W. Magnolia Ave., Fort Worth 76110; (817) 916-5333; catcitygrill.com; American; $$. Patio seating tends to be the most popular at this restaurant. Flatbreads are fine for sharing; get yours topped with chicken, goat cheese, roasted red pepper, and pecans. Layered spinach salad comes with mandarin oranges, dried cherries, pecans, mushrooms, bacon, and blue cheese crumbles with crispy wontons. Stuffed rainbow trout and peppercorn steak are among good entrees. The Sunday brunch brings in good business, and it's a good value, too. The bar business here does pretty well, thanks to fruity martinis and a good bar menu, filled with a burger, fish-and-chips, cheese fries, and fish tacos.

Cattlemen's Steak House, 2458 N. Main St., Fort Worth 76106; (817) 624-3945; cattlemenssteakhouse.com; Steak House; $$–$$$. While fancy steak houses abound, this 1947 mainstay makes no apologies for being a true throwback. Anchoring one end of the Fort Worth Stockyards National Historic District, Cattlemen's has welcomed as many dyed-in-the-wool cowboys and international tourists as the weekly rodeo that takes place a few doors away in Cowtown Coliseum. The saloon and dining rooms whisk you back to an era long, long past, as witnessed by the grainy photos of championship cattle from decades of stock show competition. Order the signature Heart O' Texas Rib Eye, a nicely marbled slab, and watch the grizzled grill man fire that baby over the open fire that serves as the focal point in the main dining room.

Daddy Jack's, 353 Throckmorton St., Fort Worth 76102; (817) 332-2477; daddyjacks.org; Seafood; $$–$$$. Opened by a New Englander whose family originally came from Nova Scotia, this is a great place to go if you're hankering for fish plates like those found on the East Coast. A Sundance Square cornerstone, Daddy Jack's offers the frequent lobster special, but it's a good bet all the time for stuffed flounder, excellent crab cakes, lobster bisque, mussels marinara, steak and shrimp scampi, and pasta fra diavolo. Warm crusty bread comes with your meal, and you'll be hooked. Other locations: Dallas and Southlake.

Dutch's Hamburgers, 3009 S. University Dr., Fort Worth 76109; (817) 927-5522; dutchshamburgers.com; Burgers; $–$$. This busy hangout across the street from TCU became such a smash hit that the owners had to build a rooftop deck just to handle all the customers. Though a favorite with the college crowd, it's also a family-friendly burger spot that consistently scores high on various "best burger" contests. All-natural beef goes into the monster patties, served atop sensational bakery buns and topped with anything from blue cheese with bacon to chili and cheese. The grilled chicken sandwich covered in freshly roasted green chiles is downright wonderful, too, as is the Greek salad. Cold beer specials happen during happy hour.

El Asadero Mexican Steak House & Seafood, 1535 N. Main St., Fort Worth 76106; (817) 626-3399; elasadero.com; Mexican; $$. Some of the city's chefs will tell you this is their favorite hole-in-the-wall. They don't come for ambience, because there's very little of that at this North Side dive. It's the food, to be sure. Green (tomatillo and chile) chicken enchiladas, enchiladas blanketed in deep, dark mole, and shrimp in butter-garlic sauce are proof. Be advised: This restaurant makes some of the hottest salsa in creation that will burn an everlasting memory in your mind. Wash that down with cold Carte Blanca and Dos Equis beers, but skip the margaritas—they're better elsewhere.

Ellerbe Fine Foods, 1501 W. Magnolia Ave., Fort Worth 76104; (817) 926-3663; ellerbefinefoods.com; American/Southern; $$$. The renovation of a 1920s gas station resulted in one of the city's favorite restaurants, and service and food are stellar. You feel as though you're at a bistro in New Orleans's Garden District. The menu changes almost daily, depending on what fresh finds chef Molly McCook discovers at the market and from her fish purveyor. Favorites have included bacon-wrapped trout stuffed with lemon and onion; creamy cauliflower soup with brie; sublime lamb chops; and hanger steak with crispy fries. Patio seating can be lovely when the weather's right. All wines sold on the wine list are offered at retail prices for taking home. See Chef Molly McCook's recipe for **Sautéed Louisiana Gulf Shrimp & Kale** on p. 239.

Esperanza's Bakery & Café, 2122 N. Main St., Fort Worth 76106; (817) 616-5770; joets.com; Mexican/Bakery; $–$$. The lunch and dinner crowd keep tables filled with people hungry for enchiladas, *cabrito,* chiles rellenos, and other purely Mexican comfort dishes. The soups are soul warming, as is *guisado de res,* tender stewed beef tips in a robust chile verde sauce with rice and beans, or for pure comfort, the *caldo de res,* a bowl of soup including big beef chunks with a pile of fresh vegetables, such as cabbage, potato, carrots, and corn. Breakfasts are enormously popular here, too. Try huevos rancheros, migas con chorizo, huevos Mexicana, and big, pretty pancakes. Second location: 1601 Park Place Ave., Fort Worth 76110.

Fred's Texas Cafe, 915 Currie St., Fort Worth 76107; (817) 332-0083; fredstexascafe.com; Burgers; $$. Grown from a little bacon-and-egg cafe, this hangout in the shadows of the Cultural District now sits surrounded by the overwhelming retail-restaurant-residential development known as West 7th. A dive joint of the first order, Fred's rose to national fame with an appearance on Food Network's *Diners, Drive-Ins and Dives* in 2009. The popular choice is the Diablo burger, incorporating chipotle chiles and topped with spicy mustard. Fred's french fries are among the best on the planet, while the portobello tacos have won fans among vegetarians, too. A big beer schooner filled with a Mexican shrimp cocktail is the choice among diners not wanting all those calories. Brunch is a happening time, when a good pick is the grilled quail and eggs. Patio dining is a blast in nice weather, especially when live music is on tap.

Fuzzy's Taco Shop, 2917 W. Berry St, Fort Worth 76109; (817) 924-7943; fuzzystacoshop.com; Mexican; $–$$. Initially begun as a little taco joint near the TCU campus, this is the little fast-casual spot that could. Today there are dozens of locations all over Texas, and Fuzzy's is spreading to surrounding states, too. The formula is simple— make good tacos with fresh ingredients at a cheap price. Our favorites have been, and will likely always be, the grilled shrimp tacos, along with the pulled pork and the beef brisket. But we're high on the salads, too, served in a giant bowl and filled with the same goodies that come on the tacos, but with lots of lettuce and any number of fresh dressings. Breakfast is big at Fuzzy's, as is the cold beer.

Grace, 777 Main St., Fort Worth 76102; (817) 877-3388; gracefortworth.com; American; $$$$. One of downtown Fort Worth's favorite dress-up places, this elegant destination effects a midcentury look that borrows sensibilities from the Four Seasons in New York. We especially enjoy the cocktail lounge—with its big windows and sleek walnut-and-granite interior—for the Women & Wine Wednesday promotions, when there are three pours for $10, plus a nice little menu of fabulous nibbles. In pretty weather, it's fun to sit outside on the patio. Good for sharing, the artisan cheese platter presents a trio of cured meats (think duck prosciutto and Berkshire pork) with a trio of American cheeses (usually something creamy, something hard, and another in-between); and the addictive little croquettes of creamy, roasted eggplant and Parmesan inside a warm, crunchy crust with a blue cheese dressing for dipping. The dining room does multicourse menus at prix fixe Monday through Thursday. Watch for lovely wine dinners, too. See Chef Blaine Staniford's recipe for **Chorizo Stuffed Dates** on p. 233.

Hacienda San Miguel, 2948 Crockett St., Fort Worth 76107; (817) 386-9923; hsmw7.com; Mexican; $$. Hugo Galvan, a native of San Miguel de Allende in the heart of Mexico, is the owner-chef of this lovely retreat in the midst of bustling West 7th. The beautiful interior brings contemporary Mexican art to the fore, and that beauty extends to the plates served. This is not Tex-Mex, be warned. Instead, you'll find fish dishes done in delicate chile treatments, pork spare ribs in exotic sauces, and the like. Brunch brings a menu with myriad egg and other specialties. The bar produces a distinctive menu of margaritas, as well. In good weather, be sure to snag a patio table.

Inzo Italian Kitchen, 2747 S. Hulen, Fort Worth 76109; (817) 924-2749; brixpizzeria.com; Italian; $$. Formerly called Brix, the name change signifies an expanded menu. For starters, there are flatbreads and wonderful Tuscan bruschetta, as well as house fries covered in creamy Gorgonzola and Tabasco sauce. Crispy calamari, Caprese salad, and a focaccia loaf stuffed with salad are more good starters. Just be sure to leave room for divine pizza from the wood-burning oven. Toppings include everything from Italian sausage and ricotta cheese to mushrooms, spinach, and jalapeños. For bigger plates, check out pork chop Marsala or Tuscan chicken paillard. Patio seating is nice in good weather. Additional location in Roanoke.

J&J Oyster Bar, 612 N. University Dr., Fort Worth 76107; (817) 335-2756; jandjoysterbar.com/; Seafood; $$. Yep, that's a remodeled Taco Bell—and it's one of the most consistently busy places in town.

That's because J&J's is the place for iced trays of Gulf oysters, platters of steaming crawfish, piles of fresh, you-peel-'em shrimp, baskets of fried clam strips, jalapeño hush puppies, and frosty mugs of beer—what more could you want? Cheap, super-casual seafood dining at its best comes with quick, friendly service and a great patio. The place gets packed at peak hours, so try to plan your visit for late lunch or early dinner.

Jazz Cafe, 2504 Montgomery St., Fort Worth 76107; (817) 737-0043; **Greek, $$.** Talk about an insiders' place—you almost have to know where this place is, because the sign on the front is so hard to see. A funky little dive in the Cultural District, the Jazz is a small, white stucco building where regulars know to expect anything. Sometimes the service is fast; sometimes it takes forever for your food to show up. But it's always worth the wait, especially if you order the black bean soup, the burger, pastrami sandwich, or the best Greek salad in town. On Saturday and Sunday, the breakfast dishes of choice are the SOB eggs (scrambled with tortillas, with black beans on the side) and the feta omelet with biscuits. Live jazz music plays on Sunday morning. It's BYOB, so feel free to bring Champagne to make mimosas. Patio seating can be lovely if the weather cooperates.

Lanny's Alta Cocina Mexicana, 3405 W. 7th St., Fort Worth 76107; (817) 850-9996; lannyskitchen.com; **Mexican; $$$–$$$$.** What a gem this is in the Cultural District, and what an exquisite place to dine on the patio when the weather's good. Lanny Lancarte II, the great-grandson of Joe T. Garcia, whose legendary restaurant is near the Stockyards, has made a name for himself with elevated Mexican cuisine. The style and sensibility will remind you nothing of Tex-Mex but will transport you to the swankiest of all Mexico City restaurants.

Among beautiful efforts are hamachi ceviche, butternut squash soup, lobster ravioli, *carne asada* in Cabernet reduction, and the most elegant desserts the mind can conceive. An inspired wine list is offered, too, and cocktails utilizing fresh juices are delightful. Ask about refreshing mocktails, as well. See Chef Lanny Lancarte's recipe for **Churros Served with Cajeta** on p. 236.

Lee's Grilled Cheese, 5040 N. Tarrant Pkwy., Fort Worth 76244; (817) 479-3220; leesgrilledcheese.com; American; $. What began as a food truck has morphed into a brick-and-mortar establishment serving excellent bread and cheese. From the classics, choose the Duke, a sandwich with baby swiss, caramelized onions, seasoned roast beef, and Dijon mustard; the Italian, with provolone, fire-roasted garlic tomatoes, salami, ham, and an Italian sauce; and the BFF, with smoked bacon, fontina cheese, and fig preserves. But oh, the Cuban Pete seduces with its swiss cheese, Black Forest ham, pulled pork, yellow mustard, and pickles. And there's the Back Breaker, a creation of macaroni and cheese, sharp cheddar, and barbecued pork—a salty and sweet back-breaking combo. All come on locally baked sourdough—yum. Fries are hand-cut, too.

Lili's Bistro on Magnolia, 1310 W. Magnolia Ave., Fort Worth 76104; (817) 877-0700; lilisbistro.com; American; $$–$$$. About a split-second before the Magnolia boom, restaurateur Vance Martin nabbed this very cool historic grocery building for a small restaurant. In 2011, he took over his next-door neighbor's space, expanding his restaurant to include a fabulous little wine bar, where live music is offered, too. The menu has something for everyone, from burgers to Asian crab cakes, beef tenderloin medallions, stuffed chicken, and sensational tabbouleh. If you don't have a reservation, plan to eat at the bar—that's as much fun as anything.

Little Red Wasp, 808 Main St., Fort Worth 76102; (817) 877-3111; littleredwasp.com; American; $$–$$$. From the owners of Grace, a block north, this casual sibling gets a chic but low-key vibe in decor from the clever use of subway tiles, barn lights, exposed industrial brick, bright red chairs, and comfy booths. A long shotgun space features an open kitchen at the far end and a bar along one wall, the latter keeping busy with guests lapping up craft beer and smart wine list offerings. Grace chef Blaine Staniford doubles his duty by turning out LRW dishes, the best of which include a burly short rib plate, knife-and-fork-required burger, lovely tomato soup, and satisfying entree salads.

Lonesome Dove Western Bistro, 2406 N. Main St., Fort Worth 76106; (817) 740-8810; lonesomedovebistro.com; American/Southwestern; $$$$. The Fort Worth Stockyards National Historic District has one fine-dining restaurant, thanks to celebrity chef Tim Love. In a neighborhood loaded with downscale steak houses, barbecue and burgers, Mexican food, and watering holes, Lonesome Dove stands out with its style and sophistication. From a great buffalo burger at lunch to a grilled quail quesadilla with goat cheese and black bean puree, barbecued duck spring rolls, braised lamb shank with sautéed spinach, and red corn-crusted halibut with cilantro-orange butter, this retreat does everything well. Cool your heels at the bar with a jalapeño margarita.

If you've not made a reservation, go around the corner to Love's White Elephant Saloon and **Love Shack** (see below), the latter a burger joint. See Chef Tim Love's recipe for **Roasted Garlic Stuffed Beef Tenderloin with Western Plaid Hash & Syrah Demi-Glace** on p. 240.

Love Shack, 110 E. Exchange, Fort Worth 76106; (817) 740-8812; loveburgershack.com; Burgers; $. Celebrity chef Tim Love's claim to burger fame is his Dirty Love Burger, a custom grind of prime

RANCH CUISINE

Before fancy cowboy restaurants came along, there was Michaels. Perhaps we could even call Michael Thomson, owner-chef of the 7th Street landmark, a visionary: In opening his dining-and-drinking mainstay about 20 years ago, he gave Fort Worth's palate a taste of contemporary ranch cuisine.

While dozens of other promising restaurants have come and gone, Michael has stuck with what he knows works. You still find on his list of classic dishes the jalapeño shrimp, pecan-crusted goat-cheese chicken, pepper-crusted beef with ancho bourbon sauce, and crab cakes with a chile cream sauce.

Thomson says that although he's stayed true to his original theme, he's become "willing, in the past four or five years, to try new things." A surprise success has been his seared sesame-crusted tuna with wasabi and ponzu accents, things he admits "you wouldn't expect to find among contemporary ranch cuisine."

Subtle interior updates have added richness to the arrangement of stone and artwork, and the Ancho Chile Bar, with its cozy banquette and corner fireplace, remains a favorite for martini gatherings. In the bar and its adjacent patio, couples and small groups gather to enjoy drinks and noshes in the abundant mild weather throughout much of the year.

Michaels Restaurant & Ancho Chile Bar, *3413 W. 7th St., Fort Worth 76107; (817) 877-3413; michaelscuisine.com; American/Southwestern; $$.*

steak and brisket that he tops with cheeses and a fried quail egg. It's a magnificent, delicious mess, perfect with a side of crinkle-cut fries and a butterscotch milk shake. Live music is enjoyed daily. See Chef Tim Love's recipe for **Roasted Garlic Stuffed Beef Tenderloin with Western Plaid Hash & Syrah Demi-Glace** on p. 240.

Lucile's Stateside Bistro, 4700 Camp Bowie Blvd., Fort Worth 76107; (817) 738-4761; lucilesstatesidebistro.com; American; $$. The regulars at this place on Camp Bowie's historic bricks know their menu so well they don't even have to look at it. Favorites include the Greek salad with grilled shrimp, pizza from the wood-burning oven, fresh lobster, grilled mahimahi, or steak Oscar with crab and béarnaise sauce. At breakfast on Saturday and Sunday, the omelets never disappoint, nor does the dutch baby, a fluffy German pancake with a lemon sauce. The bar's a popular gathering place for martinis and wine.

Nonna Tata, 1400 W. Magnolia Ave., Fort Worth 76104; (817) 332-0250; Italian; $$. The most crowded restaurant in town stays that way because there are only six tables to begin with. But this teensy bistro in historic Fairmount doubled its space last year by adding a few tables outside on a new patio. People love the food from owner-chef Donatella Trotti so much that they'll sit at those outdoor tables even in colder or hotter weather. She makes dishes from her grandmother's recipes, the foods she grew up on near Lake Como, in northern Italy. Handmade  pastas will delight, as do lighter dishes of arugula salad and sautéed chicken. This is a BYOB operation, so be sure to schlep a good bottle of wine along. No reservations are accepted, but you can leave your cell phone number and walk a few doors down to enjoy a cocktail at The Usual (p. 211) while you wait for your table. Note that Nonna Tata is only open Tues through Fri. Period.

Pacific Table, 1600 University Dr., Suite 601, Fort Worth 76107; (817) 887-9995; pacifictablefw.com; Seafood/Asian/American; $$–$$$. Owner-chef Felipe Armenta Jr. expands on the success he

enjoys at his Tavern over on Hulen Street (see p. 199). At this more contemporary space, with prolific use of cement and wood, he puts fish forward with sushi, sashimi, crudo, and grilled and roasted seafood selections. The seared scallops salad is a big hit, as is salmon in a miso treatment over soba noodles. Steak, pork, and fowl options please, as well. Healthful ideas, like brussels sprouts salad, ease the conscience enough to justify ordering coconut pie for dessert.

Piola Italian Restaurant and Garden, 3700 Mattison Ave., Fort Worth 76107; (817) 989-0007; fwpiola.com; Italian; $$. Unfolding within a charming old bungalow in the Monticello neighborhood close to the museums, this delightful bistro is a perfect place for a cocktail on the patio in good weather. Unwind there before dinner, nibbling first on a plate of goat cheese bruschetta and giant calamari or prosciutto-wrapped asparagus and an antipasti plate of meats, cheeses, and olives. For dinner, enjoy smoked chicken fettuccine, linguine primavera, rigatoni Bolognese, or shrimp-asparagus risotto. A good wine list is offered, too.

Piranha Killer Sushi, 335 W. 3rd St., Fort Worth 76102; (817) 348-0200; piranhakillersushi.com; Japanese; $$–$$$. Sundance Square's sushi place is as chic as it is enjoyable. Every kind of roll imaginable decorates this lively menu, but it's the salads that attract the most attention. Choice picks include the spicy tuna salad with avocado, tomato, and citrus chile; Caribbean tuna tartare; and sashimi salad with tuna, conch, white tuna, and veggies. Fancy martini choices, good wines, and a sake list fill a long bar menu, and the bar area is nice for catching up with friends. Other locations in Arlington.

Railhead Smokehouse BBQ, 2900 Montgomery St., Fort Worth 76107; (817) 738-9808; railheadsmokehouse.com; Barbecue;

$. You know this place has a regular following when you arrive at 2 p.m. on a Monday and the bar is completely full. That's because those giant schooners of beer are icy cold, and the attentive servers behind the bar never let them get empty. You can sit right there and enjoy lunch or dinner, or take a table—after you go through the serving line. The debate on what's better—pork ribs or beef brisket—is a lost cause so you're best advised to get a plate combining both. These hickory-smoked vittles, as well as the smoked turkey breast and chicken quarters, go beautifully with ice-crusted mugs of beer and servings of homemade potato salad and beans. There's a drive-through, too, that works well if you're just picking up a pound of brisket and a pound of ribs to take home.

Reata Restaurant, 310 Houston St., Fort Worth 76102; (817) 336-1009; reata.net; American/Southwestern; $$–$$$. Cowboy cuisine came to fame here at this Sundance Square mainstay, where grilled steak comes topped with cheese enchiladas and mahimahi gets a spicy lobster treatment. You can find lightness in a salad topped with goat cheese and candied pecans, but be assured that this is the destination for creatively sauced and generously plated goodies. Decorated in the style of the *Giant* movie ranch for which it's named, this place is a huge hit with business folks, Lone Star visitors, and locals out for a good time. Make sure to visit the rooftop patio for a cocktail, if not for your whole dinner. The view of downtown is fantastic. See Chef Juan Rodriguez's recipe for **Buffalo & Blue Cheese Meatballs with Sweet Molasses Glaze** on p. 235.

Saint-Emilion Restaurant, 3617 West 7th St., Fort Worth 76107; (817) 737-2781; saint-emilion restaurant.com; French; $$–$$$. This restaurant continues to live at the top of the local *Zagat Guide* ratings, and for good reason: It's a reliably good restaurant for quiet, elegant dining. Owner Bernard Tronche

brought French fare to town more than a quarter-century ago, and his patrons love him and it so much, they travel with him to France once a year to eat in his hometown. Upscale yet comfortable, Saint-Emilion is named for the owner's home and offers a fixed-price, multi-course meal of creatively wrought salads, fresh seafood, wild game, chops, fresh vegetables, and desserts. Look for bistro favorites like classic steak au poivre. The gracious staff can make wise recommendations from a wine list laden with thoughtfully chosen French finds.

Salata, 520 Commerce St., Fort Worth 76102; (817) 885-7720; mysalata.com; American; $. A Houston import, this fast-casual newcomer to downtown does a fine job of making the salad bar really appealing again. Restaurant chefs guide you in customizing your salad, which can be based on any of four types of greens, followed by nearly 50 topping choices from chicken breast to baked salmon, snow peas, cauliflower, carrot slices, juicy tomatoes, crunchy tendrils of bean and alfalfa sprouts, beet cubes, black or kidney beans, sesame sticks, almonds, pita chips and feta cheese. Wraps are an option, including things like chipotle chicken, marinated shrimp, or all veggies.

Sera Dining & Wine, 2418 Forest Park Blvd., Fort Worth 76110; (817) 927-7372; Spanish and American; $$-$$$. Owner John Marsh, a popular restaurant figure in town from having worked at the defunct Sapristi! and at Ellerbe Fine Foods, opened his own place in the old Sapristi space and brought on board Brandon Hudson from the staff at **Smoke** (p. 122) in Dallas. Together, they're offering tapas, such as tortilla Espanola, chorizo croquettes, littleneck clams, and roasted cauliflower and leeks; cheese boards and interesting salads, like white anchovy with heirloom tomato; and Spanish-influenced entrees, including smoked vegetables over rice, rabbit confit, and a daily fish option with mojo verde and seasonal vegetables. It's casual inside, but you'll be pampered.

Shinjuku Station, 711 W. Magnolia Ave., Fort Worth 76104; (817) 923-2695; shinjuku-station.com; Japanese; $$. The owners of terrific **Tokyo Japanese Cafe** (p. 200) over on Camp Bowie Boulevard opened a fashionable little Japanese cocktail lounge with exceptional food, and it's the nibbles that are creating a stir. Best plates to enjoy with drinks that have been infused with fresh fruit, herbs, and exotic spices include the tok fries, thick-cut potato spears dusted with spicy Japanese seasonings and served with chile mayo for dipping. There's also sushi, such as sesame-seared baby octopus, and a crazy little *okonomiyaki* (or omelet), a small skillet-sized creation that combines egg with salty-sweet pork belly, scallions, cabbage, and pickled ginger. At lunch, the mix-and-match Build Your Own Bento is fun. And delicious.

Spiral Diner, 1314 W. Magnolia Ave., Fort Worth 76104; (817) 332-8834; spiraldiner.com; Vegan; $$. Carving out a niche in an unlikely market, the owners at Spiral Diner took quite a gamble in opening a vegan restaurant in a city proudly nicknamed Cowtown. But Fort Worth's only vegan restaurant has won numerous national awards for an inventive, winning menu. Among goodies are meatless tacos, enchiladas, chili, sandwiches, and much more, all of which sworn carnivores enjoy. Breakfast is a big hit, too, and there's a great list of organic beers available. Second location: 1101 N. Beckley Ave., Dallas 75203.

The Tavern, 2755 S. Hulen St., Fort Worth 76109; (817) 923-6200; thetavernftworth.com; American; $$. Somehow, you don't expect this place to be as good as it is, and you're delighted to find that it's such an incredible find. It looks and feels like a wine bar, but the food from owner-chef Felipe Armenta is nothing short of fabulous. We visit frequently, often eating right at the bar, grazing first on grilled artichokes and bruschetta. Then, it's either the ahi tuna salad or the pan-seared scallops or the braised short ribs or the Mexico City enchiladas. Baja fish tacos are excellent, too. At brunch, served Saturday and Sunday, the *migas,* wild mushroom-spinach omelet, blue crab Florentine topped with poached eggs, and the bottomless mimosas make the weekend just perfect.

Tokyo Japanese Cafe, 5121 Pershing Ave., Fort Worth 76107; (817) 737-8568; tokyocafefw.com; Japanese; $$. What a popular neighborhood spot, brimming with youthful energy. Traditional Japanese decor—paper lanterns, bamboo screens—fills the two cozy rooms, where you can sip Ichiban, sake, or white wine while mulling over choices. Start with the salmon *crudo,* a long plate decorated with thin, velvety slices of salmon drizzled with cilantro and chile oils, scattered with cracked black pepper and topped with sprigs of micro herbs. A recent hit from the blackboard was the Stop Dropping Roll, combining smooth albacore, crunchy fresh jalapeño, creamy avocado, and spicy crab inside the sticky rice, with *tobikko,* or bright red flying fish roe, with a pleasing saltiness and a crunchy texture. Specialties we return for time and again include the yellowtail collar, chargrilled and addictive. Fried gyoza and pumpkin soup are among non-fish options.

Waters, 2901 W. Crockett St., Fort Worth 76107; (817) 984-1110; waterstexas.com; Seafood; $$$$. Owner-chef Jon Bonnell made a big splash in West 7th in early 2013 with his first seafood restaurant. A light-filled, contemporary interior finds intriguing decor elements, including columns crafted from oyster shells and a bar top featuring octopus artwork. The fish offerings change daily; our favorites have included mussels with coconut, lime leaf, ginger, and green chiles, and mesquite-grilled rockfish with asparagus and caramelized leeks. Ceviches and oysters abound, but patrons not wanting seafood can choose bone-in rib eye or portobello mushroom stuffed with herbed goat cheese, among several landlubber options.

Winslow's Wine Cafe, 4101 Camp Bowie Blvd., Fort Worth 76107; (817) 546-6843; winslowswinecafe.com; American; $$. Begun as a wine bar, one of the most popular restaurants on the West Side unfolds throughout a former 1930s gas station along the historic brick boulevard. It's where girlfriends meet to gab and graze over wine, couples reconnect over dinner, and families eat happily, thanks to a menu providing pizza (baked in the wood-burning oven on view), fillet Oscar, cedar-plank salmon, and pasta. The wine program's good, and there's now a full bar, too.

Woodshed Smokehouse, 3201 Riverfront Dr., Fort Worth 76107; (817) 877-4545; woodshedsmokehouse.com; American/ Barbecue; $$–$$$. This is not your granddaddy's barbecue joint. Owner-chef Tim Love of Iron Chef fame—also proprietor at **Lonesome Dove** (p. 193) and **Love Shack** (p. 193), both in Fort Worth—calls his riverside smokehouse eats the kind of grub he likes to serve at his own backyard parties. Popular for its open-air setting and nightly live music, Love's kitchen butchers all its meats on-site and cooks everything over live fires, fed by the Texas-grown woods stacked outside. Beef, lamb, goat, wild game birds, pork, and fish provide plentiful selections, but vegetarians are spoiled with dishes of cauliflower, kale, artichokes, and much more. Early-morning crowds like the breakfast taco service, too. See Chef Love's recipe for **Roasted Garlic Stuffed Beef Tenderloin with Western Plaid Hash & Syrah Demi-Glace** on p. 240.

The Fort Worth Foodie's Favorite Haunts

Feeling at home in a setting with good food and welcoming spirit can be the cure-all for a stressful day. Like the theme song from *Cheers* suggests, "Sometimes you want to go where everybody knows your name." Fortunately, that's the contentment I experience when patronizing favorite restaurants in my hometown.

That's the thing about Fort Worth, too: Whether you are visiting from out of town or are a local venturing out to a new restaurant, it always seems to feel like home. I am constantly in search of that place that does more than just put a delicious dish on the table, one that also shares its passion with its patrons.

Fort Worth is synonymous with family and even the restaurants are often related. I grew up going to **Esperanza's Bakery & Café** (p. 188) with my mom for Mexican sweet bread (or as I called it "turtle bread" for the shell-like sugar design). Now, my husband and I frequent the very same spot on Saturday morning for migas and burritos on the patio. The same day might include dinner at the famed **Joe T. Garcia's** (p. 204) also from the Lancarte family, where the margaritas flow and I swear it never rains in their resort-like gardens. Lanny Lancarte II's **Lanny's Alta Cocina Mexicana** (p. 191) takes you to Mexico City, which is a completely different experience than you'll find in the aforementioned Mexican places.

The Lancarte family is not the only clan making its mark on Cowtown. The Ho and Kha families are creating legacies all their

---

Yogi's Deli & Grill, 2710 S. Hulen St., Fort Worth 76109; (817) 921-4500; American; $–$$. Begun as a bagel shop with a grill in the back, this fast-casual restaurant has endured plentiful changes and massive construction issues nearby to succeed as one of the busiest eateries in the city. You'll find throngs here at breakfast, particularly on the weekend, for Yogi's phenomenal pancakes, omelets, and Benedicts.

own. **Tokyo Japanese Cafe** (p. 200), consistently packed with regulars, is our everything—it's our Tuesday night sushi take-out, weekday lunch meeting spot, and an anniversary Omakase dinner. Its sister restaurant **Shinjuku Station** (p. 199) quickly put itself on the culinary map with its Japanese *izakaya* menu full of deliciously small plates that change seasonally.

Even our newest family member, Winston the dog, gets in on the action. His Saturday often includes a stop at Cowtown Farmers Market for fresh-made dog treats for him and bread and vegetables for us. Pet-friendly patios like **Woodshed Smokehouse** (p. 201) boast a dog menu where our buddy Winston can dine on a rawhide bone covered in pit master fat. A meal there is not complete without a mouth-watering piece of chocolate meringue pie from **Black Rooster Bakery** (p. 207).

Chadra Mezza (1622 Park Place Ave., 817-924-2372) holds Pooches on the Patio Wednesdays where pups are the center of attention and owners enjoy Mediterranean fare. Chadra is also expanding its family to include a quick-service restaurant with healthy options for those on the go in the TCU area.

In Fort Worth, it's about finding the place that hits the spot, but leaves you wanting more. Luckily, that is not hard to come by in these parts.

Crystal Willars Vastine is publisher and editor of Fort Worth Foodie *magazine.*

At lunch, the sandwiches and salads are easily as good. Fried matzo with eggs, onion, and salami is as winning as the giant platters of huevos rancheros and the beef gorditas. If you walk in and find the line nearly out the door, don't worry—it moves quickly and you'll somehow find a place to sit.

Angelo's Bar-B-Que, 2533 White Settlement Rd., Fort Worth 76107; (817) 332-0357; angelosbbq.com; Barbecue; $. Sometimes there's a line nearly out the door, but fear not—it moves at a nice clip. You'll grab a tray and tell the counter staff what you want—and if you're smart, that's a plate of ribs with sides of brisket and sausage. Get some potato salad and beans, too, and be sure to order "a large"— that's a great big schooner of Budweiser, served icy cold. Or, you can have Texas's own Shiner Bock. It's all part of the ritual at this 50-year-old city favorite.

Joe T. Garcia's Mexican Restaurant, 2201 N. Commerce St., Fort Worth 76106; (817) 626-4356; joets.com; Mexican; $$. Easily one of the more famous restaurants in all of Texas, this restaurant has outlasted nearly all others in its 70-plus years of business. Begun as a little barbecue place in a family home, it's grown to cover a city block with an expansion of dining rooms and gardens that make you feel as though you're at home in someone's elegant hacienda somewhere deep in Mexico. In pretty weather, you absolutely want a poolside table for enjoying fajita salad, an enchilada plate, tortilla soup, and fabulous margaritas. Mariachis are often playing on the weekends, but every night feels like a fiesta. Lines can be long to get inside, but be patient— and enjoy a margarita while you wait.

Kincaid's, 4901 Camp Bowie Blvd., Fort Worth 76107; (817) 732-2881; kincaidshamburgers.com; Burgers; $. A Cowtown institution of the first order, this 70-year-old corner grocery on the venerable West Side has been publicized around the world for its astounding burgers. The half-pounders are hand-formed from freshly ground beef and served sizzling hot and drippy inside warm buns. Grab an order of pimento cheese–stuffed jalapeños and crinkle-cut fries, too, then eat the traditional way, standing up with elbows propped atop the wooden grocery shelves, or sitting at picnic tables in front. Other locations in Fort Worth, Southlake, and Arlington.

Paris Coffee Shop, 704 W. Magnolia Ave., Fort Worth 76104; (817) 335-2041; pariscoffeeshop.net; American; $. The reasons for dining here since the 1930s are numerous, not the least of which is the pie you want for dessert. Owner Mike Smith, whose Greek immigrant dad opened this coffee shop long ago, is the pie man, making about two dozen varieties daily. At Thanksgiving, he makes about 400 for customers. So go ahead and decide which you want, then order lunch—the chicken and dumplings, meat loaf chopped steak, baked chicken, and chicken-fried steak are all excellent. So is breakfast—get the Greek omelet and a side of grits and a side of biscuits.

Specialty Stores, Markets & Producers

Artisan Baking Co., 4900 White Settlement Rd., Fort Worth 76114; (817) 821-3124; artisan-baking-company.com. This bakery does so much special-order business that it's become a special-order-only business. But when you taste the goods made by hand here, which you can taste at the Cowtown Farmers Market on Saturday, you'll understand. Exquisite breads include the sourdough and the fruit-studded breakfast bread, pumpkin bread, all kinds of cookies and scones, granola, pies, and more. Watch for classes taught at the bakery, too, to give you mad baking skills to enjoy at home.

Avoca Coffee, 1311 W. Magnolia Ave., Fort Worth 76104; (682) 233-0957; avocacoffee.com. Fort Worth's first coffee lounge with an on-site roaster makes an exquisite, rich cup of coffee and a gorgeous

Fort Worth Dining,
a Legacy of Generations

In 1935 Joe T. Garcia and his wife established a food legacy not just for their family but for Fort Worth. Joe T. Garcia began serving barbecue out of a modest restaurant in Fort Worth's Northside that served only 16 patrons. His wife, Mama Sus, made all the Mexican dishes for the restaurant from scratch. Generations of Fort Worth diners remember fondly the experience of eating in the Garcias' front living room, serving themselves from the refrigerated beer case along one wall. At the end of dinner, one of the Garcia family members would count the beer bottles and charge diners the flat rate for supper, plus the beer.

Over the years, however, Joe T. Garcia's, or Joe T.'s as we locals call it, evolved into one of Fort Worth's most popular and visited restaurants by locals and visitors from around the world. Joe T.'s grandchildren began expanding the restaurant, gradually buying adjacent properties until the Joe T.'s spread came to cover well more than a city block. The restaurant now can seat over 1,000 folks, thanks to the addition of one of the most lush and expansive outdoor dining areas in North Texas. On busy springtime weekends, it's not unusual for the restaurant to serve 3,000 or more diners per day. And it's very common to see hungry patrons lined up around the block, for an hour or more. That's why it's a good thing that you can enjoy a margarita while you wait.

cappuccino. You need to be patient, however—this is definitely not Starbucks. Coffee is made very carefully, and the drip process for one cup takes at least 4 minutes. Beautiful, locally sourced teas are offered, too. The seating area is as hip as the coffee and the roasters. Snacks include locally made pastries and chocolates.

At lunch, a full menu laden with tortilla soup, fajita salad, chimichangas, Mexican plates, and more keeps diners sated. At night, the wait staff offers just the combination dinner, or Mexican plate (enchiladas, tacos, rice, beans, guacamole, and nachos), or chicken or beef fajitas. That's for simplicity's sake. You can actually order anything from the lunch menu in the evening, if you want. The restaurant and its traditionally great service have reached such renown that the James Beard Foundation bestowed in 1998 one of its American Classics Awards on Joe T.'s.

The heirs of Joe T. Garcia's, the Lancarte family, still run the restaurant, expanding to open **Esperanza's Bakery & Café** (p. 188). Esperanza's Bakery supplies Fort Worth with whatever Mexican sweet you desire, along with some of the best barbacoa in town. Think of a Mexican version of your favorite diner and you've got Esperanza's. They make homestyle Mexican food, and their breakfast shouldn't be missed.

The Garcia story doesn't end there. Lanny Lancarte II, great-grandson of Joe T. Garcia, traded salsa for sous vide when he attended the Culinary Institute of America in New York. Upon returning to Fort Worth, he began hosting private dinners at Joe T.'s, which led him to open his own restaurant, **Lanny's Alta Cocina Mexicana** (p. 191), in 2005. Chef Lancarte expertly combines native Mexican ingredients with French technique and Mediterranean influences, taking the rich culinary traditions of his great-grandparents and moving those forward with modernity and sophistication.

Josie Villa Singleton is the author of food blog, EatThisFortWorth.

Black Rooster Bakery, 2430 Forest Park Blvd., Fort Worth 76109; (817) 924-1600; blackroosterbakery.com. If you crave European-style bakery goods, this is your destination. The fresh French breads, the lovely pastries and scones and cookies and croissants, the friendly counter help—all will make this your regular habit. Stop in for breakfast goodies, which you can enjoy at a small counter or a sidewalk table, or for quiche or sandwiches at lunch. Special order options are abundant; just look at the tempting website. See the Black Rooster Bakery's recipe for **Cranberry Chess Pie** on p. 242.

BlueBonnet Bakery, 4705 Camp Bowie Blvd., Fort Worth 76107; (817) 731-4233; bluebonnetbakery.com. Open since 1934, this sweet operation now located inside a former church continues to please. There are gingerbread men and cupcakes to charm you, as well as a Texas fudge pecan cake that will abolish any thoughts of a diet. The pecan pies are fabulous, as are the artisan breads. Wedding cakes are done here, as are artful birthday cakes. At lunchtime, there's excellent chicken salad and assorted soups, as well as a good Reuben sandwich.

Brewed, 801 W. Magnolia Ave., Fort Worth 76104; (817) 945-1545; brewedfw.com. First and foremost, Brewed is a good place to enjoy coffee (locally roasted), tea (locally sourced), and lots of good things on tap. The latter includes local and regional beers, as well as *kombucha,* made locally by Holy Kombucha! You can sit and read and fiddle around on your computer, at whimsically arranged tables and counters inside or at a sunny patio outside, which also has a fire pit. When you're hungry, Brewed can take care of you with a lamb burger, quail and cranberry salad, pan-roasted fish with braised local greens, and pound cake topped with fruit.

Grand Cru Wine Bar & Boutique, 1257 W. Magnolia Ave., Fort Worth 76104; (817) 923-1717; grandcruwineshop.com. Relocated in late 2013 from southwest Fort Worth to the Near Southside, this smart wine shop from Karen Chu brings together the wine savvy and comfortable environs that make both veteran and novice wine drinkers feel like sticking around a while. Karen finds wines her clientele will like by doing a good job of learning what people enjoy drinking. Tasting events, wine pairing events and wine accessory shopping make lingering here a pleasure.

J. Rae's, 935 Foch St., Fort Worth 76107; (817) 332-0090; jraes .com. Holy cupcake! These little darlings are the best we've found, made in fabulous flavors like lemon, strawberry, cookies and cream, red velvet, chocolate, coconut, and more—all with sinfully perfect buttercream icing. Fabulous giant sugar cookies in cartoon shapes and colors—made for the season, made for your favorite team, made for custom parties—are too cute to be true. The cheesecakes here are to die for, in flavors that include vanilla, strawberry and white chocolate.

Magnolia Cheese Company, 1251 W. Magnolia Ave., Fort Worth 76104; (817) 945-2221; magnoliacheese.com. You expect a place with cheese in the name to source and provide excellent cheeses, right? That's exactly what this place does, but the owners go a few steps beyond that and serve exceptional meals that star those cheeses. So here, you have two places in one—a fine place to obtain cheeses to take home and enjoy, and a really amazing place to eat lunch or dinner. Cheeses come from around the state, the nation, and overseas— whatever variety you want, it's here. For meals in the very attractive little dining room, you can enjoy a Sunday brunch frittata incorporating Comté cheese, spinach, and shallots, served with a salad of quail and

blueberries; and at a weekday lunch, you can have a cheeseboard, followed by an oyster chowder with sunchokes and smoked bacon. Lovely wines and craft beer are served, too.

Oliver's Fine Foods, 415 Throckmorton St., Fort Worth 76102; (817) 744-7980; oliversfinefoods.com. Finally, the residents

FORT WORTH'S NEW SOUTH SIDE

Not so long ago, you wouldn't have thought hundreds of shiny, happy people would be cheerily lining up outside of a warehouse off South Main Street in Fort Worth. That, however, was before the twice-weekly tour-and-tasting events at **Rahr & Sons Brewing** *(701 Galveston Ave., Fort Worth 76104; 817-810-9266; rahrbrewing.com)* became among the most popular gatherings in North Texas.

In fact, only in very recent years could you find a vibrant, youngish crowd anywhere in the district called Near Southside. A renaissance not unlike that in Oak Cliff's Bishop Arts District in Dallas or Austin's South Congress has washed over the stretch of formerly neglected buildings reaching from lower downtown over to the medical district just south of Interstate 30. New energy infuses the area, and Near Southside has become the town darling.

Nowadays, you arrive at Rahr, a homegrown craft brewery on a Wednesday evening to find 250 to 300 folks queued up and on Saturday afternoon to find more than 800 preparing to storm the place. Handing over $10 each, they grab a Rahr pint glass and three tasting tickets, enter the cavernous building to tour the brewing operation and to belly up to the bar.

Over the next 2 hours, the suds sippers enjoy three ample tastes from the current selection of core brands, which include the Munich-style lager called Rahr's Blonde; the black lager, Ugly Pug; amber lager, Texas Red; IPA, Stormcloud; and signature amber, Buffalo Butt. Sometimes the selection may include one of several seasonal brews, such as the Summertime Wheat, served in early summer; Gravel Road, the German-style altbier of late summer; or the Oktoberfest, brewed for September–October release.

Since TCU grad Fritz Rahr opened the brewery in 2004, the brand has done nothing but grow, and fandom has only exploded exponentially. The abundant food truck population typically has a couple of representatives dispensing good eats here (look for **Fred's Texas Cafe** (p. 188), Bacon Wagon, Zombie, and others) during the Wednesday and Saturday tasting hours, and TCU football games on the big screen bring in droves.

As you head just a few blocks farther south, you wind up on Magnolia Avenue, the Fairmount historic district, the Near Southside neighborhood where pretty old brick buildings from the very early 1920s found new life in a recent restaurant explosion. The aging street has been pulling in customers for breakfast and lunch at **Paris Coffee Shop** (p. 205) for more than 60 years, and the venerable **Benito's** (p. 183) continues to be a good place to enjoy a late-night plate of huevos rancheros on the weekend. But additions like **Lili's Bistro on Magnolia** (p. 192), with double its original space, will keep you happy with tomato tart Provençal and green chile burgers, as well as a wine bar with live piano music. You'll be wowed, too, by **Shinjuku Station** (p. 199), a Japanese cocktail spot with sharable plates and build-your-own bento boxes.

At **Ellerbe Fine Foods** (p. 188), chef-owner Molly McCook changes the menu almost daily, depending on the fresh finds she scores at the farmers' market and from her myriad artisan purveyors. Settle into the renovated 1920s gas station space, now oozing with New Orleans-esque charm, and find the sort of rapture awaiting in bacon-wrapped trout stuffed with lemon and onion and creamy cauliflower soup with brie that earned Ellerbe an inclusion in *Bon Appétit*'s best new restaurants of 2010.

Just across the street from Ellerbe, **The Usual** has rapidly become the city's favorite cocktail destination. Owner Brad Hensarling built a name for himself and his chic watering hole by specializing in concoctions from the pre-Prohibition era and by crafting a number of newer signature drinks that incorporate only the freshest herbs, fruits, and spices. You can linger over a Montpleir, a mixture of maplewood-smoked maple syrup, bourbon, Jamaican rum, and Italian vermouth; or The Parlor, blending gin with apricot, lime, and Peychaud's, while you nosh on lamb chops or jamón-wrapped scallops from Holy Frijole, the food truck parked behind The Usual. Check out Brad's frequent cocktail classes, too.

For more information on Fort Worth South: 1606 Mistletoe Blvd., Fort Worth 76104; 817-923-1649; fortworthsouth.org.

in downtown Fort Worth have a great little market and take-out shop. Oliver's, now a popular lunch spot in Sundance Square, has an on-site butcher, a terrific cheese department, and lots of gourmet packaged goods for the condo residents to keep their pantries and larders stocked and themselves well-fed.

Put a Cork in It, 2972 Park Hill Dr., Fort Worth 76109; (817) 924-2675; putacorkinitwine.com. Wine genius Chris Keel stocks a little of this and that from everywhere, always searching for the next great find, whether for the spare-no-expense or budget-minded customer. He loves a challenge, welcoming customers to bring their wished-for wine list to his door. Each week, there's a free Thursday-to-Saturday-afternoon tasting within a particular vein, be they Torrontes from Argentina, whites from Walla Walla, Washington, or an Italian lineup that includes a Prosecco, Pinot Grigio, a Chianti reserve, and a super Tuscan. Chris can pair wines with your trickiest dinner party and toughest gift recipient, as well.

Fort Worth Suburbs

The suburbs around Fort Worth include Arlington, Colleyville, Grapevine, Haltom City, and Keller, often referred to as the Mid-Cities, as they are the municipalities lying between Dallas and Fort Worth. What were bedroom communities 20 to 30 years ago have now become busy cities unto themselves. Arlington, which lies directly east of Fort Worth, is the oldest of these, having grown to prominence in the 1960s as the home to Six Flags Over Texas. After that, Arlington's appeal grew, as well, when the Texas Rangers baseball team (formerly the Washington Senators) brought Major League Baseball to the city. In the last decade, Arlington was chosen for the Dallas Cowboys' new billion-dollar stadium, which hosted the Super Bowl in 2011.

Colleyville, Grapevine, Haltom City, and Keller—all situated in Northeast Tarrant County—have enjoyed new growth in the past two decades, particularly as Fort Worth has boomed. Roanoke, which sits in Denton County, just north of Tarrant, has quickly morphed from an old farming community to a developed city. Each offers its own share of interesting eating options.

Foodie Faves

Babe's Chicken Dinner House, 104 N. Oak St., Roanoke 76262; (817) 491-2900; babeschicken.com; American/Southern; $$. The line forms as early as 4:30 p.m. for the evening meals at this monument to home cooking. Tucked within a wonderful, 1908 rock building on the historic main road through tiny Roanoke, Babe's comforts your palate with platters of freshly fried, juicy chicken or meaty chicken-fried steaks. Served family-style, dinners come with mashed potatoes, corn, green salad, and fluffy buttermilk biscuits. At other locations, found in Carrollton, Garland, Frisco, Granbury, Burleson, Arlington, Cedar Hill and Sanger, the menu expands to include pot roast and a few other home cooking favorites.

Cacharel Restaurant & Grand Ballroom, 2221 East Lamar Blvd., Arlington 76006; (817) 640-9981; cacharel.net; French; $$$. The sophisticated dining room atop an office building in North Arlington continues to please after 25 years because there's such a consistent treatment in gems such as escargots with mushrooms, grapes, and pecans in a cream sauce, and sautéed lamb noisettes in a shallot-tarragon sauce with a wild mushroom risotto. The prix-fixe menu changes daily, but there is always a large selection of steaks, fresh fish, and fowl. The dessert and wine lists deserve praise, too. Do not consider missing the stunning soufflés.

Chop House Burgers, 1700 W. Park Row Dr., Arlington 76013; (817) 459-3700; chophouseburgers.com; Burgers; $–$$. With years of fine-dining experience as a chef, owner Kenny Mills does possibly the best burgers in North Texas at his unpretentious little shopping-center joint. He blends beef brisket with steak sauce to make a killer burger, topped with applewood-smoked bacon. He also make a 10 Pepper Burger with jalapeño Jack cheese and Tabasco mayo. The fries are ridiculously good, and there's a steak-house-style wedge salad with house-made blue cheese dressing. *Diners, Drive-Ins and Dives* found this place for its TV show, so count on big crowds coming in also for chili, gumbo, and incredible baked goods, like pie and cake. Second location: 2860 Farm Road 157, Mansfield.

Classic Cafe, 504 N. Oak St., Roanoke 76262; (817) 430-8185; theclassiccafe.com; American; $$$. Brothers Chris and Curtis Wells grew a childhood love of great cooking into a business, opening a fine-dining establishment in an old cottage in Roanoke's historic downtown. For more than two decades, appreciative customers have watched the business to grow to include a garden that produces for the restaurant and specialty menus for any low-key or high-end affair. At lunch or dinner, we're drawn to the line-caught, seared yellowfin tuna salad with fried rice noodles and the brown-sugar pork belly confit for starters, and the grilled rack of lamb and Gulf crab cakes with grilled shrimp and tomato tartar sauce for main courses. Excellent wine choices are available, too.

DeVivo Bros. Eatery, 750 S. Main St., Suite 165, Keller 76248; (817) 431-6890; devivobroseatery.com; Italian/American; $$. Terrific surprises await inside a small shopping center storefront, where you're made to feel like a regular upon your first visit. A local family of Italian descent does an admirable job of bringing handmade goodness to your plate in the form of flat-iron steak, roasted salmon, pasta, meatloaf, burly sandwiches, and compelling salads. Breakfast is an event, to be sure: blueberry pancakes, steak and eggs, and the Italian Benedict have quickly created a big fan base. Though the food is special, the setting is casual and family-friendly. And it's BYOB!

Dino's Steak and Claw House, 342 Main St., Grapevine 76051; (817) 488-3100; dinossteakandclaw.net; Steak House; $$$–$$$$. Occupying a vintage bank building along the historic main drag, this romantic newcomer positions its black granite bar area front and center. Music wafts from the piano that sits between bar and dining room. Dino's signature is the Crab Cube, a square-shaped cake that blends Maryland lump crab within a smooth crust, served on a narrow platter with Dijon-honey sauce and a red chile–apple compote for dipping. Roasted eggplant tossed with a sesame-honey-mint dressing makes for a surprisingly good salad, and grilled Texan quail in a treatment of porcini mushrooms and sherry is the perfect complement. Beef medallions in tarragon béarnaise sauce and rack of lamb with truffle rosemary polenta in a Port wine sauce make ideal main courses.

First Chinese BBQ, 2214 S. Collins St., Arlington 76010; (817) 469-8876; Chinese; $–$$. First off, you don't come here for ambience, atmosphere, or especially good service. It's all about the food, and it's exceptional. Chinese food, for whatever reason, doesn't have excellent representation in North Texas, so we're excited when we can find good-to-great versions. And that's why we come to First Chinese BBQ. It's authentic, down to the dead ducks hanging in the window; you feel like you're in NYC's Chinatown. The barbecued pork is outstanding, as is the roasted duck. The noodle dishes (beef with flat noodles—amazing) are exceptional, as well. Vegans love the crispy tofu, which is a hit with a number of meat-eaters, too—it's that good. Oh, it's a cash-only restaurant, as well.

FnG Eats, 201 Town Center Ln., Suite 1101, Keller 76248; (817) 741-5200; fngeats.com; American; $$–$$$. Easily some of the best food in Northeast Tarrant County is had at this happy surprise of a restaurant. Our favorite starters remain wasabi-spiked deviled eggs and ahi tuna tacos; and among hearty entrees, it's hard to pass up rib eye steak topped with cremini mushrooms sautéed in sherry and the Prince Edward Island mussels with chorizo and wood-grilled garlic with lemon butter and sourdough for sopping. Brunch jewels range from macadamia-crusted chicken with waffles and Veracruz Benedict, the latter a compilation of poached eggs and grilled shrimp over wood-grilled focaccia with avocado on top. Watch for special dinners pairing wine or whiskey with chef-driven creations.

J.R.'s Steakhouse, 5400 Highway 121, Colleyville 76034; (817) 355-1414; jrssteaks.com; Steak House; $$$$. Even on Monday evening, this popular gathering spot is packed and humming. A lot of the diners are business folk staying at airport-area conference hotels, but a good many are locals who know how good the steaks and chops always are here. Ask for the plump, lush rib eye to be cooked with an outer char to get proper balance for the melted butter on top and the heavy garlic-herbed mashers beneath. For sensory overload, order the pepper-crusted filet, a 3-inch-thick wonder glazed with a brandy demi-glace. A sumptuous appetizer is the bacon-wrapped barbecued lobster tail over aged cheddar grits. Champagne-brie soup is a signature, as is the avocado Caesar. Live music typically plays in the lounge.

Marquez Bakery, 1730 E. Division St., Arlington, 76011; (817) 265-8858; marquezbakery.com; Mexican; $. Each visit to this bright, tidy, unadorned dining room at the front of a tortilla factory wows us anew with its simple yet flawless plates of goodness. Our favorite breakfast consists either of huevos rancheros, two perfectly fried eggs topped with a warm, rustic, chunky ranchero sauce, shored up by cheese-topped creamy refrieds and a side of tender *barbacoa,* or *migas,* a scrambled mix of eggs, diced, sweet corn tortillas, jalapeño, onion, and tomato. Wrapped within freshly crafted supple flour tortillas, there's nothing better, except for the meat-stuffed torta, presented on *talera* bread baked on-site each morning. We can't resist taking home a half-dozen pumpkin empanadas from the bakery case, right next to the cash register. Beer is served, too.

Mi Dia from Scratch, 1295 S. Main St., Grapevine 76051; (817) 421-4747; midiafromscratch.com; Mexican; $$. Pure Mexican flavors emanate from this bright, lively, but homespun spot at the south end of Grapevine's main drag. We like starting with *quesadillas de la huitlacoche,* plumped up with roasted veggies and served with red and green chile sauces, or the tamales stuffed with pork and served with three-chile salsa, but sea bass ceviche is hard to pass up. Roasted poblano chiles stuffed with pulled pork with Oaxacan-style black beans on the side is pleasing, as is Scottish salmon wrapped in banana leaf and flavored with achiote and citrus. Sautéed chayote squash on the side with a mango-lemongrass mojo seals the deal on this treasure. Patio dining here is lovely in good weather.

Old Hickory Steakhouse, 1501 Gaylord Trail, Grapevine 76051; (817) 778-2215; Steak House; $$$$. Chef Joanne Bondy does an admirable job of making this steak-house dining experience distinctive and unlike the standard-issue hotel resort dining room. She crafts appetizers such as Atlantic mussels in Texas Shiner Bock beer broth laced with tomato and garlic; crab cakes with smoked pepper sauce; tuna sashimi with coriander, wasabi, and ponzu; and a chilled seafood platter for two. Entrees range from sautéed lemon-scented Atlantic scallops to dry-aged bone-in New York strip. Habanero creamed corn, sorrel potatoes au gratin, oven-roasted wild mushrooms, and garlic truffle fries are among sides that deserve attention. The wine program at this upscale destination exceeds all expectations.

Olenjack's Grille, 770 Road to Six Flags East, Ste. 100, Arlington 76011; (817) 226-2600; olenjacksgrille.com; American; $$. Arguably the most popular, distinctive menu in town melds comfort food with thoughtful preparation. We're mad for the salmon-crab-cake starter, a loose construction of large shreds of fish with chopped herbs and onion, lightly panfried and perfect for dredging through a pleasantly hot Creole mustard. Wood-grilled lamb chops take on a hint of Latin flavor with a spicy chorizo demi-glace, softened by polenta creamy with Jack cheese and smoky with roasted poblano. Even side dishes deserve special attention, particularly when they're as distinctive as the bacon-riddled mustard greens and mascarpone whipped potatoes. Our favorite sweet is the Valrhona chocolate cup with a chocolate-caramel-pecan mousse. An enclosed brick patio easily accommodates overflow crowds. See Olenjack's recipe for **Cod Chowder with Bacon & Potatoes** on p. 230.

Piccolo Mondo, 829 E. Lamar Blvd., Arlington 76011; (817) 265-9174; piccolomondo.com; Italian; $$. More serene than might be expected in a shopping center space, this pretty dining room, burnished by candlelight and filled with live piano music, satisfies without taking big chances. We like starting with prosciutto-wrapped melon slices, as well as a plate of escargots sautéed in sherry, garlic, and butter and decorated with a little tomato and basil, then follow up with shrimp Provençal awash in a scampi-like garlic-parsley bath. Though the arrabbiata treatment on the al dente orecchiette is milder than most, there's nothing timid about the satiny beef tenderloin coated in cracked peppercorns and lavished with a cognac-laced cream.

Potager Cafe, 315 S. Mesquite St., Arlington 76010; (817) 861-2292; potagercafe.com; American; $. Wholesome foods, prepared from locally grown products, show up on plates at this innovative dining spot. Most interestingly, you pay what you think you should—there are no prices on the menu. Obviously, you do this with integrity; a good lunch is worth at least $8 to $12. Dinner, a little more. Menu choices change daily but can typically include broccoli-mushroom soup, slow-roasted pork with salsa verde, white fish piccata, potato-rice cakes, roasted carrots, green salad, French bread, and ginger-orange trifle. Beer and wine are offered, too. It's a cash-only operation, so go with some green.

Tribeca Americana Bistro & Lounge, 62 Main St., Ste. 200, Colleyville 76034; (817) 788-3998; tribecaamericana.com/; Global Cuisine; $$–$$$. Sage Sakiri, whom locals will recognize as the gastronomy force behind the late Red Sage in Southlake and, still a destination on Grapevine's Main Street, **Dino's Steak and Claw House** (p. 215), calls his new place continental-American starring "an immigrant influence from around the world," packing a plentiful ethnic punch. An unusual but worthy salad is made with tender, silken octopus tossed with chickpeas and *fregula,* a Sardinian pasta reminding us a little of couscous. Black cod, its top seared in pork belly oil to a crisp, is augmented by Japanese yams and shallots. The Tribeca Lounge, an adjacent space with couches, offers a later-night menu of small plates. The SoHo Room accommodates private dining and business gatherings, as well.

Trio New American Cafe, 8300 Precinct Line Rd., Suite 104, Colleyville 76034; (817) 503-8440; triocolleyville.com; American; $–$$. Chef Jason Harper's tireless enthusiasm for exciting food translates beautifully to weekday lunches and weekend dinners that command reservations and wait lists envied by other restaurateurs. And no wonder: The white cheddar mac and cheese, topped with panko crumbs and applewood-smoked bacon, as well as the smoked salmon–blue corn nachos are dishes to return for, time and again. Light but satisfying, the pan-seared red fish, topped with pineapple beurre blanc and served with jicama slaw and Manchego-infused grits go a long way toward illustrating Jason's brilliance. Jason's bride, Miriam, shows pastry prowess in her coconut crème pie and tiramisu cupcakes.

Tu Hai Restaurant, 3909 E. Belknap St., Haltom City 76111; (817) 834-6473; Vietnamese; $. Far, far from fancy, this diamond in the rough is what most folks around DFW first came to know and love about Vietnamese food. Service is friendly in the small, utilitarian cafe, which can be crowded at all hours. The food is cheap and couldn't be better. Favorites, in addition to traditional pho (soup with sliced steak and crunchy vegetables), are the Saigon pancake, the vermicelli topped with grilled pork and egg roll, and the chicken lemongrass with rice. Be sure to get the Vietnamese lemonade to drink. It's cash only here.

Specialty Stores, Markets & Producers

Arlington Farmers Market, 215 Front St., Arlington 76011; (817) 633-2332; downtownarlingtonfarmersmarket.com. Open on Fri and Sat from 8 a.m. to 1 p.m., this market offers Texas-produced vegetables and fruits, honey, grass-fed meats, tacos, olive oil, salsas, breads, and more.

BreadHaus, 700 W. Dallas Rd., Grapevine 76051; (817) 488-5223; breadhaus.com. German bread bakery treats include stollen, hot-cross buns, and assorted rustic breads and sweets. Of most interest, the bakery uses only organic flours, grains, seeds, and other ingredients.

Buon Giorno, 2350 Hall Johnson Rd., Grapevine 76051; (817) 421-7300; buongiornocoffee.myshopify.com. Roasting coffee beans on-site, this coffeehouse makes a fine cup of drip coffee and espresso. Teas get dutiful attention here, too. To eat, enjoy quiche, brioche, bread pudding, shortbread, scones, palmiers, muffins, and panini sandwiches. Second location at 915 Florence St., Fort Worth 76102.

Central Market, 1425 E. Southlake Blvd., Southlake 76092; (817) 310-5600; centralmarket.com. A large gourmet grocery store, with locations around Texas, has every sort of meat, fish, vegetable, grain, cheese, pasta, wine, beer, and condiment your heart desires. All stores hold tastings and feature cooking classes (p. 50). Reservations are strongly advised; classes often sell out weeks in advance. Other stores in North Dallas, Plano, and Fort Worth.

Colleyville Farmers Market, 5409 Colleyville Blvd., Colleyville 76034; (817) 427-2333; colleyvillefarmers market.com. Specializing in local and seasonal produce, this market is your best bet in the Mid-Cities area for organic dairy, eggs, honey, artisan breads, Texas Heritage Beef, free-range chicken, and wild sockeye salmon. Open daily many months of the year.

Grapevine Olive Oil Company, 326 S. Main St., Grapevine 76051; (682) 223-1592; grapevineoliveoilcompany.com. Every conceivable infusion for olive oils and vinegars is found in this charming gourmet cook's shop. Tastings are a given, and you come away with

On The Grapevine

At 2 p.m. on a Wednesday, Wayne Turner is on the run at Into the Glass. More than a dozen patrons are perched on bar stools and at cozy two-tops at this warm and welcoming wine bar, tucked into one of the vintage shotgun spaces along Grapevine's historic Main Street. They're all happily sipping their afternoon Sauvignon Blanc and Merlot, a few of them still nibbling on a late lunch. Mostly women, all seem quite at home—especially the big guy in the cowboy hat anchoring one end of the bar.

"They're all regulars, know 'em all by name," Wayne says, as he delivers another glass to the woman in tennis togs cooing over his recommendation of a new Grenache from Australia. Guests become part of the family at Into the Glass, instantly coming to rely on wisdom from Wayne and staffers like Kyle Davis, who help in navigation through a lively wine list that changes almost biweekly.

If you want to try several of the 80 choices from California, Oregon, Washington, France, Italy, Argentina, and beyond, you're in luck—everything's available in a small pour, ranging from $3 to $7 each, as well as by the standard glass ($9 to $21) or bottle ($32 to $92).

Into the Glass has become a place also for enjoying possibly the best meals in town. The menu favorites reflect Wayne's experience working in San Francisco and Dallas. Lovely to behold and taste, his napoleon of duck confit and sweet potato pancakes, drizzled with a swirl of blackberry-balsamic *gastrique,* pairs beautifully with Costa de Oro Pinot Noir from Santa Barbara. It's no surprise that visiting winemakers like hanging out here, too.

"They know we love their boutique wines, and they appreciate our laid-back style here," Wayne says. " 'Don't overthink it, just drink it,' is our motto, and that appeals to them." And to us, as well.

Into the Glass, 322 S. Main St., Grapevine; (817) 422-1969; *intotheglass.com.*

marvelous ideas for new dishes to prepare at home. Wonderful gifts for the cook are here, too.

Keller Farmers Market, 1100 Bear Creek Parkway, Keller 76248; kellerfarmersmarket.com. Open on Sat mornings from May through Oct, this is an excellent destination for locally produced tamales, meats, eggs, produce, baked goods, chips, salsa, pasta, pickles, jellies and jams, honey, wine, coffee, pet goods, and handcrafted items.

Legacy Cakes Bakery, 120 S. Main St., Grapevine 76051; (817) 442-9999; legacycakesbakery.com. Exquisitely crafted sugary delights from pastry chef Megan Rountree include cakes in such flavors as lemon, cookies and cream, red velvet, banana, chocolate peppermint, and much, much more. Her specialty party creations have to be seen to be believed.

Main Street Bistro & Bakery, 316 S. Main St., Grapevine 76051; (817) 424-4333; themainbakery.com. Lovely craftsmanship goes into carrot cake, vanilla bean cheesecake, chocolate mousse nougatine cake, myriad morning pastries, and other sweets. There's also a lunch menu.

Market Street, 5605 Colleyville Blvd., Colleyville, 76034; (817) 577-5020; marketstreetunited.com. Though based in West Texas, this high-end grocery store has made itself indispensible to the mid-cities residents in and near Colleyville, Grapevine, and Southlake. The choices in meat, fish, produce, prepared foods, and such are more widespread than at most grocery stores, and the beer and wine department is enormous, with excellent customer service. The gourmet-to-go department offers excellent take-home meals.

Milwaukee Joe's Gourmet Ice Cream, 1417 Main St., Southlake 76092; (817) 251-1667; milwaukeejoesicecream.com. When you're ready to truly indulge, head to this place in Southlake Town Square. It's a very rich, triple-butterfat ice cream in flavors like Andes mint, black raspberry truffle, cotton candy, Dr Pepper, lemon custard, and triple chocolate. Disco Lives thrills kids—it tastes like Frutti Pebbles cereal, and it's super-blue. As in, really, really blue.

Sugar & Frosting, 126 Taylor St., Keller 76248; (817) 562-2500; sugarandfrosting.com. This sweet shop creates everything you need with sugar, and then some. Gourmet popcorn is a specialty, as are cupcakes, cakes, sugar cookies, pies, pie and cake pops, bars, brownies, and anything else that's baked with sugar.

Recipes

Here's a selection of recipes from some of the most popular chefs and restaurants in the Dallas–Fort Worth area. Cook, eat, enjoy. Bon appétit!

Beef Burgundy

Serves 6–8

1 cup bacon lardoons, cut into small pieces

2 pounds beef shoulder or boneless short rib, cut into 1½-inch cubes

Salt and pepper to taste

1 tablespoon olive oil

4 shallots, sliced

5 cloves garlic, sliced

2 tablespoons tomato paste

2 carrots, peeled and diced

2 cups button mushrooms, cleaned and halved

½ cup sliced leeks, white parts only

2 cups sliced fingerling potatoes

1 (750 ml) bottle red burgundy

1 bouquet garni (thyme, parsley, and bay leaf tied with butcher's twine)

3–4 cups beef stock, to cover

Sliced radish and parsley for garnish

Cook the bacon in a dutch oven over medium heat until done. Remove from pan with slotted spoon and set aside. Season the meat with salt and pepper. Place in the dutch oven on medium high heat, add oil, and sear the meat until it is golden brown. Do not overcrowd the pan; sear it in batches if necessary. Remove the meat and set aside.

Preheat the oven to 350°F.

Add shallots, garlic, and tomato paste and cook until the tomato paste has browned slightly. Add bacon, the rest of the vegetables, wine, bouquet garni, and the seared meat. Add beef stock to cover by an inch or so. Place the lid on the dutch oven and put in the oven for about an hour.

When the beef is fork tender, it's time to finish the dish. Remove the meat and vegetables from the broth and reduce the broth on the stovetop over medium heat until it coats a spoon. At this point add the meat and vegetables back to the reduced broth. Garnish with a little sliced radish and chopped parsley, if you like.

Courtesy of Chef Nathan Tate of Boulevardier, Dallas

Ecuadorian Shrimp Ceviche with Orange & Popcorn

Serves 6–8

4 quarts water
Salt to taste, divided
1 pound rock shrimp, peeled and cleaned
2 medium yellow tomatoes, roasted, peeled, seeded, and chopped
1 jalapeño chile, roasted, peeled, seeded, and chopped
1 small yellow bell pepper, roasted, peeled, seeded, and chopped

½ cup fresh orange juice
2 teaspoons granulated sugar
Tabasco sauce to taste
5 tablespoons fresh lime juice
½ red onion, peeled and thinly sliced
1 tablespoon chopped green onions
3 teaspoons chopped fresh cilantro
½ cup freshly popped popcorn for garnish

Bring 4 quarts of lightly salted water to a boil. Remove from the heat, add shrimp and let sit for 2 minutes. Drain and chill shrimp.

In a blender, combine the tomatoes, jalapeño, yellow pepper, orange juice, sugar, and Tabasco sauce. Blend on medium speed until smooth, about 2 minutes then season with salt to taste; refrigerate for 30 minutes.

Place the chilled shrimp in a large bowl and stir in the lime juice. Season with salt and let sit for 5 minutes. Stir in the pureed tomato mixture and add the onions and cilantro. Adjust the seasoning as necessary. Serve chilled, garnished with the popcorn.

Courtesy of Chef Stephan Pyles of Stephan Pyles, Samar by Stephan Pyles and Stampede 66, Dallas

Lobster Macaroni & Cheese with Truffle Oil

Serves 8

2 tablespoons olive oil
24 ounces lobster meat, cubed
¼ cup extra-virgin olive oil
2 pounds orzo pasta
2 tablespoons minced garlic
2 tablespoons minced shallots
2 quarts chicken stock, strained clean
2 cups heavy cream
1 cup Romano cheese, grated
⅛ cup chiffonade of basil leaves
⅛ cup chiffonade of spinach leaves
2 tablespoons chopped oregano
2 tablespoons chopped parsley
8 ounces prosciutto ham, julienned thin
2 tablespoons kosher salt
2 tablespoons cracked black pepper
2 tablespoons truffle oil

In a large pot over medium to high heat, add olive oil and sauté lobster meat until it is medium rare, about 2 minutes. Remove lobster and add the extra-virgin olive oil. Lower heat to medium and add half of the orzo pasta and sauté until golden brown. Add garlic, shallots, and remaining half of the pasta. Cover with half of the chicken stock.

Continue cooking until pasta absorbs most of the stock. Add the rest of the stock and continue cooking until all of the stock is absorbed. Add heavy cream and Romano cheese; stir until cheese is melted. Add basil leaves, spinach leaves, oregano, and parsley.

In a sauté pan, quickly sauté the prosciutto ham until crisp. Add to pasta with lobster meat. Salt and pepper to taste and finish with truffle oil.

Courtesy of Chef Kent Rathbun of Abacus, Jasper's, and Rathbun's Blue Plate Kitchen, Dallas

Cod Chowder with Bacon & Potatoes

Serves 8

4 slices thick-cut bacon, cut into ½-inch strips

4 ounces pancetta, cut into small dice

1½ cups chopped leeks, white and pale green parts only

1 sweet yellow onion, cut into small dice

2 ribs celery, cut into small dice

1 jalapeño, stemmed, seeded, and cut into small dice

1 pound fingerling potatoes, cut into ¼-inch-thick rounds

1 ounce fresh thyme, tied with string

8 ounces clam juice

4 cups heavy cream

2 pounds cod fillets, cut into pieces

Sea salt and freshly ground black pepper to taste

Cook the bacon and pancetta in large stock pot over medium heat until the fat is rendered. Add leeks, onion, celery, and jalapeño to the pot. Cook until vegetables are tender, stirring frequently, about 6–8 minutes.

Add potatoes, thyme, clam juice, and cream. Bring to boil; reduce heat to medium and cover.

Add the cod and simmer until potatoes are just tender, stirring occasionally, about 10 minutes. Season the chowder to taste with salt and pepper and serve.

Courtesy of Chef Brian Olenjack of Olenjack's Grille, Arlington

Dean's Tortilla Soup with South of the Border Flavors

Serves 4

3 tablespoons olive oil

4 corn tortillas, cut into long strips

8 garlic cloves, peeled

2 cups fresh onion puree

4 cups fresh tomato puree

5 dried ancho chiles, fire roasted and seeded (See Note)

2 jalapeños, chopped

1 tablespoon cumin powder

1 teaspoon ground coriander

1 tablespoon chopped epazote, or 2 tablespoons chopped fresh cilantro

1 large bay leaf

1½ quarts chicken stock

Salt to taste

Lemon juice to taste

Cayenne pepper to taste

Garnishes:

1 smoked chicken breast, skinless, boneless, and diced small

1 large avocado, peeled, seeded, and cut into small cubes

½ cup shredded Boyacá (Latin cheddar) cheese

4 tablespoons small-dice green cabbage

3 tablespoons small-dice red radish

1 tablespoon seeded and minced jalapeño pepper

4 corn tortillas, cut into thin strips and fried crisp

Heat oil in a large saucepan over medium heat. Add tortillas and garlic and sauté until tortillas are crisp and garlic is golden brown, about 4–5 minutes. Add onion puree and cook for 5 minutes, stirring occasionally until reduced by half. Add tomato puree, roasted chiles, jalapeños, cumin, coriander, epazote, bay leaf, and chicken stock. Bring to a boil. Lower heat and simmer for approximately 40 minutes. Skim fat from surface, if necessary. Remove bay leaf. Process through a food mill to attain the perfect consistency or use a blender (soup may become thick; thin out with additional chicken stock). Season to taste with salt, lemon, and cayenne.

Garnish each warm soup bowl with smoked chicken breast, avocado, shredded Boyacá cheese, green cabbage, red radish, jalapeño pepper, and corn tortillas. Ladle 8 ounces of tortilla soup over the garnish. Serve immediately.

Note: To roast the chiles, use a pair of kitchen tongs to hold each chile directly over an open flame. Lightly roast each chile on all sides for about 30–45 seconds. (Be careful not to blacken or burn chiles.) When chiles are cool, remove seeds and stem. This same process can be done in a preheated 400°F oven; cook chiles for about 2–3 minutes.

Courtesy of Chef Dean Fearing of Fearing's at the Ritz-Carlton, Dallas

Chorizo Stuffed Dates

Yields 50

6 dried chipotle chiles
3 dried ancho chiles
3 dried guajillo chiles
3 dried árbol chiles
¼ cup peanut oil
1 pound ground beef
1 pound ground pork
4 cloves garlic, minced

1 yellow onion, minced
Sea salt and pepper to taste
2 pounds seeded Medjool
   dates
1 pound applewood-smoked
   bacon, in slices
Toothpicks

Preheat the oven to 200°F.

To roast the chiles: Stem the dried chiles, place them on a baking sheet, and roast until crunchy, 20–30 minutes. Place all the chiles in a spice grinder and grind into powder.

Preheat oven to 350°F.

To make the chorizo: Heat a medium-size sauté pan over medium heat. Add peanut oil and heat until slightly smoking. Add both ground meats and cook until slightly brown. Add minced garlic, minced yellow onion, and ground chiles. Season with salt and pepper to taste. Reserve mixture.

To stuff the dates: Gently stuff approximately 1 tablespoon of chorizo mixture into seeded dates. Wrap each date with 1 slice of bacon and secure with tooth-pick. Place wrapped dates onto a baking sheet and bake at 350°F until bacon is slightly crisp. Serve warm.

Courtesy of Chef Blaine Staniford of Grace, Fort Worth

Crab Stuffed Jalapeños

Serves 12

3 slices bacon
12 jalapeños
3 ounces Boursin cheese
3 ounces cream cheese
8 ounces fresh lump crabmeat, picked through for shell pieces

Pinch of kosher salt
Pinch of ground black pepper
1 tablespoon chopped fresh chives

Cook the bacon slices until crispy, then break them apart into large bits by hand. Slice the jalapeños in half lengthwise, or just cut off the stems. Hollow out the inside of the jalapeño, being sure to get as much of the white veins and seeds out as possible. Combine the Boursin and cream cheese and warm just slightly until smooth and creamy. Fold in the cleaned crab meat, being very careful not to break up the large lumps of crab. Gently stir in salt and pepper.

Preheat the oven to 425°F.

Stuff each pepper as much as it will take, even overstuffing a little bit. Bake until the crab and cheese mixture is bubbling and lightly browned, approximately 7–8 minutes. Top each one with bits of bacon and fresh chives just before serving.

Note: The jalapeños can be cut in different ways. The stems can be removed, then the body of the peppers hollowed out and stuffed. They will need to be roasted in a special rack designed for roasting jalapeños vertically, which I prefer. The racks are easy to find online and make great serving pieces as well.

Courtesy of Chef Jon Bonnell of Bonnell's Fine Texas Cuisine, Fort Worth

Buffalo & Blue Cheese Meatballs
with Sweet Molasses Glaze

Serves 4–6

1 pound ground bison meat

3 ounces blue cheese crumbles

1 shallot, peeled and finely diced

½ cup chopped parsley

½ teaspoon kosher salt

1 teaspoon black pepper

Preheat the oven to 350°F.

Combine all ingredients by hand in a large mixing bowl until all ingredients are blended together. Divide mixture into 10 to 12 meatballs of roughly the same size. Roll the mixture in your hand until round. Place on cooking sheet and bake in oven for 10–12 minutes. Place on serving tray with toothpicks and finished with Sweet Molasses Glaze (below).

Sweet Molasses Glaze (makes about ¾ cup):

¼ cup dark corn syrup, preferably Karo

¼ cup ketchup

¼ cup brown sugar

¼ cup apple cider vinegar

Combine all ingredients in a large stockpot and cook over medium-high heat. Reduce the liquid until it becomes thick enough to coat the back of a spoon. Remove from heat and strain through a fine mesh strainer.

Courtesy of Chef Juan Rodriguez of Reata Restaurant, Fort Worth

Churros Served with Cajeta

Serves 12

2 cups water
1 tablespoon vanilla extract
4 ounces (1 stick) butter
Zest of 1 orange
Zest of 1 lemon
Zest of 1 lime
1 teaspoon salt
2 cups flour

4 egg yolks
2 tablespoons sugar
½ tablespoon cinnamon
Peanut or vegetable oil for frying, enough to fill a pan to a 2-inch depth
3 tablespoons cajeta sauce, found in specialty markets, for dipping

Bring water, vanilla extract, butter, citrus zests, and salt to a boil. Sprinkle in flour and beat with a wooden spoon until dough is fully incorporated. Continue to cook for a few minutes.

Transfer dough into a stand mixer with a paddle attachment and blend on medium speed. Add egg yolks, one at a time, until the dough has come back together and cooled off completely.

In a small separate bowl, combine the sugar and cinnamon.

Heat oil in a fryer to 375°F. Transfer dough to a pastry bag with a large star tip. Pipe dough to desired length into oil and snip with scissors.

Fry each churro for about 2–3 minutes, or until golden brown. Remove and place on paper towels to drain.

Sprinkle with cinnamon-sugar mixture and serve with cajeta sauce for dipping.

Courtesy of Chef Lanny Lancarte, Lanny's Alta Cocina Mexicana, Fort Worth

Apple Galette (Rustic Apple Tart)

Serves 10

Crust:

1 ¼ cups unbleached all pur-
pose flour, plus extra for
work surface

½ teaspoon salt

1 tablespoon sugar

¼ cup lard or vegetable shortening, cold (see Note)

6 tablespoons unsalted butter, cold, cut into ¼-inch
chunks

3 to 4 tablespoons ice water

Note: *Can substitute vegetable shortening for the lard and butter for vegan/
dairy-free*

*Whisk together the flour, salt, and sugar in a medium mixing bowl. Add the
lard or shortening, and mix until the fat disappears into the flour. Scatter
the butter over the flour mixture and toss well using your hands, coating and
separating the butter pieces. Add the water slowly, gently mixing the dough to
avoid breaking up the butter into smaller pieces. Add just enough water so that
the dough clumps together when gently squeezed. (You will see large pieces of
butter throughout the dough. This is what makes the crust flaky.) Gather the
dough into a ball and flatten it into a disk. Wrap in plastic and let chill for
at least one hour and up to two days in the refrigerator, or freeze to use later.*

*Remove dough from the refrigerator about 10 minutes before you need to roll
it out.*

Filling:

1 ½ pounds of Granny Smith or
other tart baking apple, or
a combination of varieties,
peeled, cored, and cut into
thin slices (about ⅛ inch
thick)

4 tablespoons sugar, divided

1 teaspoon freshly grated
lemon zest

¼ cup apricot preserves,
warmed and thinned with
a little water, if needed to
make it spreadable

About 2 tablespoons milk
(optional for vegan/
dairy-free)

Roll out pie dough between two sheets of parchment paper sprinkled with a little bit of flour
to about ⅛ inch thick and about 14 inches
in diameter. Don't worry if you still see large
chunks of butter throughout dough. Remove the
top sheet of parchment and slide the bottom sheet,
with the crust, onto a large flat baking sheet.
Chill the dough on the sheet in the refrigerator for
about 15 minutes.

Preheat oven to 450°F.

Combine apples, 2 tablespoons sugar, and
lemon peel in a mixing bowl and toss to
combine. Remove crust from refrigerator
and spread preserves on it, leaving about a
1½-inch border around the edge.

Arrange apple slices on crust, overlapping them slightly. Using the bottom
parchment paper to help lift edges of the crust, fold the plain border up and
over the apples. Pinch together any cracks, but the edges will be irregular. (It's
OK; it's rustic.)

Brush milk over the edges of crust and sprinkle the top of the whole tart with
the remaining 2 tablespoons sugar.

Bake the tart for 20 minutes, then reduce the oven to 375° and continue baking until the crust is well browned, about 20 to 30 minutes longer. Let tart
stand for at least 10 minutes before slicing and serving. Or, let cool completely
and cover.

Courtesy of Chef Gwin Grimes, Artisan Baking Company, Fort Worth

Sautéed Louisiana Gulf Shrimp & Kale

Serves 4–6

- 4 ounces applewood-smoked bacon, cut into large dice
- 1½ tablespoons olive oil
- 1 pound 16/20 shrimp, peeled and deveined
- Salt and pepper to taste
- 1 chile de árbol, cut into thin rings
- 2 garlic cloves, peeled and thinly sliced
- 2 cups kale, washed and cut into strips
- ¾ cup halved cherry tomatoes
- ¼ tablespoon kosher salt
- ⅛ teaspoon fresh ground black pepper
- 2 ounces (½ stick) unsalted butter
- ⅓ cup crumbled feta cheese for garnish

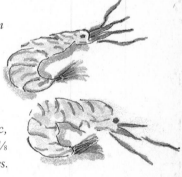

Heat the bacon and olive oil in a medium size sauté pan over low heat for 2 minutes, stirring often. Lightly sprinkle the shrimp with salt and pepper. Add the shrimp to the sauté pan and increase the heat to medium. Cook for 2 minutes and then stir, making sure to flip the shrimp. Add the chile, garlic, kale, cherry tomatoes, ¼ tablespoon salt, and ⅛ teaspoon pepper to the pan. Cook for 2 minutes. Gently stir to let the kale finish wilting.

Using a slotted spoon, transfer the mixture in the pan to a serving bowl, leaving the liquid in the pan. Add the butter to the remaining liquid and return to the stove over high heat. Continually swirl the pan over the flame until the butter is completely melted. Drizzle the pan sauce over the shrimp and kale. Garnish with the crumbled feta cheese.

Courtesy of Chef Molly McCook of Ellerbe Fine Foods, Fort Worth

Roasted Garlic Stuffed Beef Tenderloin with Western Plaid Hash & Syrah Demi-Glace

Serves 4

- **10 unpeeled garlic cloves**
- **1 cup Syrah, preferably Australian, divided**
- **2 cups veal stock**
- **4 cups peanut oil**
- **2 russet potatoes, with skins**
- **Kosher salt and cracked black pepper to taste**
- **½ cup olive oil, divided**

- **1 cup julienned red pepper**
- **1 cup julienned green cabbage**
- **1 cup julienned red cabbage**
- **1 cup julienned red onion**
- **4 (8-ounce) beef tenderloin fillets**
- **Seasonal green vegetable for serving, optional**

To roast the garlic: Place the unpeeled garlic in a cast iron skillet or a heavy-bottomed sauté pan, and roast garlic over low heat for 20–30 minutes. Shake the pan occasionally to prevent the garlic from burning or roasting unevenly. Garlic can also be roasted in the oven by placing the cloves in a 350°F oven for 20–25 minutes, until lightly browned. When the garlic is done, it will be creamy, sweet, and soft enough to squeeze out of the clove. Garlic can also be roasted ahead of time.

To make the demi-glace: In a saucepan, add ½ cup of wine, and bring to a boil. After half has evaporated, add veal stock, reduce by two-thirds, and keep warm.

To make the hash: In a 4-quart saucepan, add peanut oil and heat to 325°F.

On a mandoline or by hand, julienne the potatoes to ⅛-inch strips and rinse in cool water to remove some starch.

When oil reaches 325°F, carefully drop the potato strips in oil, stirring frequently. Cook for approximately 4 minutes, or until golden brown. Remove potatoes from oil, and place in a bowl. Season with salt and pepper.

In a large, hot iron skillet or flat grill, add ¼ cup olive oil, peppers, cabbage, onions, and garlic. Cook until cabbage is wilted, adding salt and pepper to taste. Add remainder of wine to cabbage mixture and simmer. Reserve and keep warm.

Preheat the oven to 350°F.

To prepare steaks: Make a small slit in the side of each tenderloin with a paring knife, squeeze 1 large clove of roasted garlic in each, and set aside. In a hot sauté pan, add ¼ cup olive oil. Season fillets by liberally rubbing salt and pepper into the top and bottom of the steak. Place all 4 steaks in the pan, sear on high for 1½ minutes each side, and place in the oven for 4 minutes for medium rare to medium.

To serve: Place potatoes in center of plate, and add the cabbage on top. Place tenderloin on top of the cabbage, and pour demi-glace on top of the steak. If desired, garnish with a seasonal green vegetable like grilled asparagus or green beans.

Courtesy of Chef Tim Love of Lonesome Dove Western Bistro,
Woodshed Smokehouse, and Love Shack, Fort Worth

Cranberry Chess Pie

Serves 8

6 tablespoons (¾ stick) unsalted butter, at room temperature

1 cup granulated sugar

2 eggs, separated

3 tablespoons all-purpose flour

1 tablespoon fresh lemon juice

½ teaspoon freshly grated nutmeg

¼ teaspoon salt

1 cup buttermilk, at room temperature

1 (9-inch) piecrust, baked

1 cup fresh or frozen cranberries, chop some in half

Preheat oven to 350°F.

Combine the butter and sugar with an electric mixer until smooth. Add the egg yolks and mix to combine. Add the flour, lemon juice, nutmeg and salt. While your mixer is running, slowly add the buttermilk. Whip the egg whites till soft peaks form. Gently fold the egg whites into the buttermilk mixture until just combined. Pour into piecrust. Gently drop your cranberries on the top, evenly covering the top of the pie, and bake 45–50 minutes until the pie is lightly browned. Cool and serve at room temperature.

Courtesy of Chef Marche Ann Mann of Black Rooster Bakery, Fort Worth

Appendix A:
Eateries by Cuisine

Coded for Corresponding Regional Chapters:
(DD) Downtown Dallas & Surrounding Districts
(DE) Deep Ellum–East Dallas
(FW) Fort Worth & Suburbs
(ND) North Dallas
(OC) Oak Cliff
(PC) Park Cities
(U) Uptown

Tillman's Roadhouse (OC), 123
Tried & True (DE), 65
Trio New American Cafe (FW), 219
II Brothers Grill & Bar (ND), 174
T/X Restaurant & Bar (U), 99
Urbano Cafe (DE), 67
Village Kitchen (PC), 141
Whiskey Cake Kitchen (ND), 175
Winslow's Wine Cafe (FW), 201
Woodshed Smokehouse (FW),
    201, 203
Yogi's Deli & Grill (FW), 202

Asian
Abacus (U), 102
Chan Thai (OC), 109
Five Sixty by Wolfgang Puck (DD), 43
Pacific Table (FW), 195

Bar
Lee Harvey's (DD), 32

Barbecue
Angelo's Bar-B-Q (FW), 204
Baker's Ribs (DE), 56
Lockhart Smokehouse (OC), 116
Pecan Lodge (DD), 39
Peggy Sue BBQ (PC), 137
Railhead Smokehouse BBQ
    (FW), 196
Sonny Bryan's Smokehouse (DD), 46
Woodshed Smokehouse (FW),
    201, 203

Burgers
Burger House (PC), 142
Chop House Burgers (FW), 214
Dutch's Hamburgers (FW), 187
Fred's Texas Cafe (FW), 188, 210
Goff's Hamburgers (PC), 146
Hunky's Hamburgers (OC), 114
Kincaid's (FW), 204
Lee Harvey's (DD), 32
Love Shack (FW), 193
Maple & Motor (DD), 33
Twisted Root (DE), 66

Cajun
Wicked Po'Boys (ND), 176

Chinese
First Chinese BBQ (FW), 215

Coffee Shop
Mecca Restaurant, The (DE), 61

Delicatessen
Carshon's Delicatessen (FW), 185

Farm-to-Table
Smoke (OC), 122

French
Bistro 31 (PC), 130
Bonnie Ruth's Café Trottoir et
    Patisserie (ND), 155
Boulevardíer (OC), 108

Southwestern

Bonnell's Fine Texas Cuisine
(FW), 183
Fearing's at the Ritz-Carlton (U), 102
Lonesome Dove Western Bistro
(FW), 144, 193
Michaels Restaurant & Ancho Chile
Bar (FW), 194
Reata Restaurant (FW), 197

Spanish

Cafe Madrid (U), 80

Steak House

Al Biernat's (PC), 141
Arthur's Prime Steaks and Seafood
(ND), 154
Bob's Steak & Chop House (U), 78
Capital Grille, The (U), 81
Cattlemen's Steak House (FW), 186
Chamberlain's Steak & Chop House
(ND), 177
Dallas Chop House (DD), 28
Del Frisco's Double Eagle Steak
House (ND), 178
Dino's Steak and Claw House
(FW), 215
Dunston's Steak House & Bar
(ND), 178
J.R.'s Steakhouse (FW), 216
Nick & Sam's (U), 91
Old Hickory Steakhouse (FW), 217
Pappas Bros. Steakhouse (ND), 179

Perry's Steakhouse & Grille (U), 93
Place at Perry's, The (U), 94
Ranch, The (ND), 169
Randy's Steakhouse (ND), 170
SER Steaks + Spirits (DD), 41
Steve Fields' Steak & Lobster
Lounge (ND), 172
III Forks (ND), 173

Tex-Mex

Digg's Taco Shop (PC), 131
Primo's (U), 94

Thai

Chan Thai (OC), 109
Malai Kitchen (U), 88
Royal Thai (DE), 63

Upscale

Mansion Restaurant, The (U), 103
Oak (DD), 36
Village Kitchen (PC), 141

Vegetarian & Vegan

Cosmic Cafe (U), 82
Kalachandji's (DE), 60
Spiral Diner (FW), 199

Vietnamese

Bistro B (ND), 154
Malai Kitchen (U), 88
Tu Hai Restaurant (FW), 220

Appendix B:
Dishes, Specialties
& Specialty Foods

Coded for Corresponding Regional Chapters:

(DD) Downtown Dallas & Surrounding Districts

(DE) Deep Ellum–East Dallas

(FW) Fort Worth & Suburbs

(ND) North Dallas

(OC) Oak Cliff

(PC) Park Cities

(U) Uptown

Bakeries

Artisan Baking Co. (FW), 205

Black Rooster Bakery (FW), 203, 207

BlueBonnet Bakery (FW), 208

Bonnie Ruth's Café Trottoir et
    Patisserie (ND), 155

BreadHaus (FW), 220

Crème de la Cookie (PC), 148

eatZi's Market & Bakery (U), 104

Empire Baking Company (U), 105

Esperanza's Bakery & Café (FW),
    188, 202, 207

Frosted Art Bakery & Studio (DD), 48

Tu-Lu's Gluten-Free Bakery (PC), 150

Village Baking Co. (PC), 150

Zaguán Bakery (U), 101

Breakfast & Brunch

Benito's (FW), 183, 211

Bonnie Ruth's Café Trottoir et
    Patisserie (ND), 155

Esperanza's Bakery & Café (FW),
    188, 202, 207

Fernando's Mexican Cuisine (ND), 161

Index